MICHAEL SMITH AND JONATHAN FRANKLIN

CABIN FEVER

TRAPPED ON BOARD A CRUISE SHIP WHEN THE PANDEMIC HIT

A true story of heroism and survival at sea

ENDEAVOUR

Originally published in the United States by Doubleday,
a division of Penguin Random House LLC, New York

First published in Great Britain in 2022
by Endeavour, an imprint of
Octopus Publishing Group Ltd
Carmelite House
50 Victoria Embankment
London EC4Y 0DZ
www.octopusbooks.co.uk

An Hachette UK Company
www.hachette.co.uk

ISBN (Hardback): 9781913068738
ISBN (Trade paperback): 9781913068745

A CIP catalogue record for this book is available from the British Library.

Printed and bound in UK

1 3 5 7 9 10 8 6 4 2

Typeset in 12.5/18pt Garamond Premier Pro by Jouve (UK), Milton Keynes

This FSC® label means that materials used for
the product have been responsibly sourced.

CONTENTS

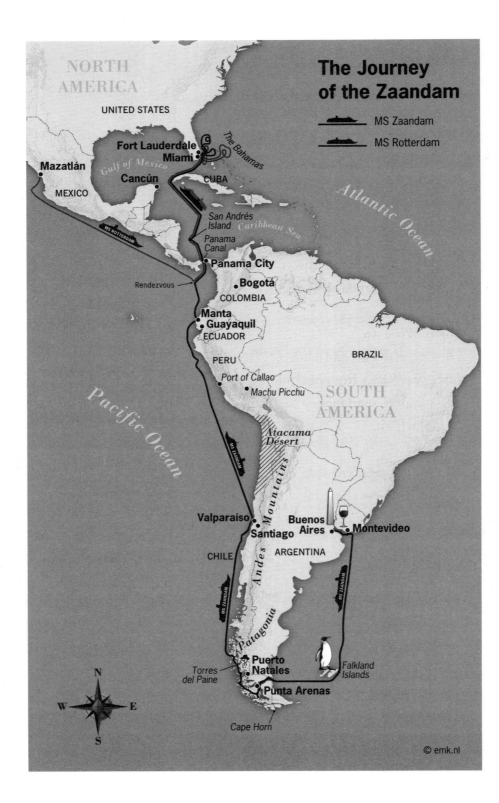

THE CHARACTERS

Ane Smit
Captain of the *Zaandam*. A skilled navigator and soothing leader, Captain Smit brings a quarter century of experience on the bridge of cruise ships around the world.

Wiwit Widarto
A dedicated worker and manager of the ship's laundry who has spent nearly thirty years away from his Indonesian family, laboring in the bowels of cruise ships to send money back home. Wiwit finds strength in his deep Christian faith.

Erin Montgomery
Sanitation officer aboard the *Zaandam*, Erin is among the first to identify and track a cluster of strange viral outbreaks on board the ship.

William Burke
Chief maritime officer for Carnival Corporation, Burke is a thirty-five-year veteran of the U.S. Navy. Now he's in the battle of his career.

Lance Hutton

After decades working as an educator in Missouri's public schools, Lance is ready for his lifelong dream—a visit with his wife to Machu Picchu, the lost Incan city hidden in the Andes.

Carl Zehner

A Vietnam vet and longtime white-water rafting adventurer from Nashville, Tennessee, Carl has enjoyed dozens of cruises. But this one is special: He's here to celebrate his fortieth wedding anniversary with his husband, Leo.

Leo Lindsay

After working in hospitals for years, Leo knows all the tricks and skills of a nurse. He's been on many cruises, but this one is the most special of all, to celebrate four decades with Carl.

Dr. Cindy Friedman

A scientist at the Centers for Disease Control and Prevention in Atlanta, Dr. Friedman's specialty is epidemics.

George Covrig

This burly and gregarious Romanian manager of shops aboard the *Zaandam*'s sister ship, the *Oosterdam*, soon volunteers for one of the most challenging jobs of his career.

Claudia Osiani

A psychologist from Argentina who is determined to celebrate her birthday at sea.

Anne Weggeman

Stressed to the max on her first cruise job, the young Dutch woman plans to quit once the *Zaandam* reaches dry land.

Amanda Bogen

The ship's bubbly twenty-seven-year-old entertainment host in charge of keeping her elderly guests busy with water-aerobics classes, trivia contests and other activities.

CHAPTER 1

CHOOSE FUN

MARCH 6, 2020

Quinquela Martín Cruise Ship Port,
Buenos Aires, Argentina

Wiwit Widarto walked down the gangway of the MS *Zaandam* and into the bustle of Buenos Aires, another twelve hours in the cruise ship's sweltering laundry behind him. He'd worked relentlessly, enduring all day on his feet in the bowels of the ship. In one marathon shift, Wiwit and his crew had cleaned dirty sheets, towels, and linens from the ship's 716 cabins, making way for a new cruise with a slew of fresh passengers—more than twelve hundred in all—from all over the world.

For a precious few hours, Wiwit was free. He walked along the dock, the 781-foot-long ship towering above, the navy blue hull topped by a glimmering white superstructure. With an oversized funnel and lights along the railings that twinkled against the darkening sky, its elegant silhouette evoked the golden era of transatlantic travel, that of the *Titanic*. Another couple of decks were set at or just above the waterline; it was in this cramped underbelly, with little natural light, where Wiwit worked, slept, and lived.

Wiwit joined up with six friends—fellow Indonesians and coworkers—all eager to explore the city's famous nightlife before embarking the next day on a monthlong voyage around the tip of South America. En route to dinner, their taxi wove around the city's leafy Parisian-inspired boulevards, and manicured squares. It was 10:00 p.m., early for *porteños*. The crowds were starting to parade by the tango bars, white-tablecloth restaurants, and baroque cafés with irresistible pastries displayed in glass cases as if they were jewels. Traffic crawled along streets lined with mansard-roofed neo-Parisian mansions, Art Deco apartment buildings, and quaint Tudor-style homes—built a century ago by waves of European immigrants. The city felt far removed from the ominous warnings about a deadly virus that had spread out of China, to Italy, then Spain and the rest of Europe, and now the United States. Argentina had registered perhaps a dozen cases and one death, hardly a blip on most people's radar.

Wiwit and his fellow coworkers settled in for dinner and chitchat. Life on the *Zaandam* was tribal. There were dozens of nationalities aboard, and they gathered to speak in their native tongues, prepare their traditional foods, and share communal prayers. Hundreds of citizens from Indonesia, the Philippines, and Thailand worked aboard the *Zaandam*, many employed in housekeeping and hotel services. They rarely had a free day on land. They were responsible for making the beds, cleaning the toilets, washing the linens, and responding to the summonses and whims of the passengers aboard the *Zaandam*. Throughout the day, the housekeeping staff checked each room, tidying up messes, folding towels into animal figures, all the time speaking English with the guests. But now, they could briefly forget about those duties. It was time for a burger at a bar in Palermo, one of the more elegant of four dozen neighborhoods in the sprawling city of fifteen million. This was their last weekend on land before more seven-day workweeks and the twelve- and often fourteen-hour shifts they were used to.

From their table, they looked out at the bars and restaurants packed around the square. Families strolled the well-lit streets, locking arms. Couples sipped wine at outdoor bistros; friends crowded together, all seeming to yell at once, gesturing wildly, enjoying a beautiful evening together.

A compact, balding man with closely cropped black hair and a deeply etched smile, Wiwit had worked on cruise ships for almost thirty of his fifty years. God's will and an evangelical Christian faith had guided him. On every cruise, he organized Bible-study groups for coworkers and was known for his mastery of applying the Word to the difficult life he and his fellow workers all led at sea. Lately, however, Wiwit was worried this volatile virus spreading from Wuhan, China, would find its way into his family's home in Batam, Indonesia. Now Wiwit was on the *Zaandam*, traveling to the end of the world, near Antarctica, but he worried about the medical care back in Batam. Would this disease strike down his wife? His two sons?

It was a rollicking, end-of-the-austral-summer weekend in Buenos Aires. On Saturday night, after the slew of new passengers had filled the *Zaandam*, the Backstreet Boys brought their hits to a packed open-air crowd on the Campo Argentino de Polo. A.J., Howie, Nick, Kevin, and Brian crooned, "When the cold air starts filling up my lungs!" and the largely female crowd echoed the chorus throughout: "My lungs ... Oh, I breathe." For the entire duration of the concert, thirty thousand fans were on their feet, screaming, singing, shrieking.

Across town, adjacent to a neighborhood of pastel-colored wooden shacks known as La Boca, an even larger crowd of 54,000 people crowded into the football stadium, La Bombonera, for a crucial match on the home turf of Boca Juniors. In Argentina, football is religion. A Boca win against Gimnasia that night would eliminate archrival River Plate from the championship. The crowd went wild during the pregame show. Maradona, the former Boca midfielder and Argentine national hero, limped slowly onto the field. The legendary U-shaped stadium vibrated as if rattled by an earthquake. Euphoric fans stomped their feet, launched fireworks, and unfurled massive banners in the stands. Holding court, Maradona reigned supreme, hugging and kissing player after player, like a priest giving his blessing. Maradona paused, then raised both arms to the crowd, beckoning them to scream louder, as he used to when he ruled this same pitch thirty years earlier. Boca honored Maradona's legacy and triumphed 1–0, taking the championship. Fans flooded the streets of Buenos Aires, waving flags, chanting victory songs, and mocking distraught River fans. As hundreds of travelers continued to board the *Zaandam*, promises of heightened medical checks didn't materialize. Some passengers were questioned about their travels. Many simply showed up from the United States, France, Italy, the United Kingdom, and Australia and walked aboard, few questions asked.

The *Zaandam* catered to seniors; more than three-quarters were over sixty-five years old. Many passengers were in their eighties. They'd all spent thousands of dollars for an exotic voyage to penguin colonies and glacier fields, and through the Strait of Magellan. Ten stories tall and the length of two football fields, the *Zaandam* promised elegance, but it was a little worn-out. This would be one of the last cruises before the ship's once-every-few-years maintenance overhaul. Holland America planned to send the *Zaandam* into dry dock not long after this cruise ended in Port Everglades, Florida. Welders, painters, and cleaners would come aboard, clambering through its crevices like worker ants in a frenetic mission to overhaul everything from the small infirmary to the sealed porthole windows in the cabins.

Passenger Lance Hutton noticed the *Zaandam* could use a face-lift as he boarded, but he didn't care. Cruising was comfortable, predictable, and educational. Just how he liked to travel. He'd been on eighteen cruises since retiring two decades earlier after a career as a teacher, principal, superintendent, and administrator of public schools in Missouri. He'd seen a lot of the world from the deck of a cruise ship. But there was one adventure he still craved, a hike up the Andes Mountains to Machu Picchu. Lance was a straightforward man. He'd lived in Missouri much of his life, mostly in small towns. But for reasons he couldn't explain even to himself, he couldn't shake the dream of visiting the shrouded Incan city, high above the Peruvian jungle. Six months earlier, he'd booked passage on the *Zaandam* with Sharon, his college sweetheart and wife of fifty-six years. They'd paid thousands extra for the excursion to Machu Picchu, and finally Lance Hutton was going to explore the famed hidden city.

Stocky, soft-spoken, with intense brown eyes and full head of hair that belied his age, Lance wasn't easily flustered. He'd mastered keeping his calm, carefully choosing his words, working through a problem before making a decision, acting resolutely and without hesitation so that his teachers and kids would follow. But he worried about Sharon, not because she was seventy-nine, just a year younger than he was. It was her lungs. Her bronchiectasis, a chronic respiratory condition, put her in the high-risk category for those susceptible to this strange new virus. It seemed to prey on people like her. But ten days before the *Zaandam* was set to embark, Holland America Line, which operated the *Zaandam*, made it clear to Lance that refunds were not an option. The cruise line sent him an email specifying that refunds were limited to customers with proof of direct contact with someone who had tested positive or who'd traveled to China. From what Lance understood, the preexisting medical condition that made Sharon more susceptible did not qualify them for a refund.

Lance had checked his email again before boarding the long flight to Argentina, but there were no new communications. Throwing away twenty thousand dollars felt too extravagant. Lance wasn't a rich man, never had been. He'd raised his family on an educator's salary. Sharon did secretarial work here and there. They'd practically built their own house and lived frugally. They couldn't bring themselves to toss away that kind of money. So they rationalized away the fear of the new disease, and the worries about Sharon's lungs. Aboard the *Zaandam*, they settled into their cabin on Dolphin Deck, the entire room only slightly bigger than a queen-size bed. If it were too dangerous, he told himself, Holland America would not have let them aboard. *Whatever is going to happen will happen,* he thought. *No sense worrying anymore.* It was a gamble—Lance knew that—and he wasn't a gambler. But it was too late to turn back.

Down the hall, Carl Zehner and Leonard Lindsay began to settle into their cabin, unpack their bags. Leo mentioned that check-in had been fast. He'd expected that heightened medical protocols would slow boarding. News broadcasts were awash with stories of cruise ship outbreaks. Two Holland America ships—the *Grand Princess* and the *Ruby Princess*—were suffering COVID-19 outbreaks off the Pacific coast of the United States and Sydney, Australia, respectively. Weeks earlier, the *Diamond Princess* had been hit hard in Japan, with at least nine passengers dead and hundreds infected. But on the *Zaandam*, in another hemisphere, there seemed to be little more of a medical screening than normal on a cruise, a short questionnaire, asking whether they'd had a cough or fever or recent contact with China. The only novelty he noticed was a quick temperature check.

Carl and Leo had been planning this cruise for a special occasion: their fortieth anniversary. Leo, a retired nurse, was concerned about boarding a cruise ship with a pandemic spreading. But Holland America had issued statements and sent emails, explaining all the care they were taking to prevent just such outbreaks. It felt like they were being encouraged to get on the ship, especially after the company awarded them four hundred dollars in ship credits. But Leo, a slightly portly man with a full head of dark hair, was a worrier by nature, especially when it came to health issues. Carl, a wiry, white-haired Eagle Scout and Vietnam War veteran, put Leo at ease, as always. They'd been on fifty cruises together, including a dozen on Holland America ships. The cruise line was their favorite and would take care of them, as usual. "We trusted them, because our outcomes have been good with Holland America," said Leo. "We felt like they had our safety and our health most in their minds."

Two decks above, Claudia Osiani sat in her cabin, looking out the window at a bulkhead and life raft as she sought to dismiss her anxieties. Claudia had worked three decades as a psychologist, and it was her job to analyze what was behind these feelings, but she couldn't pin it down. This cruise was a birthday present from her husband, Juan Henning. Aboard the *Zaandam*, in a few days, she would celebrate her sixty-fourth birthday. She couldn't bring herself to let that inner voice get in the way of enjoying the trip, much less cancel it. So Claudia did what a psychologist shouldn't do when it comes to feelings—she ignored them. *I won't tell Juan that I am worried,* she told herself.

On the five-hour drive to Buenos Aires from their home in Mar del Plata, they had discussed at length the recent deadly virus outbreaks on several cruise ships in other parts of the world. "This cruise is different; it will be packed with locals," they reassured each other. It made them feel safer. Juan had sacrificed deeply to provide Claudia this present. She loved him too much to let on that she was worried. They had been together for forty-two years and complemented each other. Claudia was a stickler for detail and liked to dress well, keep in shape, make sure her hair kept a blond hue and that her makeup was just right. She was the gregarious, rather emotional half of the marriage, prone to speaking her mind, making grand gestures. Juan, a soft-spoken accountant, was in many ways her opposite. His mother was an English immigrant; his father hailed from the Netherlands. But they'd made it work, raising three kids who'd already given them nine grandchildren. "We're going so far south," she told Juan in the car. "It's going to be a bunch of Argentines on that ship, maybe some Chileans."

They spotted the *Zaandam* as they arrived at the Port of Buenos Aires. Christened in May 2000, the Dutch-flagged *Zaandam* had the feel of an ocean liner of a bygone age. It was steeped in the 147-year history of the Holland America Line, born in an era of transatlantic passenger ship travel. Known as "the Spotless Line," Holland America was for decades the industry leader in service and style. As a sister company of the White Star Line, Holland America steamships were related to the *Titanic*.

As the couple boarded the ship, they were shocked. Almost none of the passengers came from Argentina or South America. Their hopes of cruising with people from places where COVID-19 hadn't yet taken hold were shattered. Aboard the *Zaandam* were 305 Americans, 247 Canadians, 229 UK citizens, 105 French, and 131 Australians. The passengers crowded around one another, leaning in, talking, hugging, laughing. No social-distancing protocols were visible. Claudia heard a cough, then another, and wanted to hide. "All those people were from where the pandemic was," she recalled. "It was kind of scary."

Donna Mann and Jorge Hill, her seventy-nine-year-old partner, were discussing just that as they settled into their cabin. "Wasn't that strange," Donna commented. She was sure Holland America had warned in an email that it would be examining every passenger's passport to see where each person had traveled. COVID-19 was spreading massively in China and more recently in Italy. Surely, they would want to flag people who had been to those places recently, at least for a tougher medical screening. "Yes," Jorge replied. "They didn't even go through the pages."

The couple had worried about COVID-19, even thought about canceling the trip. Jorge tracked the *Zaandam* online, and he was relieved to see the ship had been in South America since autumn. Together, they watched the news, and prior to leaving their home in California, they noted with calm that just one COVID-19 case had been logged in Brazil, and it was someone who had traveled through Italy. But what swayed them was Dr. Anthony Fauci, the director of the National Institute of Allergy and Infectious Diseases, located in Bethesda, Maryland. He'd been their voice of reason since this epidemic began. Donna had known about him since the 1980s, when he led the national response to fight HIV. Shortly before they embarked, they caught snippets of interviews in which Fauci seemed to say that international travel was "safe." But the lack of much real scrutiny while boarding rankled Donna. No one had even checked her temperature. Donna and Jorge didn't know that temperature checks were not mandatory aboard the Holland America fleet until March 15, more than a full week later.

MARCH 8, 8:00 A.M.
Buenos Aires, Argentina, Aboard the Zaandam

The main crew hallway on B Deck buzzed with activity. Workers jokingly dubbed it "I-95," after the interstate highway. At the stern end of the corridor that ran the length of B Deck, Wiwit Widarto was at his post inside the laundry operations center, working amid the whir of the huge washers and dryers. He had everyone coming at him—typical for the beginning of a cruise. The housekeeping staff needed linen napkins, tablecloths, and perfectly pressed sheets by the hundreds.

The laundry operation was like the crowded floor of an old-world factory. Sixteen people moved amid a patchwork of windowless rooms crammed with oversized washers, dryers, and pressers. Next door, three tailors were mending a stack of crew uniforms. Wiwit oversaw it all. He'd first worked for Holland America when he was barely twenty years old. His job included free room and board, so expenses were limited. Every month, Wiwit sent roughly fourteen hundred dollars to his family. This was far more than he could save working at a hotel or restaurant back in Indonesia. It was a grueling schedule. Wiwit worked seven days a week; he was always moving. There were few days off during his contracts, which typically ran from six to ten months.

Wiwit missed many Christmases with the family because of his job. When he returned home, sometimes it was only for a month; then he would head back to join the next ship. He'd first joined the cruise industry to recoup the costs of his wedding, sending home a bit less than five hundred dollars a month. "This job is temporary", he told his young wife. But work opportunities in Indonesia were limited.

After leaving the cruise ship industry in order to work closer to home, Wiwit spent two years in Indonesia. Then he returned to sea, this time to fund the down payment on the family home. Over the years—and then decades—there were always reasons to return to sea, to continue the sacrifice, to pay for a better life for his family. Wiwit rarely complained. He believed that this is where God wanted him to be. That's what he told the Bible-study group when they met Sunday evenings aboard the ship, after everyone was done with their shifts.

A year earlier, in 2019, Wiwit received a major promotion to supervisor and was running the laundry. He could now work on a six-month contract. In June, he could go home to Batam, Indonesia, across the strait from Singapore. He wanted to spend as much time as possible with Anny, his wife. Working ships, Wiwit had missed so much. Anny had raised their two sons, Matthew and Bryan, often alone. The previous July, when Wiwit celebrated his fiftieth birthday, he'd promised Anny that he'd retire soon. Then he would be home to stay. They could open the restaurant they had long dreamed about. "Just a couple of years," he told Anny, "and it will all be different."

But now Wiwit was busy getting his crew to finish dealing with the carts filled with dirty linens. They had to get through them all, and fast. Complaining wasn't an option, and besides, they all knew that this is how cruise ships operated.

Worldwide, nearly 200,000 men and women kept these massive floating hotels running. On the Holland America Line, two-thirds hailed from Indonesia, the Philippines, and Thailand. On the *Zaandam*, most of the six hundred employees worked, ate, drank, and slept on A Deck and B Deck, an unseen village out of sight of any passenger and not mentioned in any glossy brochure. Most workers bunked two to a cabin in windowless spaces and shared a bathroom among four mates. They ate in the crew mess, mid-ship on A Deck, drank in the adjacent crew bar. They made it up to the upper decks only when passengers needed them.

The captain, his top officers, and those who ran the food, beverage, entertainment, hotel, and medical operations worked and lived on the upper decks. Most of these men and women were grouped by nationality. The Dutch tended to run the bridge. The Europeans and Americans ran the entertainment side of the operation. Medical staff came from South Africa. Many of these employees were privy to benefits, including individual cabins with windows, private bathrooms, and, in some cases, open-air balconies. They had their own bar and minimal restrictions on mixing it up with the passengers.

None of that bothered Wiwit. What he did worry about was this virus. He had talked about it with Anny when she texted and said she was concerned about his safety on the ship. "Don't worry," he'd assured her before the cruise began. "We are on the other side of the world from all that. The cruise line says we are fine." Wiwit had reason to be concerned. But for now, he didn't have time to dwell on that. Work called.

Erin Montgomery sat inside her small office on Lower Promenade Deck, reviewing the sanitation protocols one more time. There were so many details. Were the refrigerators clean? Was the pool sterilized? Erin understood the dangers of viral transmission in such a high-density environment.

Erin had worked cruise ships for three years. A divorced mother of five, she had gone through a lot to get there. She started working in restaurants at fifteen, moving to teaching culinary arts in California so that she'd have more time to raise her kids. When her youngest daughter finished school, Erin sought adventure, and scored a job producing and hosting the shipboard version of PBS's *America's Test Kitchen* cooking show. Erin had cooked on nine Holland America ships and loved it. Her blond hair, bright blue eyes, and contagious laugh made Erin seem younger than her fifty-six years. She was funny, forceful, and full of confidence, which helped when she had to cook and perform for hundreds of passengers simultaneously, day in and day out. Erin loved dressing in her chef's whites, cooking for the camera, making people happy. But one year earlier, she had heard about a newly created job: sanitation officer.

This was a position born out of a 2016 criminal case that federal prosecutors had successfully brought against Holland America's Princess Cruises (as well as its parent company, Carnival Corporation), for years of dumping oily wastewater from its ships into U.S. waters and the pristine seas around the Bahamas. Carnival sought to conceal the pollution from federal regulators, resulting in a forty-million-dollar criminal penalty and a five-year term of probation. That massive fine was followed in 2019 by an additional twenty-million-dollar criminal penalty after the company was found guilty of violating the terms of the probation by falsifying ships' logs and "illegally discharging plastic mixed with food waste in Bahamian waters." Court-ordered oversight determined that Carnival held "a culture that seeks to minimize or avoid information that is negative, uncomfortable, or threatening to the Company, including to top leadership (i.e., the Board of Directors, C-Suite executives, and Brand Presidents/CEOs)."

In order to remedy the repeated lawbreaking, the monitor declared that "Top [Carnival] leadership must own its role in having historically fostered a culture that minimizes or avoids difficult information." Despite the clear instructions, Carnival continued to run foul of the law. The court-appointed monitor declared that the company held "a culture of excess frugality."

During the multiyear probation, Carnival CEO Micky Arison was repeatedly brought before federal judge Patricia Seitz, who, after multiple probation violations, vented her frustration in open court. "But, Mr. Arison, this company—this is not the first criminal proceeding that this company has gone through. It's not the second. It's not the third. And you have been at the helm of the company throughout. I almost feel like I'm talking with a chronic drug addict in that they come in and they are all remorseful, they say the right things, but it doesn't translate into walking the walk."

Seventy-two ships from the Carnival Cruise Line, Princess Cruises, and Holland America Line were placed under federal court monitoring to literally clean up their act, and they needed employees to police what was being dumped into the sea, especially from the kitchens. Erin liked the job description because she could do her part to protect the oceans and keep people healthy.

In January 2020, Holland America sent Erin to a sanitation course in Miami run by the Centers for Disease Control and Prevention (CDC). She was taught the sanitation regulations, including protocols to combat disease outbreaks. With a population density akin to a prison, cruise ships were prime breeding grounds for contagious diseases, sometimes foodborne and in other cases spread from person to person. Over the years, Holland America had many outbreaks, and the *Zaandam* was not immune.

From 2006 to 2019, the ship reported five disease outbreaks, an unusually high number.

When Erin boarded the *Zaandam* in early February 2020, she was assigned to supervise two dozen dishwashers and garbage workers spread among the ship's seven kitchens. They worked in a variety of eateries, ranging from the modest crew galley on A Deck to the kitchen inside Pinnacle Grill, the ship's high-end restaurant. The sanitation officer's job was a demanding one. Erin was in charge of coordinating numerous health and safety protocols and assuring a web of complex systems worked to perfection as the ship cruised some of the most remote places on Earth.

In the previous month, the *Zaandam* had made runs to Antarctica, through the Strait of Magellan, to the far reaches of the South Atlantic, to the Falkland Islands and beyond. Erin was confident that they'd kept the virus off this ship, and not because of some romantic trust that they were too far from the epidemic. There'd been no known cases of anything remotely like the virus, and had there been evidence, Erin Montgomery, sanitation officer, would have been among the first to know. Part of her job was to assure medical records were precise, which included strict rules for reporting any kinds of flulike illnesses. Failure to do so would expose the cruise lines to huge fines and a lot of heat from the CDC. Erin's job was to ensure that didn't happen.

Her day, so far, had been overflowing with unpleasant tasks: She'd checked the nasty grease traps, the food-waste grinders, and the rat guards—devices designed to keep vermin from climbing up the lines to get on (or off) the ship during port calls.

Awaiting the final preparations for embarking, Erin relaxed at the Lido Deck dining area, imagining what she was going to eat for dinner. She'd gone over everything in her head, time and time again. They'd ratcheted up the protocols for disinfecting, assigning frequent wipe-downs of surfaces, including elevator buttons, and other simple tasks like that. They'd scavenged Plexiglas sheets to install along the buffet tables and assigned more stewards to serve food, as a precaution against any stray germs.

A friendly French woman, alone and in her seventies, asked if she could join Erin for dinner. The passengers were exploring their new world, and they often liked to meet the officers. As they chatted, the woman mentioned to Erin that she was feeling a little under the weather. Had she picked up a bug on the long flight from France to Argentina? A man sitting nearby on the airplane, she mentioned, had coughed nonstop during the flight. After everything they'd done on board, Erin felt confident the *Zaandam* was as protected as it could be from any virus.

Erin knew a disease outbreak when she saw one, and it wasn't going to happen on her watch.

Seattle, Washington

As the *Zaandam* prepared to leave Buenos Aires, the virus was still seen as a problem for the Chinese, the Italians, and the Spaniards. Global hot spots were half a world away from the *Zaandam*, or at least that was the opinion of Orlando Ashford, president of the Holland America Line.

Ashford was no mariner. He held decades of experience in human resources and management consulting when he was tapped to lead Holland America by Carnival CEO Arnold Donald in late 2014. Eternally smiling, Ashford knew how to talk the corporate language. He'd led Holland America through a period of astounding growth. Fiscal year 2019, with twenty billion dollars in revenue and three billion dollars in earnings, was the most profitable year ever for Carnival, and Holland America Line was a key part. Global passenger numbers had tripled, from ten million people cruising in 2004 to thirty million in 2019. Not only was cruising becoming ever more popular but a growing club of cruisers were deeply loyal to the experience, the ships, and even specific crew members. Aboard the ship, passengers and crew often spoke about how it felt like "a big family."

Ashford understood these ships were floating resorts, and a fantasy space where hospitality reigned supreme. In the days leading up to the sailing of the *Zaandam*, his staff had checked with the ports, the U.S. government, the CDC. No one was prohibiting the ship from setting off. In fact, few places on Earth felt safer than South America. "We're trying to protect and deliver a wonderful guest experience, a wonderful vacation experience. That's what this business is engineered to do," he explained to *Bloomberg Businessweek*. The government wasn't ordering him not to sail, the ports were buzzing, and the passengers arrived in droves. The *Zaandam* would set sail, as planned, the afternoon of March 8. "We felt like we could deliver a great guest experience," Ashford proclaimed.

Meanwhile, another Carnival executive, Dr. Grant Tarling, was working overtime from his offices onshore. As chief medical officer for Holland America owner Carnival Corp., he'd been dealing with severe outbreaks for over a month. At least twenty-one passengers were dead or dying from COVID-19 on Carnival ships. Hundreds more had been infected. One of the deadliest outbreaks had been on the *Diamond Princess*, in January in Japan, but there were others, as well.

To help passengers better understand the risks, Dr. Tarling delivered updates in cheery three- to five-minute videos that seemed aimed at easing fears of COVID-19 on a cruise. "Given recent events and general inquiries we have received about travelers' health," said Dr. Tarling, looking into the camera in one video released in late February, a map of the world behind him, "you may want to bring your own thermometer." It sounded like an offhand remark, devoid of any urgency. The lead M.D. also mimicked the correct position to sneeze, bringing his bent arm close to his nose. "If you cough or sneeze, do it into a tissue or your bent elbow." His third piece of advice was, "Buy travel insurance." The doctor suggested passengers read the insurance coverage closely to "make sure it is the kind 'cancel for any reason' and covers many unexpected travel situations, such as medical care and evacuation."

Washington, D.C.

Five thousand miles north of the *Zaandam*, in the West Wing of the White House, Olivia Troye sat in her office and pulled up a spreadsheet. Since May 2018, Olivia had worked as a homeland security and counterterrorism adviser to Vice President Mike Pence, briefing him about bombings, natural disasters, and school shootings. Beginning in January 2020, COVID-19 outbreaks on cruise ships began to show up on her radar. And since early February, when President Trump placed Pence in charge of the White House Coronavirus Task Force, cruise ship outbreaks and how to deal with them became a growing part of Olivia's day-to-day work. So many ships kept reporting cases that the White House needed a spreadsheet to keep track of them all. Olivia, a forty-three-year-old brunette with intense brown eyes and a passion for government service, felt overwhelmed with the logistics of bringing each and every one of these massive ships to port. Her boss also seemed swamped, and that was unnerving to her, considering he was vice president of the United States.

But for a few hours in early March, Olivia needed to help the veep focus on the latest outbreak on the *Grand Princess*, nearing San Francisco Bay. The vice president was just back from Port Everglades, a cruise ship hub north of Miami, where he'd met with cruise line CEOs and Florida political leaders, including Republican governor Ron DeSantis. The cruise lines had been lobbying the White House to allow them to continue operating, usually calling Pence, which meant the calls went through Olivia first. The ongoing cruise ship outbreaks had set the industry on the edge of a catastrophic financial abyss that no one could have imagined even a few weeks earlier. Epidemiologists and public health experts at the CDC were pressing to suspend cruises—all of them. The CDC, however, was under intense political pressure to hold off making an announcement until *after* the vice president's meetings, but it had the legal orders ready to go, and the cruise lines were terrified. Without swift help from Pence, they knew that soon no one would be permitted to board a ship and the industry would be plunged into an unprecedented financial crisis.

Olivia wrote the talking points for Pence, expressing the administration's unwavering support for cruising; she'd hoped Pence would like them. Watching the vice president live on CNN, she received her answer. Pence walked into a conference room at the port, flanked by politicians and government brass. As the cameras rolled, he emphasized that the White House was backing the cruise industry. "American people value our cruise line industry. It brings great joy and great entertainment value for Americans," Pence declared. "We want to ensure Americans can continue to enjoy the opportunities of the cruise line industry."

Buenos Aires

Late afternoon on March 8, after all passengers and final provisions were brought aboard the *Zaandam*, Claudia Osiani strolled Promenade Deck. Clouds were starting to roll across the skies above Buenos Aires, and droves of passengers lined the railings to catch a last glimpse of the magnificent city laid out below. But Claudia was trying to quash the worries that had stalked her even before this cruise began. Like all passengers, she'd filled out the cursory five-question health survey when boarding. She saw no mention of COVID-19, and despite repeated company promises to screen passengers during enhanced boarding procedures, no one had stopped her or Juan to monitor their temperatures. Maybe the virus was another of those terrestrial problems everyone could leave behind as they walked up the gangway and were greeted with trays of champagne and fine wine, a twenty-two-foot-high pipe organ in the atrium, and a soundtrack of classic rock tunes. Maybe she was overthinking the risks.

On the *Zaandam*'s high-tech bridge, Captain Ane Smit, a twenty-five-year veteran of Holland America with a soothing voice that imbued a sense of calm and security, went over his final preparations for a challenging route through some of the world's most notoriously rough waters. His command center was loaded with electronic maps, sonar, depth finders, multiple GPS systems, and panels lined with buttons, switches, and thruster and throttle controls. Spread across several consoles, there were endless streams of data sorting out the complex operations aboard the ship.

In the medical center was Dr. Warren Hall, a South African obstetrician and the ship's chief medical officer. They'd filled out their "formularies," listing the medicines and medical supplies they needed for the voyage ahead, based on a master list of inventories drawn up by Holland America's onshore medical department. Most of the cases on the Holland America ships were cardiac or trauma. Slips and falls led to frequently painful but rarely grave injuries, which was fortunate, given that the medical center on the ship was unable to deliver long-term intensive care but rather was designed more like a basic emergency room with the ability to stabilize patients in the few hours it usually took to reach port and, soon after, a proper hospital. On the rare occasion when the ship was more than twenty-four hours from port—near the Antarctic Peninsula, for example—Dr. Hall had a stock of emergency oxygen tanks to cover those crucial few hours.

Dr. Hall had one other physician aboard, Dr. Sonja Hofmann, a South African who was lead doctor for the crew. Dr. Hall would focus on guests. Between them, they shared four nurses to care for the 1,243 passengers and 586 crew members. The *Zaandam* carried a meager health detachment, roughly one medical provider for every three hundred people aboard the ship. The casino staffing was far more generous, with eighteen full-time employees, but in a way it all made sense. Passengers tended to flock to the casino and avoided the med center, where even a simple visit might run into the hundreds of dollars in extra charges.

One key medical item wasn't stocked: tests for COVID-19. The corporate office had determined that tests were hard to get (and unreliable). There were a few boxes of surgical masks and a dozen oxygen tanks, enough to run the ship's sole ventilator for about five days. The cruise line was betting that COVID-19 tests wouldn't be necessary. "Based on the information we had, based on the commitments that we had from the ports, and based on the guests' desire to go," Ashford would later explain, "we had every expectation to be able to go around South America."

Claudia Osiani and Juan Henning were dubious about their safety aboard the ship once they saw the slew of foreigners carousing and congregating. They immediately decided they would try their best to steer clear of the other guests on this trip. The couple was booked only on the first leg of the cruise, so in just thirteen days they would get off the *Zaandam* in Chile and take a ninety-minute flight home to Argentina. They decided to self-isolate to the degree possible aboard a cruise ship.

Down in the holds of the *Zaandam*, the quartermasters went over the stores for the long trip. It takes army-like logistics to keep a cruise ship supplied. Most of the nonperishable goods stacked in the *Zaandam*'s holds had been gathered months earlier at the cruise line's warehouse in Miami, where supplies were packed into containers and shipped to Chile. The result was packaged in the holds in neat shrink-wrapped pallets, which were lashed down to prevent spillage during the inevitable rough seas. The bosun's mates had been busy over the last two days in port, loading enough fresh produce and meats from the local markets for the first two-week leg of the cruise. To feed all passengers and crew on a ship like the *Zaandam* would typically require 130,000 pounds of vegetables, 40,000 eggs, 20,000 steaks, 16,000 cans of beer and soda, and hundreds of cases of wine. They'd topped off the *Zaandam*'s massive tanks at the port with hundreds of tons of diesel and bunker fuel, enough to keep it running even longer. In the overpriced gift shops, clerks were tallying the big-ticket items: Hermès scarfs, Calvin Klein suits, and twenty-two pounds of diamond jewelry worth almost a million dollars. With plans to restock fresh produce, fuel, and water along the route, these supplies would keep the ship running until it reached San Antonio, the Chilean port where the first leg of the cruise would conclude. The *Zaandam* was ready to set sail.

In addition to the carefully itemized manifest items, one extra traveler was aboard the ship. The crew was unaware of its presence. It was never cataloged or ordered and had not purchased a ticket. This stowaway, likely hiding in the lungs of a passenger or perhaps a crew member, was microscopic in size yet capable of overwhelming this gargantuan ship. As the *Zaandam* prepared to leave Buenos Aires, Holland America executives told the world that the *Zaandam* was immune to such threats.

CHAPTER 2

MYSTERIOUS STOWAWAY

MARCH 8, 5:32 P.M.

Río de la Plata, off Buenos Aires

A few minutes before dinner was served in the ship's dining rooms, Captain Ane Smit handed over command of the *Zaandam* to the local harbor pilot. It was a constant in every major port: No cruise ship went in or out without a certified local harbor pilot aboard who knew the secrets of winds, currents, and shipping patterns. In Buenos Aires, Roberto Fuchs was the one. It was Smit's job to keep quiet and follow orders. "Pilot on the bridge," Fuchs announced, formalizing the command handover as he scanned the path through the broad windows that framed the *Zaandam*'s bridge.

A bank of light clouds, broken by muted rays of the waning late-summer sun, bathed the seemingly endless Buenos Aires skyline in a deep pewter patina. Scattered light showers were falling farther out, in the great expanse of the world's widest river, the Río de la Plata. But conditions overall were excellent.

Fuchs ordered into action the two tugboats that were lashed by steel cables to the *Zaandam*—one port and one starboard. From the bridge, it was a hundred feet down to the waterline, where dockworkers cast off the mooring lines and the 61,396-ton ship pulled free of land. Aided by two propulsion engines and the power of the tugs, the *Zaandam* eased ahead at three knots. It towered high above pedestrians ambling along the piers.

Within minutes, it was making twelve knots in the turgid, ocean-like river, headed northeast toward Uruguay.

The *Zaandam* was already a buzzing little world that included ten decks, eight bars, two pools, a casino, a mini tennis court, an art gallery, a library, and a performance hall with a capacity for five hundred. In the privacy of their cabins, dancers stretched, magicians rehearsed, guitarists tuned instruments, members of an a cappella choir belted out songs, and a team of masseuses was busy kneading away knots from that stressful life on shore. Few passengers were monitoring the news channels that would have alerted them that forty-eight minutes before the *Zaandam*'s departure, the U.S. State Department had posted a warning about COVID-19 that was as unprecedented as it was unambiguous: "American citizens, especially with underlying conditions, should not travel by cruise ship." Aboard the ship, the musicians were headed to the stage.

With a ratio of one crew member for every two passengers, the *Zaandam* was a promise to pamper. Passengers booked travel for a minimum of fourteen days, with many staying on for a full month. The ship catered to what cruise booking agencies dubbed "a mature audience," which meant many grandparents and couples in their sixties or seventies, well into retirement, many of whom planned to celebrate a special anniversary or a gentle adventure.

A chartered jet from Paris made the fourteen-hour flight, allowing one hundred French retirees to experience South America's wild southern lands while sipping at wineries and imbibing local culture. This was no Caribbean island-hopping bacchanal cruise. There were educational lectures led by experts, who described the fjords, glaciers, and wildlife appearing magically as the ship sailed through some of the most exotic settings on Earth.

As the harbor pilot guided the *Zaandam* through the treacherous currents of the Río de la Plata, its speed approaching twenty knots, a clutch of guests gathered poolside on Lido Deck for a tradition: the departure cocktail. White-gloved waiters filled glasses with sparkling wine. Hors d'oeuvres circulated on plates decorated with fresh flowers. There were people from dozens of nations aboard, and the mix was energizing. Conversation flowed easily; laughter abounded. There was a feeling they were all on a collective adventure. This would be the chance to walk the Falkland Island battlefields, where, in 1982, Margaret "Iron Lady" Thatcher counterattacked Argentine dictator Gen. Leopoldo Galtieri as the UK and Argentina battled over the clutch of sheep-infested islands.

Farther south, they would navigate the Strait of Magellan and the Beagle Channel, following Darwin's route, and then cruise up the west coast of South America to relive the excitement of Hiram Bingham's 1911 discovery of Machu Picchu, high in the Peruvian Andes. The passage through the Panama Canal was always memorable, and from there it was a lovely sun-drenched finale to Florida. This cruise aboard the *Zaandam* had been receiving positive reviews and had pleased guests by the thousands for years.

This South American route offered glimpses of Eden for nature lovers. Navigating south, the *Zaandam* would encounter striped dolphins, humpback whales, pods of orcas, and penguin rookeries. Massive icebergs calved off the glaciers, and sooty albatrosses with seven-foot wings would draft upon the winds flowing off the ship's broad wake. Wine tasting along the route offered a sampling of South America's finest grapes, including Chile's smoky Carménère and Argentina's silky Malbec. Bookworms would be inspired by the same lands in mythical Patagonia that writers Bruce Chatwin and Paul Theroux had explored, then exalted. Along the rocky coastline of central Chile, they could tour Pablo Neruda's remote hideaway, where between visits from his *amante*, the Chilean poet could be found at his desk facing the crashing Pacific surf. As the *Zaandam* left Río de la Plata and prepared to head out to the South Atlantic, the passengers aboard the *Zaandam* were certain they would soon escape drudgery, routines, and the day-to-day normalcy of life on land. It was to be, everyone agreed, a memorable cruise and an unforgettable trip.

*

Amanda Bogen loved her role as entertainment host aboard the *Zaandam*. Athletic, full of verve and the excitement of being twenty-seven years young, Amanda had worked a dozen jobs on cruise liners. Her role on this ship was keeping her passengers busy. As fitness instructor on Lido Deck, she drew crowds in the open-air pool with her water-aerobics classes, usually held after lunch but before the evening winds whisked across the deck. Amanda was adept at tailoring her routines to the abilities of the guests, be it an eighteen-year-old slacker or a spry eighty-year-old grandpa. By the end of her forty-minute classes, she had her charges exhausted, half from exercise and half from laughter. During the evenings, she became Amanda the Trivia Queen as she continued working inside the Crow's Nest bar, running the twice-nightly competitions with questions so complicated that guests regularly surrendered and pleaded for a clue. Funny and friendly, she ran the show with a ringmaster's finesse.

Amanda understood that many of the guests (as Holland America trained its employees to call passengers) boarding in Buenos Aires were repeat cruisers. They understood the *Zaandam* vibe, and what to expect. This was the generation that had come of age with Aerosmith, Led Zeppelin, and, if they were older, Jimi Hendrix. With a seventies rock 'n' roll theme, the *Zaandam*'s wood-paneled walls featured guitars used by Iggy Pop and one signed by members of the Rolling Stones. Where else could passengers flirt and kiss in front of a display case holding Bill Clinton's saxophone?

Every night at sea, the crew of the *Zaandam* presented an entertainment smorgasbord. Dance troupes prepared for energetic performances every evening. The intense routines led to frequent injuries. On the previous cruise, a broken ankle had forced one dance troupe to re-choreograph entire scenes overnight. Despite the hectic schedules, there were also moments for the crew to organize their own impromptu performances, like the nights Amanda took over as DJ at the crew bar to mix it up.

A seven-man production crew from the Philippines kept the shows running. These pros rigged the equipment to hold fast during roaring storms. They could dramatically silhouette a dancer with a perfect spotlight, even during intense rocking of the ship caused by massive swells. They could reconfigure the stage from a venue for a cello concerto to that for a magic show in twenty minutes. And they knew to mute the audio instantly if Captain Smit needed to broadcast an urgent announcement over the shipwide intercom.

The *Zaandam* was also a stage for guests, officers, and crew to shed landlubber life. A strange phenomenon occurred when people walked up the ship's gangway. Going out to sea provoked a flowering of personality, an alternative existence, a chance to temporarily redefine the contours of expectations, if not reinvent oneself completely and slip into a new personality. "There are parties at night, with these beautiful women that show up, and they're not women at all—but men you work with every day," said Erin, the sanitation officer, laughing in admiration as she described drag queens, whom she called "wild." Veteran crew members knew the tradition of married officers literally taking off their wedding rings as they boarded the ship. It seemed many cheated. To those crew members looking for it, the *Zaandam* upheld the cruise ship cliché of "more sex than in college dorms."

Aboard the *Zaandam*, Amanda felt she was part of a tight community. At times, she called it her family. She thrived within the bonds forged among those who work on ships. Life at sea had an intensity not often found on land.

In an instant, a ship might suddenly pitch, roll, and even sink, and to survive, everyone was obliged to work together. Teamwork wasn't a concept, but a way of life.

In the hundred years since the *Titanic* disaster, passenger safety, navigation technology, and lifeboat procedures had vastly improved. Yet aboard the *Zaandam*, as on any other cruise ship, evacuation drills, fire alarms, and warning sirens remained a constant. Warning tones regularly shattered the airwaves as yet another safety exercise commenced. Though Amanda had heard the alarms a hundred times, it always felt like a reminder to look around, to realize that everything was moving, everything was in flux—the wind, the weather, the sea, even the sense of time. Despite the often grueling hours, she had to admit that life on a cruise ship was a constant rush of adrenaline because of all the new experiences, all the new surprises.

As the *Zaandam* guests settled into their cabins, the medical crew and safety officers prepared for contingencies ranging from seasickness to suicidal tendencies. Occasionally, stressed guests would explode (alcohol being the most common trigger) and security officers were called in to calm the waters. "Every ship has a brig. If anything happens, that's where they have to lock people up. Ours is a padded blue room," Amanda explained as she mused about past "incidents" aboard the *Zaandam*. "Ships have everything you can think of," she continued. "It's crazy. Every ship has a morgue. . . Ours is the same room where they keep the fresh flowers."

MARCH 9, 5:33 A.M.
Montevideo, Uruguay

As the morning sun prepared to light up the port of Montevideo, the *Zaandam* came to the docks. The journey across the coffee-colored Río de la Plata had been brief. So, too, this stop in Uruguay. The passengers would have only a few hours before the *Zaandam* headed back out to sea, and most of the crew would not disembark. Erin Montgomery was among the lucky ones scheduled to leave, and she couldn't wait to get off the ship. She hadn't stepped foot on land since her contract began on the *Zaandam* five weeks earlier. Erin was pretty sure she was the first woman at Holland America to hold the title sanitation officer, so she felt a continual obligation to excel. Those self-imposed standards meant she worked nonstop, all to demonstrate that she—and any equally qualified woman—could handle the workload. Erin hadn't allowed herself a moment to relax, until now.

The stop in Montevideo included an excursion for passengers to visit a historic Uruguayan winery twenty-five miles outside the city, but first Holland America had arranged a sneak peek for a select group of crew members. As a manager, Erin needed to be there. New staff had just been rotated in for this cruise, and corporate tradition required a "relaxed" outing to kindle a spirit of camaraderie and teamwork. The new crew members needed an opportunity to get to know one another, to work out any kinks.

A cruise ship was no ordinary workplace. A thousand things could go wrong; colleagues had to trust the person next to them, sometimes with their lives. A few hours of frolicking around a winery could go a long way toward breaking down prejudices and cultural barriers. Erin understood all this. She knew this cruise would be an exhausting month, probably without a real break; most likely, she'd be working seven days a week. A little wine wasn't a bad idea, she concurred as the bus pulled into Establecimiento Juanicó, a three-hundred-acre vineyard that dated to the early 1800s.

There were thirty-three crew members from various areas of the ship sitting on the bus, including some of Erin's staff. Everyone seemed eager for the wine tasting to commence. But first, they endured the obligatory tour, visiting the wine-making plant, exploring the dark cellar with its arched stone ceilings. As they began the wine tasting, another bus pulled up. Twenty-four passengers stepped off. For years, Holland America had been sending busloads of customers to this vineyard for the $184-per-person excursion. The owners laid out an impressive selection to taste, starting with their top-of-the-line Atlántico Sur Reserve, a sauvignon blanc, followed by a dry red made from Tannat, the national grape of Uruguay. As Erin sipped her glass of Tannat, the passengers wandered in, checking out the tasting area before heading out on their own tour.

Among the crowd were Donna Moran and Jorge Hill. They were looking forward to this excursion, to take in the country air, smell the *terroir*. The grape harvest had ended, and the 2020 wine was beginning to age in giant tanks, some in oak casks. By the time Donna and Jorge returned from the tour, Erin and the rest of the crew were heading out. They had a ship to run and couldn't stay for the far longer lunch offerings. Establecimiento Juanicó offered a well-rehearsed show, especially the barbecue lunch. All that meat, expertly grilled over a huge wood-fed fire, was delicious. Uruguayan beef is legendary, and the *colita de cuadril* steaks and *matambre* sausages kept coming. A sensual tango demonstration followed. But for Jorge and Donna, the conversation was even more entertaining.

Donna had befriended a gregarious American from Florida. She laughed as the man held court at the table, passing meat to everyone, boasting about his exploits. Single, in his early sixties, and brash, he was clearly on the make. He publicly outlined his plan to hunt for a partner on this shipload of seniors. Donna found it amusing, watching him showcase his adventures. But one story stuck out, especially later. "I just got off a cruise ship in China," he boasted between refills of Tannat. Donna and Jorge looked at each other, hesitating to pass judgment, not making much out of it. Later, Donna would think often about this man from Florida and his trip to China and the fact that all their food had passed through his hands as he bellowed out his stories.

MARCH 10, 10:03 A.M.
South Atlantic, 126 Miles Southeast of Montevideo

The following morning, cruising in the open Atlantic Ocean for a first full day at sea, the *Zaandam* steered south toward the Falkland Islands, vapor trailing from her single smokestack.

Carl and Leo headed to the card room, on Lido Deck. The bridge setup was nothing special, just a cordoned-off section of an events room with a few tables, coffee and cookies off to one side. But this was what they lived for on cruises, and they arrived early. The couple had been playing bridge at sea for years. The games were part of their daily cruise routine, and they usually met players who'd hang out with them for the duration of the journey. The best bridge games were found on Holland America's ships, probably because they attracted the type of older folks who still played.

As soon as they walked in, Leo noticed a curious scene unfolding. A man in his sixties was waiting, rather impatiently, to play. A far younger, vivacious woman at his side was giggling. What an odd couple, Leo thought, a man of his age with a woman so young. Leo was intrigued, and, more important, he wanted to play, so he and Carl each took a seat. The man was a character, brash and funny. Clearly, this Swedish gentleman was having a good time showing off his young girlfriend. But after a few hands, he began coughing. It was subtle at first. He brought out a soiled cloth when he coughed, then stuffed it back in his pocket. Leo was aghast; he imagined all the germs festering on that handkerchief. The man's hacking worsened as time went by, and Leo felt like he had to say something.

"You know," he said rather diplomatically, "that seems like a pretty bad cough."

"Oh, I got it on the airplane," the Swede replied nonchalantly. "I always get a cough on the airplane; it's from the air-conditioning."

"Oh. Well, can I get you a glass of water?" asked Leo. Yet he knew, drawing on his years as a nurse, that wouldn't help much. *That cough,* he thought, *it isn't going away anytime soon.*

In the evening, hundreds of guests headed to Mainstage, the ship's theater. It was time for the Welcome Gala, a signature social event on every Holland America cruise. The official capacity was five hundred, but by the time the show kicked off around 7:00 p.m., the crowd was standing room only and the cocktail tables were crowded with wineglasses and champagne flutes.

Big-band show tunes warmed up the crowd, followed by a Copacabana-style dance revue. Then Captain Smit walked in, smartly dressed in his Holland America officer's uniform with his four-star rank marked on the jacket cuffs and repeated on the epaulets gilding his shoulders. Smit had earned each of his four stripes by rising up the Holland America ranks: cadet, fourth officer, third officer, first officer, staff captain, and, finally, captain. He'd worked for Holland America his entire career, making captain by demonstrating the aplomb, nautical skill, leadership, and coolness under pressure that Holland America demanded from its top officers. Entering the theater, Smit had all present raise their flutes of champagne. He proposed a toast: a communal cheer for the exotic sights and experiences that lay ahead on the journey.

After the Welcome Gala wound down, the passengers explored the decks, finding their favorite spots to wonder at the immensity of the dark ocean, watch the ship's wake on the expansive fantail, or marvel at thousands of sparkling stars. The night was pleasant but chilly; the air felt ever colder as they advanced farther offshore and deeper into the South Atlantic. Land was nowhere in sight, and as they searched to find their way back to the right deck and exact room number of their cabins, many got lost. *Zaandam* crew members were prepared for this and staffed the halls with extra helpers to usher guests into their new quarters.

Few passengers complained about the Lilliputian dimensions of their accommodations. Rooms were for changing clothes, sleeping, and intimacy. Every evening, stewards slipped a list of activities under the guests' doors; entitled "Where and When," it showcased offerings that began at the crack of dawn. Even if a guest never left the ship, never took a single shore excursion, there was so much to do on board: a professional photographer teaching how to shoot portraits, a chef sharing kitchen secrets. Experts invited by Holland America lectured one day on wildlife, the next on true crime. Then in the late afternoon, the schedule slowed, allowing guests to settle in for one—or perhaps both—of the happy hours, at the Lido and Crow's Nest bars. Evening dinners were often formal affairs, with dresses and jackets, and special necklaces, ties and heels.

Carl and Leo skipped the gala for something far more interesting, the mixer at the bar up on Lido Deck. These mixers were a cruising tradition, one that the couple never missed. They'd been going on cruises for forty years now, and there was something like this on every ship. Many years earlier, when you had to be discreet, it was known as "Friends of Dorothy," after the character in *The Wizard of Oz*. If you didn't know what that meant, you didn't belong there. Leo remembered one cruise, going way back, when a straight couple at their dinner table overheard them talking about the mixer. "What's this group, the Friends of Dorothy?" they asked. Carl and Leo looked at each other and grinned, feigning ignorance.

A lot had changed since then; the gay mixer was no longer a secret. Leo and Carl were surprised when they walked into the bar for the happy hour meet. There were more than thirty people gathered, men, women, nonbinary folks. They had a blast. There were two women from Tasmania, Australia, a couple of men from England, another from Scotland. Leo looked at Carl, intrigued. They'd expected a shipload of old fogies who preferred an early bedtime over mixing with the other gays on board. But this crowd was lively. They would definitely be back the following night.

As the *Zaandam* headed farther out to sea, everyone aboard seemed destined to leave behind some parts of life on land. Life aboard the *Zaandam* was like stepping onto a moving stage, an alternative reality set upon a seascape, where time slowed down and emotions ramped up. Relationships were built, fragmented, and reinvented. Friendships were founded, marriages were invigorated, lovers separated, and lovers reunited. Living inside a tiny room yet sharing experiences together with eighteen hundred other souls aboard a massive ship reinforced the strengths, and exposed the faults, of every relationship.

*

Four decks below the main stage, sanitation officer Erin Montgomery was miserable. She couldn't remember the last time she'd felt so ill. Her head pounded, the nasal congestion was intense, and a bone-racking pain swept through her body. Erin went through her CDC training in her mind repeatedly, trying to figure out how she'd become sick. She had labored to ensure this ship was safe from disease, especially from the novel virus. They'd raised this cruise to a heightened sanitation status, designated as level four. Every hour, surfaces were wiped with disinfectant. They had installed extra hand sanitizer stations. Yet, despite all these precautions, Erin was trembling and weak. Increasingly, she was also scared. Every movement brought pain. When she tried to breathe, her chest felt like someone was sitting on her, crushing out the air.

Erin made her way up to the medical center, located at the bow end of Dolphin Deck. Dr. Sonja Hofmann, one of the South African physicians on board, looked Erin over and concluded that she didn't have a fever. She advised taking Tylenol and cough syrup and getting rest to regain her strength. Erin was shocked. "I don't have to have a fever to have something serious," she pleaded. The doctor smiled, told her she'd be fine, and sent her back to her cabin.

Erin worried she had COVID-19. All the lessons from her recent classes at the CDC came tumbling back. Excessive cough? Shortness of breath? Chest pain? She had them all. Erin attempted to finish her shift, inspecting the ship's kitchens, picking through refuse in the trash, measuring the chlorine levels in the hot tub and the temperature in the refrigerators. But when she moved, everything hurt, and she couldn't stop coughing. Erin recalled the experts at the CDC, and how they'd described, even back in late January, how ships were vulnerable to this virus. She racked her brain. Where had she picked up this bug, COVID-19, or whatever it was? She felt wiped out, and no one wanted to take her seriously.

All she could do was return to her cabin and worry. As she rode the crew elevator, Erin tried to stave off panic. She had seen photos of this new virus in her training. During breaks, the CDC epidemiologists spoke ominously about its fearsome killer traits. She envisioned how the spiky "crown" of the virus embeds in the human lung. Was it now inside her? Was it now aboard the *Zaandam*?

MARCH 12, 7:08 A.M.
Blanco Bay, Port Stanley, Falklands

Three days out of Montevideo, around dawn on March 12, the *Zaandam* anchored in the harbor off Port Stanley, the capital of the Falkland Islands, a remote archipelago in the South Atlantic. Passengers awoke to find the small port buzzing with activity. Inflatable Zodiac boats serving a small National Geographic cruise ship skipped across the harbor. More stable transport boats, known as tenders, lowered from the *Zaandam*, shuttled passengers to the pier. Some tourists settled into vans headed to the penguin rookeries. Others walked into town to check out the proper stone walls, British signage, and quintessential English phone booths painted that rich red. The worn double-decker bus in town claimed lineage to London, and a corner pub with craft beers did a brisk trade selling pints of ale. Tea shops decorated with lace and tables piled with scones provided snacks and respite from the gusty winds.

Claudia Osiani knew where she would go first. The Argentine psychologist needed to visit the battlefields and tour the museum recounting the 1982 war in which 649 Argentine military personnel were killed during the UK counterattack on this archipelago that Argentines know as Islas Malvinas. Osiani had formed her image of the Malvinas in the early 1980s, as a young resident completing her mental-health rounds at a naval hospital in her hometown of Mar del Plata. Osiani had treated Argentine war veterans for a slew of post-traumatic stress disorders. They had described hellish battle scenes, watching in horror as friends were shot to pieces, maimed, and killed by British bullets and bombs. Osiani had long wondered about these moments. What, actually, had her patients been through? Why were the psychological scars so deep, so permanent? She had long sought to visit the islands to better understand the root of their trauma. "They described such horrible things, things that destroyed their youth, that it haunted me," Osiani said. "I had to see this place. That was the whole reason to get on that ship."

As Osiani and her husband stepped off the tender, an old friend who lived in Port Stanley awaited on shore. They spent the day driving around the island, climbing into the forty-year-old trenches, inspecting the battlefields, marveling at the quaint town with its strange English customs. Sitting in a café, drinking hot coffee, Osiani felt fulfilled. The visit to the museum, with its crude videos of the war and scenes of suffering, had been painful to watch, but the mystery was gone. She could now better visualize the trauma of those young soldiers. After so many years, she felt liberated from the weight of that tragedy.

A few miles away, on the rocky coast of the Falkland Islands, Bengt Wernersson, a seventy-nine-year-old widower traveling alone on the *Zaandam*, was amazed at what he saw. Thousands and thousands of penguins squawked and waddled in a raucous display of nature's abundance. Wernersson, a retired corporate accountant from Stockholm, was well traveled and adventurous, yet this was his first trip to South America and his first time aboard a cruise ship. He was traveling alone for the entire trip, no partner., no family. Just him and his camera. When he'd left home a week earlier, his daughter Shanty Dahl harbored a sense of foreboding. She helped her dad take precautions against the deadly new virus. Shanty made sure her dad traveled with hand sanitizer and a medicine kit packed with Paracetamol, all the while crying, pleading for him to be careful. As Wernersson explored the penguin colonies, he snapped photos of the birds, taking in the exotic scene. The tour operators on the Falklands were nervous about the visitors. They had limited medical facilities on the island and faced extreme logistical challenges when attempting to reach the mainland. Like people in many isolated communities, they also held a well-established and long-standing fear of infections arriving from the outside world by ship. Windswept and sparsely populated, their isolated island felt like a shield against this new sickness. There were no cases of COVID-19 on the islands, and locals worried the disease might arrive by cruise ship.

Historically, plagues were spread in part by rats that climbed down ropes and left the ships, bringing disease to shore, which is why part of Erin's duties included assuring that rodent barriers were properly in place along the mooring lines. But to many locals, these tourists packed into minivans were the most dangerous vector for infection. The specter of COVID-19 was far off, but the van drivers on the Falkland Islands were far stricter than the international authorities in setting rules for the *Zaandam*. The clearly rattled drivers feared passengers might infect them, and as a result, they were hyperaware of every sniffle and cough. If a guest needed to blow his nose, the drivers insisted the soiled tissue be sealed in a plastic bag. "When we were leaving, my boyfriend and I wondered, What happens if they ever get a case?" said one of the *Zaandam*'s shore-excursion guides. "Because if they did, no one from South America was going to help them out. It was weird. They were their own little community, similar to the cruise ship, which was our little bubble."

As the sun sank toward the horizon, the *Zaandam* pulled out of Port Stanley harbor. The ship steamed south, then prepared to turn west, toward Cape Horn and the southernmost tip of South America, with the famous passage to the Pacific Ocean, the Strait of Magellan. The *Zaandam* faced two days of open ocean before the next port of call. Passengers lined her decks, watching the Falklands melt away.

Erin Montgomery had no view of the fading Falklands. She lay agonizing in her small bed in the crew quarters on A Deck, just above the waterline. She tried to find a position to sleep that didn't overwhelm her with pain. As she fought this illness, whatever it was, alone in her tiny cabin, she feared the worst. If indeed she had been stricken with COVID-19, the entire ship was now also at risk.

CHAPTER 3

UGLY VIBE AT THE ENDS
OF THE EARTH

MARCH 14, 5:45 A.M.
Punta Arenas, Chile

Forty-eight hours after leaving the Falklands, the *Zaandam* prepared to disgorge nearly a thousand passengers onto the streets of Punta Arenas. This Chilean city, located on the Strait of Magellan, had long thrived by hosting ships approaching Cape Horn and making the perilous crossing between the Atlantic and Pacific Oceans. But Claudio Radonich, the mayor of Punta Arenas, was particularly worried about the *Zaandam*. Mayor Radonich usually relished the sight of ocean liners towering above the port. Before the Panama Canal was built, Punta Arenas, one of the southernmost cities on Earth, was a key lifeline in the era of clipper ships. But after the Panama Canal opened in 1914, ship traffic withered to a trickle and so, too, the city's prosperity. Now, a century later and with little to no local industry and a population topping 120,000, cruise ships were a cog in the local economy. Every year during the October to March cruising season, up to a hundred ships docked, bringing thousands of foreigners with dollars to spend. Cruise ships pumped millions into the local economy. The *Zaandam* called many times a year and was widely beloved for hosting a courteous and generous clientele. But for the mayor, this port of call felt different.

At 5:45 a.m., as a pair of tugboats finished easing the *Zaandam* against the Mardones Pier, a frigid gray pall hung over the city. A brisk late-summer wind whipped across the Strait of Magellan, rain seemed certain, and

Mayor Radonich imagined an army of tourists infected with the dreaded coronavirus assaulting his city.

Punta Arenas is a remote outpost, even in the southern hemisphere, and it was about as far as possible from the plague erupting in China. The city is closer to Antarctica than Santiago, and the desolate expanses of Tierra del Fuego are visible from the promenade along the strait. Traveling to the next city means traversing miles of mountains, grasslands, or insanely rough seas. But now, as the *Zaandam* towered above the pier, Radonich kept thinking, *This looks like a floating epidemic waiting to happen.*

Once dockworkers tied the ship down, a Chilean government delegation walked up the gangway to enforce a series of hastily drawn up biosecurity protocols. Dr. Hall, the ship's lead doctor, led the officials to a conference room. Inside, a table was piled high with documents, far more than the usual paperwork. Typically, one or two inspectors would board the *Zaandam*, but now there were three officials from the Ministry of Health, led by chief epidemiologist Rosa Paredes. Joining Paredes was an immigration agent, an agricultural specialist, a naval officer, and the cruise line's local shipping agent.

The visit had nothing to do with checking passports. Immigration police had boarded the ship overnight for that, as it steamed through the strait toward Punta Arenas. The Chileans were looking for signs of COVID-19. They worried the *Zaandam* might be harboring sick guests or crew, and if those people disembarked, they might bring the disease to these remote shores. They were particularly concerned about the number of European passengers on board. How many had come from hot spots in Spain and Italy? How much risk were the hundred French passengers aboard the ship? They immediately set some ground rules. If a passenger was sick, he or she had no business setting foot on Chilean soil. Dr. Hall politely answered Dr. Paredes's questions as she perused the medical records on the table.

Eight passengers and two crew members had traveled through Spain or Italy en route to the ship, but they'd had layovers only at airports. They seemed safe enough, Paredes concluded. The doctor assured Paredes that not a single passenger was displaying COVID-19 symptoms, and no one had a fever. One American had come down with what seemed to be mild influenza. Two others, from Indonesia and the United States, respectively, also had reported feeling sick. But these three were isolated. The Chileans were given indications that the ship was under control and free of COVID-19. Even so, they were extremely cautious. In the two days since the *Zaandam* had left the Falkland Islands, unease about cruise ships coming to dock had intensified exponentially.

One week earlier in Punta Arenas, a small ship known as the *Silver Explorer* had docked and unloaded passengers for shore excursions. An adventurous eighty-three-year-old British man took a walk, pausing in the Plaza de Armas to chat up the folks at the city's tourist kiosk. By the time the *Silver Explorer* reached the next port of call, the tiny fishing village of Caleta Tortel, the British tourist had come down with a fever, a nonstop cough, and shortness of breath. A Chilean navy helicopter medevacked him to a hospital, where he tested positive for COVID-19. It was the first known case of COVID-19 in Patagonia and the second in all of Chile.

On the day the *Zaandam* arrived at Punta Arenas, the Chilean Ministry of Health had imposed a full fourteen-day lockdown in Caleta Tortel. Armed soldiers blocked the only road into town, hoping to seal the virus inside this remote village of about one thousand people, ringed by impassable glacial fields, jagged peaks, and rough, icy waters. The Chilean health inspectors aboard the *Zaandam* were under tremendous pressure to avoid a repetition of that unfortunate outbreak. But finding no evidence of COVID-19 or any suspicious illness, the Chileans declared the *Zaandam* to be free of COVID-19, and the passengers were cleared to hit the town and explore.

*

After another round of temperature checks and a long wait, Claudia and Juan walked off the ship with hundreds of others to explore Punta Arenas for the day. Braving a light rain that made the dull chill that much worse, Claudia again experienced the sense of foreboding she'd struggled with back in Buenos Aires.

Punta Arenas is a quaint little city with red, blue, and green homes spreading out from the banks of the Strait of Magellan. But the vibe suddenly felt dark, unwelcoming. For the previous five months, Chilean citizens had been waging a massive uprising against the government. There were signs everywhere of protests, which were jarring to the unwitting passengers of the visiting cruise ship. The city felt like it had been recently overrun by a mob. Bus stops had been destroyed, buildings torched, and rebellious graffiti scrawled across walls. The glass facade of a shop selling mobile phones was pocked with dozens of impacts from what appeared to have been shotgun blasts.

Twenty miles away, more than a hundred passengers from the *Zaandam* began a sightseeing expedition to the penguin breeding grounds of Isla Magdalena. They'd left the ship just after daybreak, the wind buffeting the sides of their buses as they approached a rickety landing where a ferry awaited. The clouds darkened as they took their seats, four guides accompanying them. Some passengers paid extra to zip ahead on a speedy catamaran to the island. It was a tricky walk down the narrow path to the water's edge, through forests of old-growth beech and evergreen. The cruise ship guests marveled at lagoons with piles of bleached driftwood tossed on the shore. Then the expansive pebbled coastline opened up to an area where an estimated 120,000 penguins nested. The visitors snapped pictures, amazed at the stunning, exotic spectacle of natural beauty at the ends of the earth.

Claudia and Juan skipped the penguin trip. Juan had a friend from Argentina who ran an eyeglass shop in Punta Arenas's duty-free market. Their friend was nervous, scared. He shared gossip about the *Zaandam* that was ricocheting all over town. Locals feared the ship's passengers would bring the plague to their city, he explained. He urged his friends to escape, find a way back home to Argentina. Act quickly, he advised, before the port shuts down and the *Zaandam* became stuck at sea. On the stroll back to the ship, Claudia sensed the tension. "It was ugly," she noted. "You could feel people staring, wanting us out. It wasn't pretty." Walking through the city, the psychologist in Claudia sensed that people were on the verge of a mental tipping point. Fear, perhaps panic, was closing in. It was palpable. "It's like we are bringing the plague to their town," Claudia told Juan. "We need to get back on that boat."

Anne Weggeman was flustered as she sorted out the daily barrage of passengers' complaints, questions, and worries. Days with shore excursions were always like this, a buzz of activity that made grabbing a meal practically impossible. As a young musician from the Netherlands, Anne had sought a way to earn money to pay for musical instruments and figured a year at sea would be an adventure and a means of raising money. Maybe six months would be enough if she really saved. Yet, after just two months, Anne was exhausted by the seven-day-a-week, ten-hour-a-day grind at the guest reception desk. She'd made a load of friends, but the rising warnings about COVID-19 were hammering home a message: It's time to abandon ship.

"I got the sense that maybe I wouldn't be able to get off the ship. And I was thinking of resigning. I thought, maybe I want to go home.

Maybe I cannot handle all of this," admitted Anne. "I got an anxiety panic attack. I ended up in medical."

The medical staff calmed her fears, explaining that life on the ship was often stressful, that it was common for workers to be overwhelmed. Anne shared drinks at the crew bar with Dr. Hall, and he boosted her courage. When Dr. Hall discovered that she was fluent in French, he invited her to volunteer in the med center by translating for the elderly French passengers, who tended to have limited English. Dr. Hall made her laugh, reinforced her stamina with his positive charm, and for a bit longer, Anne was able to ignore the fears building inside her.

Leo and Carl had stayed aboard the *Zaandam*, and thus missed the tension in Punta Arenas. They were taken aback when they saw a well-dressed couple lugging their suitcases through the reception area just before dinner. The woman seemed frantic, as if the ship's gangway could be pulled up at any moment. Leo was so baffled, he had to stop them to ask, "Are y'all getting off the ship?" She looked at Leo, then Carl, and, unnerved, replied, "Yes, we're getting off the ship." Carl watched them walk away, suitcases in tow. "Gosh, why would you get off now when you've still got another two weeks of this trip?" he asked, incredulous. It made no sense. It couldn't be that virus. That was so far away. The cruise line had assured them that this was a clean ship. No one was sick, as far as he could tell. It made no sense. Who could be so nervous that they felt the sudden need to abandon ship?

MARCH 14, 6:10 P.M.
Strait of Magellan, off Punta Arenas, Chile

At 6:10 p.m., with all guests back on board, a Chilean harbor pilot on the bridge ordered tugboats to pull the *Zaandam* away from the dock and into the Strait of Magellan. The pilot, one of two on board, would navigate the ship for days through the strait and north, into the treacherous Pacific Ocean waters along the shattered spine of Chilean Patagonia and beyond.

As the guests settled back in, and unbeknownst to most people on board, Captain Smit faced the most daunting challenge of his career. Three hours earlier, Holland America had suspended cruises worldwide due to the threat of COVID-19. Shortly afterward, U.S. health authorities took the unprecedented step of issuing an industry-wide "No Sail Order," warning that cruise ships' closed spaces and older clientele formed a fertile environment for the transmission of COVID-19. One of the CDC's highest-ranking scientists, Dr. Martin Cetron, told *Bloomberg Businessweek*, "If you had to design the most efficient system for spreading COVID, it wouldn't look much different than a cruise ship."

The world's cruise lines ordered all ships back to port and individual nations were taking precautions a step further. Captain Smit used the ship's intercom to break the news. He appeared to choose his words carefully, aiming to be honest, calm, and resolute. He needed to ease the stress of the nearly two thousand people aboard this vast ship in perilous seas, many of them far from home. "Our itinerary will be cut short," he explained slowly, deliberately. "The *Zaandam* will head to our next stop in Puerto Montt," another small Chilean city, which, he explained, would take four days to reach by sea. Smit was a master at making momentous events sound almost routine, and this was no exception. This was the first time in modern maritime history that the global fleet of cruise ships had been called back to port. Hundreds of ships were crisscrossing the world's seas, seeking safe refuge. It was an astounding escalation of the mass fear of the virus that was sweeping the planet. Changing the route of a cruise ship at the last minute was a complex logistical challenge. Suddenly ending a cruise, with no real evacuation plan, could easily explode into disaster. For now, Smit explained calmly in English shaped by his Dutch accent, the *Zaandam* would head toward San Antonio, a Chilean port near Santiago. That would be the end of the journey. The cruise line's travel desk would do what it could to help, Smit explained, but the passengers would need to find a way to get home.

San Antonio was already the final destination for many passengers. Hundreds would disembark, so most passengers, including Claudia and Juan, didn't need to worry about arranging travel plans home. But hundreds of others, including the Huttons and Carl and Leo, had planned to stay on for the second leg of the cruise, from Chile, through the Panama Canal, all the way to Florida. That leg, Smit revealed, was canceled.

Leo knew what that meant. He was the planner, and Carl followed along. It was a bad break, an abrupt, disappointing end to their anniversary cruise. But they were such veterans of cruising that they knew surprises did happen, sometimes bad ones. Leo rang up a friend back in Nashville to help find them some flights. Meanwhile, Carl suggested they try to have all the fun they could, make the best of it. For everyone's troubles, Captain Smit had a surprise. First, he explained, they would weave through one last natural wonderland—Glacier Alley, a cruise amid icebergs, where chunks of glaciers the size of apartment buildings collapsed into the frigid southern Pacific. For photographers and even experienced travelers, a calving glacier and the wind-sculpted icebergs presented a memorable spectacle.

Smit searched for the right tone. He needed to describe this unprecedented situation yet maintain his firm hold as the ultimate authority. "As the global community works together to stop the spread of COVID as soon as possible, it is a powerful demonstration that we are more alike than different," he said slowly, allowing his words to sink in. "We all want to stay healthy, protect our families, our parents and our children, and to be able to return to normal life as soon as we are able." In isolation, such a statement could sound contrived. But not to anyone on board who knew Smit. He believed what he said, or he wouldn't say it at all. Smit had a gift for winning the confidence of those he commanded, as well as that of passengers. When he spoke, passengers sensed his honesty, empathy, and genuine desire to provide details. Among the crew, he was liked for being approachable, whether it be a work issue or a personal challenge. The engineers admired him for getting his hands dirty with them. If something needed to be replaced down below, Smit would ask to see for himself, so he could understand the needs of his ship. He'd diplomatically call out subordinates if they were in the wrong, while demanding excellence. But he always acted with respect and fairness. Smit tended to remember personal details, like the names of his crew members' partners or pets. And if someone needed to talk, the door to Smit's quarters alongside the bridge was always open. Not all captains were so approachable. And in the most trying times, character mattered.

As Captain Smit faced down crisis, entertainment host Amanda Bogen was busy developing plans to keep the passengers entertained, distracted. Fortunately, a huge celebration, known as the Orange Party, had already been scheduled. This hokey standard event on the *Zaandam* commemorated Holland's national color and heritage. As the passengers filed in, the crew went to work. Waiters served fried pork rinds and egg rolls, greasy Dutch snacks, and a signature cocktail strong enough to numb any dark thoughts.

Up on the bridge, Smit honed his plan. He would provide the guests with a quick tour of the glaciers, then steer due north, unload the passengers in central Chile, and return the ship to Fort Lauderdale along with the crew. Smit had the credentials for the task at hand. Making captain in the cruise ship world can take well over a decade as the mariner slowly rises in the ranks, much like a navy cadet gains command of a ship. Cruise ship captains must first show merit as rookie mariners, fresh out of the nautical academy, before being promoted up the chain of command. Only a select few ever have a shot at captain. "It's a long route; it takes experience to get there. To be captain, you have to prove that you are able to withstand the pressures of the job," explained Henk Keijer, a master mariner and marine engineer who worked ten years as a captain for Holland America ships. For a stint, Keijer commanded the young Smit. Even then, he recalled, Smit showed promise, especially as a navigator. He had what the fighter pilot crowd described as "the right stuff," which is why Holland America trusted him at the helm of the *Zaandam*, a ship carrying thousands of lives and a construction cost of three hundred million dollars.

Three hours out to sea, Smit received an urgent email from Victor Oelckers, Holland America's shipping agent in Chile. The Chilean Ministry of Health was shuttering the country's ports at 8:00 a.m. the next day. The *Zaandam* had to get back. In an email to Smit, Oelckers pleaded, "Please return to Punta Arenas!"

Oelckers coordinated with Ben Atherly, the port operations director at Holland America headquarters, in Seattle. Atherly calculated the logistics. They could have the *Zaandam* turned around and back to Punta Arenas by 2:30 a.m., well within the government's deadline. But then they would need time to let the passengers disembark. Some of the older guests were in their eighties. They couldn't get off the ship quickly in the dead of night, unprepared, without help. It was a complex logistical undertaking. The agent promised to work his government contacts, do everything he could to buy time. But the *Zaandam* needed to turn around immediately. The few passengers watching the GPS tracking screen on the in-room TV station noticed a sloping turn as the ship reversed course.

Two decks below, in the Mainstage theater, Amanda noticed the ship tilting. But Amanda knew the night was clear, the seas normal. Why, she wondered, had the *Zaandam* made a U-turn? She went to the officers' bar, which was abuzz with news. At 11:27 p.m., Chile's maritime authority had announced that the port of Punta Arenas would shut down for foreign ships at midnight. Not at 8:00 a.m., but in thirty-three minutes. Even at full speed, the *Zaandam* had no chance of making it back in time to dock. The *Zaandam* had no available port. The only option was to lay anchor at Bravo Point, one mile off the city's shoreline. "Considering that we are now having to anchor, I suggest we arrive at 7 am at the position," Captain Smit emailed his shore agent in Punta Arenas. Smit faced an avalanche of logistical hurdles. He was stuck at sea, with nowhere to dock. No matter how well provisioned, the *Zaandam* needed food to serve six thousand meals a day. Without a port, without refreshing supplies ranging from fresh water to crucial medicines, no cruise ship could endure long at sea.

As the *Zaandam* made the U-turn, Lance Hutton awoke, unable to go back to sleep. He and Sharon had skipped the Orange Party. Boisterous celebrations weren't their thing, especially for Sharon, who was a little shy. Lance stared out the fixed window, trying to process it all. First, the captain had announced a global shutdown of cruising, then the news that the entire trip would be cut short. Lance tried not to dwell on the hit to their whole vacation plan. There would be no hike to Machu Picchu, which was the principal reason he'd risked so much to board the *Zaandam*. A note slipped under their door outlined their new itinerary: five days at sea, then final docking in San Antonio, a city two hours from the international airport in Santiago.

Then a second note from the captain came under their cabin door. Chile was closing all ports. Now the captain was heading back to Punta Arenas. Lance had no idea how they were going to book a flight home once they disembarked in Punta Arenas. Lance was upset. He and Sharon had just spent six hours touring Punta Arenas, walking the windswept promenade along the coast, the cemetery with its manicured cypress hedges and ornate marble mausoleums, the central square. "Why hadn't Holland America ended it all right there, when everyone was on land, close to the airport, close to going home?" he asked. "They should have closed down then, before they pulled out of that port."

MARCH 15, 7:13 A.M.
Bravo Point Anchorage, Strait of Magellan

Before first light, on March 15, Lance dressed, left the cabin quietly to avoid waking his wife, and walked up to Promenade Deck to see for himself what was happening. The sun was over the horizon, breaking through the clouds, casting a warm glow upon Punta Arenas. The bay was smooth, the frigid water bluer than usual. It was magical, until Lance noticed the Chilean naval cutter that blocked the *Zaandam*'s path, guns raised. "That's when I started to realize this might get really bad," he said. "That's when the world turned upside down."

Captain Smit interrupted breakfast by announcing that the cruise was over. Holland America was ending the voyage immediately. It was too perilous to continue. Holland America officials were trying to convince Chile to allow them to disembark. In the interim, the *Zaandam* would lay at anchor. "So much has changed in the last twenty-four hours that to go on farther would only present substantial operational challenges and no assured port for your disembarkation," Smit announced on the intercom. "The world is rapidly shutting down its borders. We simply have no choice."

Then a third note appeared below the door. It was three pages of fine print, signed by Orlando Ashford, Holland America's president. Bottom line: Passengers would have to find their own way home. And pay for it. Lance stormed back to Promenade Deck, heading to the big circular customer service desk. The place was awash with confused elderly passengers. How would they make it home from a remote city near the South Pole?

The receptionist looked unreceptive. Lance sensed she wasn't happy to see him, and he hadn't even opened his mouth. Lance politely demanded Holland America pay for the expensive flight home. It didn't go well. By the end of their discussion, the receptionist was practically yelling at Lance, adamantly sticking to the company's refusal to pay for air travel home. But Lance Hutton was not backing down. He knew he was right. He'd bought a ticket that promised to deliver him back to Fort Lauderdale, where he'd already booked and paid for the flight back to Missouri. No way was he going to pay for another flight. And from southern Chile, of all places. Lance was indignant as he walked away, trying to sort out his options and discover a possible solution.

On the bridge, Smit had growing hope he'd find a way to dock the *Zaandam* and allow all these people to disembark. Around 11:00 a.m., Mónica Zalaquett, Chile's undersecretary of tourism, reviewed a detailed evacuation plan for the passengers, including confirmation of their flights leaving Chile. That was a good sign, thought Captain Smit, but nothing was certain. Holland America's travel offices were frantically booking buses and flights to shuttle people to the Punta Arenas airport, then home. But they needed more time, and the clock was ticking. Over the next two hours, they seemed to have mapped out what was essentially an evacuation plan. Corporate sent the plan over to the government while the port agent and a team of assistants scurried to arrange transport to the airport, secure face masks, book flights, arrange bag lunches, find a crate of hand sanitizer. The list kept growing.

Captain Smit fretted. He emailed the agent for an update but received no immediate response. Then the Chilean government requested documents attesting that all the passengers were healthy. So he had Dr. Hall email over a statement. "It is the opinion of the two doctors on board that based on the information available there are no guests on board that would be considered high risk," Dr. Hall's email read. "I trust this statement provides reassurance."

At 10:45 p.m., they received their answer: The Ministry of Health would let the *Zaandam* dock in the morning, along with three other cruise ships waiting in the bay. "This is great news," the ship's hotel director emailed the shipping agent. Smit seemed assured his ship would soon be out of this mess. But on land, an angry crowd began to gather.

As the night wore on, rumors flashed across Punta Arenas: A cruise ship defied government orders and docked anyway! Tourists are entering the heart of the city! The cruise ship is filled with people from Italy and Spain, where COVID-19 is raging!

At Prat Pier, two small Chilean passenger ships, the *Stella Australis* and *Venta Australis*, docked. Passengers filed down the gangways. The cramped pier was packed with people trying to find a way home. Clearly, there was no organized plan. Most passengers were Chileans, but there were also foreigners with no plane tickets home, no transport to the airport. A crowd of protesters began to gather outside the gates leading to the docks. Locals arrived in cars, taxis, and by foot. Truck drivers began to park their rigs and blast their horns. A few protesters arrived carrying clubs, sticks, and rocks. Tension was mounting. The lost passengers seemed desperate, while many locals feared these outsiders were bringing disease, maybe death. "This is sovereign Chilean soil and no way I am going to allow any foreigner to step off that ship," said one man angrily, gripping an ax handle.

The crowd grew; the chants picked up. In the distance, the *Zaandam*'s lights flickered in the night, a gigantic symbol of danger. While those aboard were too far away to observe the fury brewing at the port, on the bridge, the officers were growing alarmed. They were following reports on social media about protests at the dock, and clearly cruise ships were in the protesters' crosshairs. The *Zaandam* was hundreds of meters away from the older docks, where the protesters, gathering in the pitch-black night, were screaming across the harbor. Ever more frequently, blinding spots of red light cut through the windows of the bridge. Protesters were aiming laser penlights their way. None of it made sense. Chile had given the go-ahead to dock, which was all Captain Smit and his superiors in Seattle needed to worry about.

By dawn, protesters blocked the gates of the port, demanding the ships stay away. The Ministry of Health sent a ranking official to the city in an effort to calm the crowds, to explain that the port was closed. The port director also addressed the crowd, now numbering in the dozens. But it didn't work. Health and port officials feared the protests would spiral out of hand if more ships docked, especially a cruise ship filled with foreigners.

On board the *Zaandam*, the mood remained hopeful. The ship's cruise director came on the PA to ask all passengers to venture down to reception to fill out a health screening form and have their temperatures taken, as required by Chilean authorities. They were preparing to get off the ship. The waters of the strait were calm, save for a gentle roll of the sea that had more of a soothing effect than anything else.

Soon, a line of passengers snaked up, around, and down corridors on two decks. Claudia and Juan worried about crowding together so tightly. It was impossible to keep a distance from the person in front of or behind them. Many didn't seem to care.

When Juan and Claudia finally arrived at the head of the line inside the Vista Lounge, two crew members sat at a table, a box of neatly arranged passports before them. As passengers handed in their completed health forms, they received their passports and instructions to leave luggage outside their cabin doors, ready to be carried off the ship. The corridors of the ship were soon lined with bags. Their escape from this frightening situation was imminent.

On the bridge, Captain Smit emailed the shipping agent, asking for additional supplies of drinking water to replenish dwindling stocks. He also needed to empty the nearly full garbage and wastewater holds. Smit hinted that time was running out for the *Zaandam*. Would the authorities allow them to do these essentials? Could they at least get water?

There was no answer, and then the agent, Victor Oelckers, broke the news. Chile had declared a maximum health alert due to the coronavirus outbreak. All borders—sea, land, and air—would shut in forty-eight hours. In Punta Arenas, the port was closed immediately because of the dock protests. The government gave them one option: The *Zaandam* *might* be permitted to unload passengers, but only after it lay at anchor for a minimum of two weeks, under an enforced quarantine.

Smit began searching for a way out: Did this new shutdown mean they had forty-eight hours to dock in Punta Arenas and get everyone off? The agent knew there was no chance, so he summoned up the best advice he could for Smit: "No, Captain," he said by email. "Suggest you leave Punta Arenas."

Smit faced many options. Should he head northwest, to the Pacific, or go east, back through the strait, to the Atlantic? Where would he find provisions? To make it all the way north, to reach the United States, he'd need literally tons of supplies. They were due to restock in San Antonio, and they had pre-positioned shipping containers of stores—everything from potatoes, carrots, and eggs to bottled water, wine, Coca-Cola, and beer.

Any chance for negotiation had been scuttled by the volatile events the virus had provoked on land. Chile had shut ports, not only here but for 3,500 miles north, all the way to the Peruvian border. Farther north, throughout Peru, Ecuador, and Colombia, ports were also slamming shut. Captain Smit's options narrowed dramatically, and they were all bad. But sticking around for two weeks in the Strait of Magellan would be too risky. The currents were ferocious, the weather notoriously rough, and there were no assurances that passengers would ever be allowed to disembark.

When Smit received his orders from corporate, the guessing game was over. As captain, he was in command of the ship, according to the laws of the sea. But when the ship is owned by a multinational corporation, the rules are different. A captain, just like the doctors and other top officers, defers to his superiors on shore and to the owners of the ship. They would plot the route, make the plans. He would execute their orders.

The leadership at Holland America operations centers in Seattle and Santa Clarita, California, decided to make a run for it. They plotted a course four days north, to Valparaíso, where they would need to take on supplies and mull over their options. Maybe the Chileans would let them dock. It would put them close to the international airport in Santiago.

Smit prepared for this uncertain journey. He needed water. But once he started steaming, he could make drinking water from the sea, so that wasn't so urgent, as cruise ships have onboard plants to remove the salt from seawater. For now, Smit could endure the port's denial of the request to fill his tanks with water from land. On shore, Holland America had two hundred staff members on the payroll to handle the task of resupplying ships, from warehouse workers to experts who kept the complex web of logistical support operating. At the heart of this system were shipping containers packed with staples: food, drink, and spare machine parts. Emergency medical supplies were usually flown in.

For the *Zaandam*, the critical supply port for this voyage was San Antonio, where they originally planned to restock the *Zaandam*. Any break in that supply chain would snarl shipping schedules and quickly disrupt the smooth functioning of the ship. Holland America hadn't been prepared for ports to close just as the *Zaandam* needed them most. Luckily, the cruise line had topped off the *Zaandam*'s fuel tanks in Buenos Aires, so they had enough to last until San Antonio, the next planned stop. "I think they underestimated how fast this disease could spread," said a U.S. diplomat who negotiated with corporate leadership at Holland America. "They thought they'd be okay."

*

Down on A Deck, Erin Montgomery wondered, did she have COVID-19? Thinking it over, she suspected that she had first become sick at the wine tasting in Uruguay. Now she felt so sick that any movement brought intense pain. Erin feared that her body was shutting down, giving in to the virus, and that she was going to die. She was desperate to wake her body up. So she made herself move, pacing her room, walking the decks when she could, knocking out push-ups, and for weights using a pair of thick cookbooks.

"It feels like an elephant is standing on my chest," she told the nurse. She'd heard others were coming down with something and were too weak to work. She could see them every time she went to the medical center. Personnel there gave her Tylenol and sent her back to her cabin. She started jotting down the cabin numbers of sick crew members on a notepad. Her gut told her something was spreading. The numbers were rising.

Steering the *Zaandam* north, Captain Smit was in search of a port. The sea, calm after a rough few days, was his only refuge. As the *Zaandam* traveled down the Sarmiento Channel toward the open waters of the Pacific, a travel agency in Sweden made contact with the ship. Bengt Wernersson, the seventy-nine-year-old widower from Sweden, had not checked in with his family for two days. His daughter Shanty, back home in Stockholm, was worried. Her father had a habit of texting every day, morning and night, but there had been nothing. Her dad was traveling alone, so there was no one to ask to check up on him.

Shanty had been terrified before her dad even left Stockholm for Buenos Aires. He was a lifelong traveler and was quite fit for his age. Even now, so late in life. But COVID-19 was spreading across Europe. As her dad rode alone to the airport in a taxi, they spoke on the phone, and she hadn't been able to hold back. "I felt like I was going to cry. I felt like I was seven years old, and my dad was going so far away," she later said, describing the conversation in Sweden with her father.

Shanty knew her pleas wouldn't do any good. Bengt couldn't get a refund, and he was a man who'd lived eight decades by taking calculated risks. He had a long career as a corporate controller, so he knew odds better than most. In his mind, the risks were not big enough to warrant abandoning this trip. He was traveling so far from this virus, and he promised to take care. "Honey, you don't have to worry," he told Shanty by phone as he approached the Stockholm airport. "Everything will be fine."

Shanty's emergency calls to the travel agency worked. A member of the ship's crew went to her dad's cabin and found him alone. He'd been coughing for days. The doctors ordered Bengt quarantined in the cabin and began checking on him twice a day, but there wasn't much they could do to ease the cough. When Shanty reached her father, he tried to calm her, telling her it was a little fever. He had been healthy, strong, and athletic all his life, he said—no need to worry so much. "A man of his age and generation, he was thinking that this will pass," Shanty said. "It was just a fever. It will pass."

CHAPTER 4

CRUISE TO NOWHERE

MARCH 16, 9:41 P.M.
Sarmiento Channel, Chilean Patagonia

As the *Zaandam* headed toward the calm waters of the canal, a sudden—and bizarre—air of normalcy enveloped the ship. The angry mobs, the glaring townspeople, the protester with an ax handle, and the cold refusals of aid were replaced by full-on cruise fantasy. By morning, passengers leaned over the rails to record videos as a pod of black-and-white dolphins—dubbed "panda dolphins"—darted through the inky-gray waters. They photographed the towering forest walls that hemmed in the channel. Passengers relaxed in chaise lounges and sat at the poolside bar, the glass roof closed halfway to minimize the late-summer chill.

Holland America executives thousands of miles north, in the United States, ordered all hands on deck—not to deploy an emergency virus lockdown but to flood the ship with so many activities that passengers might forget all the *unpleasantness* in Punta Arenas. "We are trying to pack every day with as many fun activities as we can, anything to keep them, I guess, happy and distracted," said Amanda, responding to her boss's requests to ramp up the entertainment. Then she reported to the Crow's Nest. It was time for her twice-nightly trivia contest at the coolest bar aboard.

Amanda had four years' experience in the business of distracting cruise ship passengers. She started work right out of college and had notched visits to dozens of countries on cruise ships. That included two trips to the Antarctic Peninsula after boarding the *Zaandam* in January. Now she had no excursions, no port calls, and more than twelve hundred passengers expecting entertainment for the remaining six full sea days that lay ahead. Amanda fell back on the silly stuff that passengers loved, especially the older crowd on this ship. She prepared talent and magic shows, twist-off sixties dance parties, a scavenger hunt, and a shipbuilding competition, with prizes awarded by officers on the bridge. Amanda worked the crowd inside the Crow's Nest bar as the sun dipped below the horizon, brushing the Patagonian sky with a magenta pall. She scanned the room and took the pulse—all well. Everyone seemed to be having a good time.

Donna and Jorge watched the scene from a table near the bar, amused. The place reminded Donna of the bar from *Star Wars*, full of bizarre characters, all making a move. The American man they'd befriended early on at the winery was up at the bar, casing the room, then talking up a noticeably older woman. He was not young, Donna noted; he was in his sixties, she guessed. But most everyone else was far older. When he caught Donna looking, he walked over and sat at their table to chat. Donna cut in, starting the conversation: "How are you doing?" He liked to talk, and he leaned in to share rich morsels about his escapades. Donna and Jorge thought he was entertaining, sure. But she couldn't stop thinking about how he'd boasted of coming straight from a cruise in China. Since the winery, it had become glaringly clear to Donna that this voyage wasn't as far from COVID-19's reach as they all imagined. Had this man come into contact with the virus, unwittingly, in China? And now he was here, talking loudly in this tiny bar, getting close, laughing, sharing food. Donna didn't want to obsess about this; they all felt fine. But with the alarming turn of events back in Punta Arenas, people were tense and getting scared. Donna couldn't help but worry.

Inside the Mainstage theater, dancers limbered up for the night's show. Headliner Lee Bradley, known as "the Golden Tenor," had flown in from the UK and just boarded in Punta Arenas, prepared for two performances slated for that night. The Mainstage would be packed with five hundred guests—each show was sold out. Bradley, a celebrated opera star, didn't disappoint. During his show, the crowd cheered and drank. A comedian joked that the cruise felt like a hostage situation. One singer acknowledged the shadow of COVID-19 as he belted out Frank Sinatra's rendition of the Cole Porter tune "I've Got You Under My Skin."

MARCH 17, 8:13 A.M.
Miami, Florida

Nearly six thousand miles north of the *Zaandam*, Carnival's Fleet Operations Center in Miami was abuzz, like a military command post. Off the coast of Sydney, Australia, a fresh outbreak was raging through the cruise ship *Ruby Princess*, where more than a hundred passengers were infected with what the company designated as ILI, or an influenza-like illness. The company was trying to convince skeptical Australian health authorities it was not COVID-19, according to internal documents from an Australian parliamentary inquiry investigating the outbreak that culminated with 1,242 passengers and crew on the *Ruby Princess* being infected by COVID-19. Hundreds recovered, yet an estimated twenty-eight passengers died.

There were rows of cubicles for specialists, before a seventy-four-foot-long patchwork of LED screens across the wall that were capable of tracking the speed, nautical bearing, fuel, and supplies for each of the nearly one hundred ships Carnival Corporation had at sea. Around the world, roughly 120,000 employees kept this fleet staffed, maintained, and filled with paying tourists every day of the year. Carnival was the world's largest cruise ship operation. They operated more vessels than the British Royal Navy.

Carnival had two other command posts, in Seattle and Hamburg. As live data flashed across the screens, engineers and officers monitored the weather and sent instructions to change course when conditions looked dodgy. They scheduled deliveries of stores, and, in rare cases, dealt with passenger medical emergencies by organizing air ambulance evacuations. Deep in the Southern Hemisphere and so far from initial COVID-19 epicenters in China and Europe, the *Zaandam* had been low on their risk radar.

William Burke, a retired United States Navy vice admiral who ran Carnival's fleet operations, would take point on this crisis. Admiral Burke, as he was called even six years after leaving the navy to work at Carnival, conveyed the confidence of a military commander. Burke had graduated from the U.S. Naval Academy and earned an advanced degree from MIT. During his thirty-five years in the navy, Burke had risen through the ranks to become commander of the USS *Toledo*, a nuclear submarine. High-stakes logistics at sea were nothing unusual for Admiral Burke. For a stint, he'd been on the board of trustees at CNA, a military think tank that focused on solving fast-moving logistical challenges, like the 1990 invasion of Kuwait by the U.S. Marine Corps. Now Burke faced a quandary he'd never confronted.

On the screens, Burke could pull up the *Zaandam*'s position, the rate of fuel consumption, the status of safety systems, the weather conditions, and mechanical data from the engine room. All the vital signs were right there. Carnival Corporation had spent millions to build the 35,000-square-foot center in an office complex near the Miami airport. There were proprietary software systems, named Argos and Neptune, designed to run ships more efficiently. The promise was that big data would find efficiencies that human brainpower couldn't. But the *Zaandam* now faced a challenge that all the technology in the world couldn't solve. It was a civilian ship with no port. The Chileans had deployed warships to discourage the *Zaandam* from coming anywhere close to the mainland.

For now, the *Zaandam* was navigating north, cutting the distance home by the minute. Burke and other executives didn't know exactly where the *Zaandam* would end up, so they had drawn up plans A, B, and C. The *Zaandam*'s navigational team plotted three routes: one to Puerto Vallarta, in Mexico, another to San Diego, and a third, the preferred option, to Port Everglades, just north of Miami. But they had time; it would take at least ten days for the *Zaandam* to reach any of those ports.

Carnival needed to lobby governments at the highest levels. It was a language in which the cruise lines were well versed. The son of Carnival's founder, largest shareholder, and board chairman, Micky Arison, had the political connections to get that done. He'd stoked ties with Donald Trump long before Trump was elected president of the United States. Carnival sponsored episodes of Trump's TV show, *The Celebrity Apprentice*, and Arison invited Trump and his wife, Melania, courtside to a Miami Heat game—not difficult, given that Arison owned the team.

Carnival retained a network of powerful lobbyists, including Pam Bondi, the former Florida attorney general. One of the most influential GOP lobbyists in America, at the 2016 Republican National Convention, Bondi led "Lock her up" chants. Later, Trump hired Bondi for his impeachment defense team. In 2017, Carnival hired Bondi's sister-in-law Tandy as vice president of public affairs. For years, Carnival had made hefty investments in the political favor bank. Now they needed to call in those IOUs.

When a diplomat from the U.S. embassy in Chile called Burke, asking what he could do, it was clear that the offer came directly from D.C..

Washington was starting to realize that they had a PR nightmare on their hands—U.S. citizens were stuck at sea on cruise ships, including the *Zaandam*. The diplomats set up an ad hoc coronavirus war room inside the U.S. embassy in Santiago. State Department officers began to map, track, and calculate possible ports for the *Zaandam*.

Diplomats along Latin America's entire Pacific coast, including from England, Holland, France, and the United States, began working their sources, trying to convince countries from Peru to Panama to allow the *Zaandam* to dock. Ramon "Chico" Negron, a veteran diplomat forced to abandon his post in Beijing because of COVID-19, helped lead a task force on cruise ship outbreaks. Negron and his team made little initial headway. World leaders were panicking in the face of this pandemic, and cruise ship passengers had a proven record of bringing the virus ashore. No country wanted to let them dock, diplomatic cables show.

Burke informed the State Department that Carnival had decided to keep the *Zaandam* moving north, which was far better than being anchored or trapped at a distant foreign port. There was no talk, though, about passengers and crew who were falling ill aboard the ship.

What Carnival needed, Burke explained to the diplomats in Santiago, was help convincing Chile to permit the *Zaandam* to anchor offshore and take on supplies. The ship was running out of food and water, and would need fuel within a week. They had the shipping containers stocked with stores that were pre-positioned in San Antonio. All they needed was permission to move those supplies a few miles up the Pacific coast to Valparaíso, load the *Zaandam*, refuel, and continue north.

The logistics of finding a port and resupplying the ship were daunting, given the current circumstances. But a far more dire situation was developing aboard the *Zaandam*. More passengers were becoming sick, and fevers were rising. The tiny silent stowaway was making itself known.

MARCH 17, 11:32 A.M.
Sarmiento Channel, off Puerto Natales, Chile

Claudia Osiani was shocked at the scene playing out before her eyes. Hours earlier, Captain Smit had essentially declared a state of emergency on board. The world was shutting down to slow the spread of the most dangerous viral outbreak in a century. Cruises were banned worldwide. But aboard the *Zaandam*, the response looked like what she—as a psychologist—would classify as full denial. Everywhere she glanced, she saw evidence of Carnival Corporation's efforts to fulfill its trademark slogan, Choose Fun.

Claudia walked the ship, unnerved by all these older Europeans, Americans, and Canadians gathering, seemingly oblivious to the threat of this disease. She had read about the horrific outbreaks on the *Diamond Princess* and the *Grand Princess*. These were all ships owned by the same multinational corporation that owned Holland America, yet here they were. The gym, spa, and hair salon were open, packed with people. *This makes no sense,* Claudia thought.

Crew members made attempts to protect against an outbreak. They seemed to be everywhere, gently and politely suggesting that passengers wash their hands or make use of the hand sanitizer stations. The self-serve buffets were shielded by Plexiglas, and servers were posted every few feet to ladle out the portions to minimize contact with food. But few employees wore face masks. When Osiani asked one steward why not, he said, politely, that there weren't enough to go around. "Everything is so normal, even after announcing a pandemic," she angrily told her husband, Juan. "There's a total lack of conscience." They'd befriended two couples, one from Argentina and another from Uruguay. Collectively, they made a pact to stay away from the crowds. "We didn't close ourselves into our rooms, but, yes, we stayed to ourselves."

Two days out of Punta Arenas, Osiani was eating breakfast in the Lido restaurant when she noticed the coughs. They seemed to be everywhere. *I can see that these people are sick; anybody can,* she thought. After breakfast, Osiani marched down to the front desk, by the huge pipe organ. She sought out someone who looked to be in charge. "How can the captain allow this? Allow people to gather in groups, so close to each other, if there is a pandemic all around?" she asked. Claudia urged the staff to take precautions, to protect the ship from COVID-19. "Why should we do that?" the front desk manager replied. "How can we stop people? The boat is clean and safe. How can we stop people from having fun?"

At the afternoon bridge game, Leo Lindsay was alarmed. The Swede couldn't stop coughing. Sometimes he'd catch the cough inside his handkerchief, but not always. It was impossible for anyone at the table, or in the room, to avoid the microbes coming out of him. The fits of coughing were repeated every day, so Carl and Leo had discussed a plan. Leo, who had specialized in public health during his career as a nurse, wanted to report the man to the doctors. After they all had their temperatures checked in Punta Arenas and were declared a symptom-free ship, they figured they were okay. But the man's cough seemed worse. Leo was convinced he had to report this.

Leo took a break from the game, walked into the medical center, and sidled up to the reception desk. The nurse asked how she could help, and Leo explained his background and the symptoms he'd been observing, day after day, at the card game. "You know, I just am not comfortable being in contact with this person," he said. The nurse thanked Leo but never called him. Never followed up.

Beneath the veneer of cruise-life fantasy, the virus roamed the ship, infecting ever more passengers and crew. Erin could see it with her own eyes. On her most recent visit to the medical center, a woman lay on the examination table, looking even sicker than Erin. Down in the crew kitchen, another woman was slammed by shortness of breath and fever, so Erin convinced her to stay in her cabin. Then one of her dishwashers came to her. "Chef," he called out to Erin, using the moniker that had stuck ever since her *America's Test Kitchen* days, "I've lost my sense of taste."

The worker felt awful. Erin told him to stay in his bunk, to nurse himself back to health alone, using the cough syrup she'd scrounged up for him. Erin knew from her CDC training that the best protocol was to isolate the sick in their cabins for a few days. But up at the medical center, the doctors were giving crew members Tylenol and cough syrup, and many were going back to work. Erin thought this was foolhardy. People were getting sick, but the ship had no way to test patients for the virus. There were no test kits aboard. All the symptoms lined up with COVID-19. So Erin started taking things into her own hands. "I started hiding employees in their rooms so they wouldn't expose others," she later commented.

*

Fifteen-foot swells crashed into the hull as the *Zaandam* headed north, into the open waters of the Pacific Ocean. The cruise director came on the intercom to announce that the night's shows were canceled, as unusually rough seas made it unsafe for the dancers and singers to perform. There would be no tenor cracking pandemic jokes, no big band playing the Vista Lounge.

But it was Saint Patrick's Day and heavy seas were not enough to prevent a proper celebration of the Irish patron saint, which was a tradition on Holland America's ships. No way would they cancel the Saint Patrick's Day Pub Crawl. A group of diehards gathered in the Crow's Nest for the first round, then moved to the next bar and the next, sampling different drinks at every stop. As the crawl advanced, coughing echoed along the corridors. Down on A Deck and B Deck, where most of the crew was quartered, two to a room, they heard the festivities and the new soundtrack for the voyage: a chorus of coughs.

MARCH 18
Santa Clarita, California

Patient symptoms suggested to the doctors that an unidentified respiratory virus was spreading on the *Zaandam*. Yet several weeks earlier, Dr. Grant Tarling, Carnival's chief medical officer, had seemed to make a very public point of downplaying the risk of COVID-19 on Carnival cruises. He suggested that the virus was not that dangerous for most people. "In fact, about 80% of those with the illness only have mild symptoms just like that of a common cold," he wrote on a corporate blog. "As long as you wash your hands and take care not to sneeze or cough on others, the odds are you will be fine."

Since the early days of the epidemic, Carnival seemed to be gambling that it could beat COVID-19 on ship after ship—and it was losing. Internal emails show that Tarling had followed the disease's deadly advance closely for months, even disseminating detailed "Instructional Notices" with the latest science and advice on preventing and controlling COVID-19 aboard the corporation's huge fleet of ships. Tarling was well aware of how vulnerable cruise ships were to a deadly and contagious virus like COVID-19. In 2017, he coauthored a study in the *Journal of Travel Medicine* that demonstrated how difficult it is to prevent and combat viruses in the close quarters of a cruise ship.

On January 20, 2020, when Tarling informed Carnival CEO Arnold Donald of his concern, the two talked. Tarling warned that COVID-19 was spreading fast and could be transmitted from person to person, emails show. Yet, on January 26, Dr. Tarling and other top executives emailed the latest policy to managers of another of the corporation's lines, Princess Cruises, suggesting there was a "low risk" of COVID-19 outbreaks on cruise ships and that crew members should be discouraged from using face masks on board. Managers should make it clear that masking up around passengers was prohibited, they said.

By the time the *Zaandam* set sail, Carnival was well into its third major COVID-19 outbreak on its ships, this time on the *Grand Princess*. At least two passengers had died, and many more were sick. The ship was en route to Hawaii, but with the virus outbreak raging, the *Grand Princess* suddenly doubled back and returned to California. State officials banned the ship from docking, forcing it into a holding pattern off San Francisco. On March 4, four days before the *Zaandam*'s departure, Tarling pushed back on CDC recommendations to confine passengers to quarters and serve meals in their rooms, in an attempt to contain the virus's deadly assault, emails show.

That night, Tarling called Dr. Cindy Friedman, the CDC's point person on cruise ship outbreaks, to argue that it would be too complicated to serve three meals a day to 2,400 passengers in their cabins. Friedman and a sixteen-person team were crammed into a room in Building 21 at CDC headquarters in Atlanta, surrounded by corkboards, whiteboards, and evidence of a burgeoning body count from the multiple cruise ship outbreaks. With cruise ship deck plans taped to the walls, they sought to map the outbreaks of this new disease. Were there clusters? Was sickness spread airborne? Face-to-face? Through touching surfaces? Warnings on their office door kept out anyone with a cough, fever, or shortness of breath. There were signs of their marathon sessions inside the conference room: Empty bags of potato chips, used hand wipes, and empty bottles of hand sanitizer lay scattered on the gray carpet under the long desks.

Tarling was adamant in his talk with the CDC leaders: The *Grand Princess* didn't have enough face masks and other protective gear for the servers to wear, even if it were possible to quarantine guests and serve food via a makeshift delivery system. He also argued that disrupting the meal routines might put passengers at risk by interrupting their schedules for taking needed medicines, which, he insisted, presented even more of a health risk than COVID-19. Dr. Tarling offered to isolate a few dozen passengers who'd been suspected of having contact with the sick on the previous *Grand Princess* cruise. But the outbreak became so severe that the U.S. Coast Guard was called in to fly a helicopter that would hover just above the deck of the *Grand Princess* while rescue workers lowered a cooler of COVID-19 test kits and the CDC personnel needed to administer them.

Five days later, on March 9, the *Grand Princess* was given emergency permission to dock in Oakland, California, and more than 2,400 passengers were sent into two-week quarantine under armed guard at four military bases, spread across the country. At least 159 passengers eventually were stricken with COVID-19 and eight died.

Now, as the *Zaandam* languished off Patagonia, Carnival quietly began to prepare for the worst. On March 18, the company ordered 6,000 surgical masks, 600 surgical gowns, and 4,800 pairs of protective gloves for the *Zaandam* from a marine medical supplier on Staten Island, an internal invoice shows. Getting the supplies on board could take many days because no country was allowing the ship to dock.

But beyond the medical center and the cabins where the sick languished, the cruise had to continue. The global pandemic shutdown was advancing on land—universities, offices, restaurants, and schools were closing across the world. Towns, cities, and entire nations were imposing curfews and the mandatory use of face masks. On the *Zaandam,* the opposite was occurring. The crew, following corporate's mandate, tempted passengers with group activities.

Waiters prepared a magnificent spread for the Lido buffet, including eggs and bagels with smoked salmon and capers, and passengers packed the place for hours. Up on Sports Deck, the poker tournament continued into a third day. Players crowded around the tables, playing their hands. At the Explorer's Lounge, guests curled up on the couches to read in the afternoon, and lectures drew a crowd. And in the Crow's Nest, guests pressed close together by the front windows to watch a pod of orca whales swimming ahead of the ship. But the big event on board was Formal Night. By 7:00 p.m., hundreds packed into the Mainstage, crowding the banquet tables, waiting to take a whirl around the dance floor. This was a rare chance to show off sequined cocktail dresses, flowing chiffon gowns, and smart suits or tuxedos. Unlike back home, there were no social-distancing mandates to get in the way as the band played on.

MARCH 19, 10:18 A.M.
Pacific Ocean, off Puerto Montt, Chile

By midmorning on March 19, diplomats were working frenetically to convince the Chilean government to provide relief for the *Zaandam*. The ship was full of foreigners, including hundreds of Australian, French, UK, and U.S. citizens, and they all needed to be repatriated. Inside La Moneda, the presidential palace in Santiago, President Sebastián Piñera's top advisors were on the receiving end of the intense diplomatic campaigns to allow the ship to dock. The Americans had helped Chile by flying home hundreds of Chilean citizens on a chartered jet. The government of Chile owed them a favor, and they were trying to cash it in.

Chile had long been one of the United States' most stable allies in South America, but President Piñera wouldn't budge. Like nearly every head of state around the world, he was under tremendous pressure to show he was doing everything possible to protect his populace from the onslaught of this terrifying virus. Given the precedent of the elderly Brit infected with COVID-19 who disembarked in Caleta Tortel, President Piñera was stuck. Allowing a cruise ship full of foreigners to dock would create yet another political crisis, and his popularity was already at a record low of 7 percent. He was going to have to tell the foreigners: No one would be allowed to disembark.

After intense U.S. lobbying, the Chilean authorities would permit the *Zaandam* to moor outside Valparaíso to take on supplies at sea, which is what Captain Smit announced when he came on the intercom. Docking was out of the question, he quickly established. No one would go ashore in Chile, or anywhere, in the foreseeable future: Peru, Ecuador, and Colombia had also shut down their frontiers as well as seaports, the captain explained. For the first time in memory, the world had turned its back on a cruise liner in distress.

The lockdown news did little to crimp life on board. The ship was humming with memories of Formal Night and so much still to come. People worked out in the gym, and lines formed outside the beauty salon as guests waited for a manicure or massage. During dinner at the Pinnacle Grill, one of the fancier dining rooms on board, there were no signs of crisis. The night's menu included lobster bisque, filet mignon, and candied bacon, but only for those who had a reservation. All tables were booked.

MARCH 20, 10:47 A.M.
Pacific Ocean, off Valparaíso, Chile

Midmorning, the *Zaandam* was moored in Valparaíso Bay, about a mile offshore. The ship was so close that passengers could see people walking along the docks, while cars and buses meandered down a coastal road. The water was calm, the sky cloudy as the *Zaandam* came to a halt.

Lance Hutton arose at dawn, anxious to figure out what was happening. They'd been at sea three full days since the debacle in Punta Arenas, so stopping anywhere was a relief. *At least we can get supplies,* he thought as he headed out to take a look. *Maybe we'll be able to get some people off this ship.* Lance was trying to be optimistic in a situation that seemed increasingly hopeless. The last few days had been bizarre. Around the world, fear of this virus was palpable. But here, they tried to make it all seem so normal. Lance and Sharon tried to keep to themselves. They stayed away from the pool, preferred reading in the cabin or on a deck chair to attending a packed show. But they had to eat, and two nights earlier they'd gotten a scare at dinner. A man paused beside their table and coughed. "It was a deep cough," said Lance. "The kind that makes you notice." Lance and Sharon tried to turn away, as if that would help. But the man was close and kept coughing, only partially covering his mouth. "That made me take a pause," Lance said. "Made me worry."

On deck, the morning was glorious, the sun peeking through a thick bank of clouds, the land so close that it seemed possible to swim ashore. Then Lance trained his gaze on the water below. Two Chilean naval boats patrolled a couple of hundred feet away. *No one is going to get off the ship,* he realized. *That's for sure.*

On the docks, an impressive load of supplies awaited: pallets of Heineken, Coca-Cola, and Fanta and crate upon crate of carrots, red onions, avocados, and oranges. There was wine, milk, flour, and an entire pallet of Corona beer.

A tanker ship, the *Don Pancho*, pulled alongside to fill the *Zaandam*'s tanks with fuel. Once the maneuver began, an elephant seal climbed atop the vessel's bulbous prow, begging for food from the passengers who were watching from the *Zaandam*'s decks. Then a barge with a crane appeared, and two men maneuvered supplies into a hatchway on the starboard side of the *Zaandam*. The barge pitched perilously close to the big ship as heaving swells hampered the operation. The crane operator struggled to control the heavy pallets. A load of Coca-Cola almost crashed into the *Zaandam*'s side as the sea rolled. Quietly, some unloading was also coordinated. A few hours into the maneuver, a small launch came alongside, the pilot wearing head-to-toe protective gear—mask, gloves, gown, and safety glasses. The French embassy had cut a deal with Chile to allow two of its citizens off the ship. They showed no signs of respiratory illness but were in desperate need of medical treatment and could die without their specialized medicine. The launch headed toward the port. Another launch picked up six Chileans—four passengers and the two channel pilots who'd guided the ship since the Strait of Magellan. At the port, a pair of government vans picked them up, the drivers dressed in hazmat suits. The pilots were then made to exit the van at a random highway crossing outside Valparaíso, abandoned to call a cab. "They dumped us," one of the pilots recalled, "like stray dogs."

MARCH 21, 11:02 A.M.
Pacific Ocean, Anchored off Valparaíso, Chile

Twenty-four hours later, as the massive resupply operation continued, Wiwit Widarto, the laundry supervisor, felt a panic growing inside him. He called his wife, Anny Doko, at home in Indonesia, via a WhatsApp video call, as he did every day. The couple's two sons, twenty-year-old Bryan and eighteen-year-old Matthew, had been raised, housed, and educated thanks to his salary from Holland America. Their talks usually centered on Wiwit's concern for Anny and the kids. For days, he'd been worried that his family in Indonesia would fall sick with COVID-19. But now Wiwit was worried about the dangers he faced on the *Zaandam*.

For three consecutive days, he'd felt tired, his muscles aching. Wiwit assumed it must be his workload, or maybe a common cold. He and the rest of his crew were working nonstop, ten to twelve hours a day, in the sweltering confines of the ship's three cramped laundry rooms, trying to keep up. Ever more passengers and crew were confined to their cabins, which translated into more soiled sheets, towels, and napkins. When passengers rang for special services, Wiwit made a point of going to their cabins to personally change their sheets or exchange towels. Some guests were clearly sick, but he would help them as best he could. Adding to the workload, several of Wiwit's staff members were also ill. Wiwit ordered them to return to bed, to rest, which meant he and the remaining workers had to work even harder. After roughly three decades on cruise ships, Wiwit was a perfectionist, and that drove him to work harder at times like these.

Anny felt Wiwit's voice was different. He was worried.

"You have to go to the medical center," Anny said, growing more concerned. "You have to get some help."

Wiwit explained that he'd gone to the medical center but all they had been able to offer him was Paracetamol. The stronger medicine was about to run out, and Wiwit told her it had to be saved for passengers. Anny was shocked. "You need to stay strong, focus on yourself, get better," she said, attempting to raise his spirits. Wiwit told her he'd do his best, but right before hanging up, he shocked his wife. "Anny," he said. "Please pray for me."

The extent of the spreading infection was clear along the crew corridor outside Wiwit's cabin. Door after door of the shared crew rooms, far from passengers' eyes, were marked with a red sticker. These were the cabins of the sick, the little red dot warning those in the know to stay away.

In the medical center, Dr. Hall needed to understand who was sick so he could contain this outbreak before it spun out of hand. So he called a meeting of the crew who handled shore excursions. For the last six days, they'd had little to do, since no port calls meant no excursions.

Dr. Hall asked for their help. He had hardly slept. The nurses aboard were equally exhausted, but the excursion teams were free. Could they volunteer to monitor the temperatures of crew members? When one colleague said she wanted to wear a face mask as protection, a supervisor said no. They didn't want to alarm or upset the passengers. They were instructed to start their new assignment immediately. They were to report to the medical center, pick up thermometers and lists of crew members to be examined, then fan out to take their colleagues' temperatures.

The *Zaandam*'s medical staff was accustomed to treating life-threatening illnesses while far from land. Fatal heart attacks and falls were common among the older passengers. The medical center was carved out of the bow end of Dolphin Deck and was well equipped. At the entrance, there was a reception desk, not unlike the arrangement in many doctors' offices, and two examination rooms off to the right. The medical center had surgical tools at the ready for emergency procedures and a medicine closet packed with drugs, ranging from Viagra to adrenaline-filled vials, used to stimulate a faltering heart. Down a hallway, there were four inpatient rooms, outfitted like those in a hospital. One room was a mini intensive care unit, complete with a ventilator to take over a patient's breathing, a vital signs monitor, and an X-ray machine.

Sickened passengers and ill crew members now lined up in the corridor, waiting their turn to enter the medical center. Some looked so weak, as if they might topple over. Inside, passengers and crew crowded into the tiny white reception area. And in each of the three examination rooms, a patient lay prone on a hospital bed. Everyone seemed to be coughing incessantly. The two doctors and four nurses were overwhelmed.

There were approximately eleven tanks of oxygen on board, and the ventilator was going through the five-foot-high cylinders rapidly. Dr. Hall knew that a flood of elderly patients with respiratory issues would require far more oxygen. Without more tanks, these patients would suffocate, then die. They would worry about the next patients later.

In an adjoining room, Bengt Wernersson, the Swedish widower, was fighting for every breath, as well. The virus had sapped his energy, leaving him with a fever and cough that only seemed to get worse. Medical personnel diagnosed Bengt with ILI.

With no training in COVID-19 prevention, the shore-excursion crew embarked upon a dangerous mission. They came face-to-face with crew members working in the most exposed areas: the housekeepers and food servers. It was their job to take each worker's temperature, so that Dr. Hall could understand who was sick enough to require isolation in a cabin. It was scary yet critical work.

By evening, the number of documented cases of this flulike illness skyrocketed. Forty-six passengers and crew were diagnosed with ILI, a serious ailment defined by a sustained fever above one hundred degrees. Another twenty-seven had less-serious symptoms and were classified as having ARI—acute respiratory illness. There was no way the doctors could know what virus was spreading throughout the ship. They had not been stocked with tests for COVID-19. Those testing kits available at the time were unreliable—the CDC's own test failed at least a third of the time. Dr. Hall had no way to know for sure what was ravaging those aboard the ship.

Two decks up, Erin Montgomery had no doubt what was taking place. As sanitation officer, she was copied on the emails that medical personnel sent whenever they officially ordered a person into isolation. The fines for failing to isolate sick patients were stiff, and it was Erin's job to ensure compliance. With every email, she jotted down the cabin number of the patient on her legal pad. There were dozens of numbers scrawled across the page, and when she color-coded the symptoms, Erin panicked. Like a jigsaw puzzle taking shape piece by piece, Erin's crude homemade sketch revealed contagion patterns for the viral outbreak. Staring at the data, analyzing the patterns, she didn't notice her boss standing behind her; he was also looking at the list.

He looked at Erin and asked, "What's that?"

"Those are all the cases we have," said Erin. "See how they are clustered together? We have a real outbreak on our hands."

High above the tense scene in the medical center, the Crow's Nest bar was packed yet again for happy hour. The weather was sunny and bright. The gym, pool, spa, and library were open. But what caught most passengers' attention were things happening around the ship.

Spread out along the railing of the broad decks that wrapped around the upper levels, passengers gawked at what was taking place below them during the final hours of the two-day resupply operation. At 5:30 p.m., the captain came on the intercom and the ship went silent. All the supplies were loaded, he announced, and it was time to continue the journey. The *Zaandam* set course for the Panama Canal, five days north. The plan was to negotiate passage through the canal and return home to Port Everglades, in Fort Lauderdale. They could arrive by the final days of March, or sometime in early April. Smit told the passengers in no uncertain terms that what had happened was unfair, unprecedented, and unacceptable. The Chileans had abandoned them. At dinner, he announced there would be free wine as they collectively hit the open seas. And to great applause, he added, "I can assure you no Chilean wine will be served."

MARCH 22, 7:11 A.M.
Pacific Ocean, off Vallenar, Chile

By morning, there were subtle signs of trouble on the *Zaandam* as the ship headed north under a brilliant morning sun, the sharply angled keel slicing through the calm Pacific waters. The breakfast buffet wasn't as rich as usual, despite the resupply operation in Valparaíso. The gym was busy, but something felt different. Crew members were poised to sweep in and clean equipment as soon as a guest finished a set. As she headed into the Lido for lunch with Juan, Claudia Osiani noticed people disinfecting handrails, elevator buttons, bathroom door handles, and pool chairs more frequently than before. Juan and Claudia had reserved a table for lunch with their Argentine friends, and after the previous evening's announcement, Claudia felt encouraged. At last, they had a plan to return home. Meanwhile, she planned to hunker down, keep her distance from all those coughing people, and make the best of a tense situation. *Being trapped on a luxury ship isn't a bad place to wait out this sickness*, she thought.

*

Unlike Claudia Osiani and most of the passengers, members of the officer corps were all too aware that something was amiss on the *Zaandam*. The day before, word had gone out that people were getting sick. But that came with the territory. The officers knew firsthand how ships were a breeding ground for viruses, especially stomach bugs. The more experienced officers knew the ship inside out, and many were good friends. They took care of each other. If something was going around, they thought they could handle it. It didn't initially occur to them that the virus might be COVID-19. Resting on the deck, taking a moment to recoup energy, Amanda Bogen was sunbathing with a ranking officer when a friend arrived with news: "Guys, I think we're going to go into a lockdown."

The man laughed. As second officer, he figured he was in the know and played down the idea. "No, I don't think so."

MARCH 22, 2:17 P.M.
Pacific Ocean, Due West of Copiapó, Chile

Claudia, her husband, Juan, and friends from Argentina were drinking tea in the Lido dining room as they gossiped quietly, hoping those at the next table over could not hear. They were discussing COVID-19 and how best to avoid the crowds on the ship. They were sitting near the sweeping main staircase—the one that always reminded Osiani of the staircase aboard the *Titanic*—when an announcement startled them.

"Good afternoon. This is your captain speaking from the bridge with an important announcement," Smit began, addressing the entire ship. "I ask that everyone please listen closely." The news was grim. An influenza-like respiratory virus had sickened many passengers. "Out of an abundance of caution, we must ask that you return to your staterooms as soon as you are done with lunch," the captain ordered, "where, regrettably, we are going to have to ask you to remain."

The *Zaandam*, now due west of Copiapó, Chile, and heading north, was locking down. The ship's public areas emptied within minutes. Fearful passengers hurried to their rooms. "It was so abrupt," said Osiani, "like they didn't have a plan."

Carl Zehner was in the middle of a bridge game in the card room, sitting across from the Swede and his young, vivacious date. The man had been coughing all morning, right at Carl. The handkerchief didn't seem to be enough to keep it all to himself. Carl also had felt under the weather the last couple of days, a little tired, a little congested. But he'd convinced himself it wasn't anything to worry about. He'd be fine. He didn't tell Leo because he knew he'd worry, the nurse in him and all.

Carl had always considered himself invincible, even at seventy-four. He'd lived on the edge for a long, long time, all the way back to Vietnam, when he served in a helicopter support battalion. Then the extreme sports, like rafting, kayaking, all of that for decades. But with the captain's announcement that people were sick with some kind of viral-type flu, whatever that was, the situation was deteriorating. The assumption that the *Zaandam* was out of COVID-19's reach, all of a sudden, didn't stand up. Carl looked at the Swede and suggested they continue the game later. He stood up to leave, wishing the coughing Swede and his companion good luck.

*

The *Zaandam*'s quarantine had begun. Passengers retreated into their cabins, most with less space than a one-car garage. Dozens of rooms were windowless. Claudia Osiani felt an overpowering force closing in. It had only been minutes since lockdown began, and the gravity of it all was already sinking in. She sat in the cabin with Juan, nervously switching between staring out the window and watching television. It was as if she could feel the teeming outbreak on the other side of the door. Relying on her training as a psychologist, Osiani knew that anxiety, fear, and depression were all rising. It was the uncertainty that ate away at her. "That lack of knowing, lack of anything, made it so much worse," she said. Surrounded by more than a thousand people, she felt quite alone.

CHAPTER 5
LOCKDOWN IN THE PACIFIC

MARCH 22, 2:31 P.M.

Pacific Ocean, Northwest of Copiapó, Chile

Amanda Bogen had never seen Lido Deck so empty. The deck chairs by the pool were askew. With no one talking or laughing, the humming of the ship's engines and the whisper of a breeze were the only sounds. A lone waiter appeared and began dumping never-to-be-finished cocktails, beers, and coffee. It was all so sudden. Half an hour earlier, a hundred guests had lounged lazily next to the sculpture of frolicking dolphins. She took a final stroll around the deck, and the sea breeze felt like a luxury. "I never walked so slow," she said. "I didn't want that lap to end." Amanda knew the impending lockdown meant everything was set to change, and she wondered, *How long will it be until I get fresh air?*

Reluctantly, she walked down staircase after staircase to her cabin, nine decks below. Even without a highly contagious disease aboard, Amanda was loath to use an elevator and prided herself on jogging up and down the stairs. When she ran into crew members, it was surreal. Some folks were already wearing face masks, gloves, and gowns. Gone were the smiles and hellos she always received—and gave—when passing someone in the narrow hallways. *It's like a creepy ghost ship,* she thought.

Despite adding a few twists and turns, avoiding a direct route, finally she was facing her cabin and confronting what she so sought to avoid: isolation. Amanda used her key card to open the door to her coveted private room.

She glanced around. This was going to be her life. Alone. Her boyfriend, the only reason she'd abandoned working on a round-the-world cruise for this South American cruise, was now her ex.

A crew announcement shook her from these dark thoughts as the boss summoned the entertainment department to an urgent meeting. Nonessential crew would be confined to quarters just like the passengers, as they were not needed to help run the ship. With the venues darkened, the entertainers figured they'd be stuck in their cabins for the duration. But now, gathering in the Mainstage theater, the performers listened grimly to their new assignments. With lockdown restrictions, there would be no live magic shows, no song and dance routines, no line dancing. At best, they might film a piano solo and pipe the act to passengers via one of the in-house TV channels. But for now, and the foreseeable future, live entertainment was over.

The hotel director asked for volunteers. He was preparing for a wave of anxious phone calls from guests now that they were all confined to their cabins. In the seven weeks since the first COVID-19 cases had erupted at sea, Holland America executives had seen a spike in calls for help. Amanda and several of her friends agreed to work the phones. It was a justification to escape the claustrophobia of a tiny room and an opportunity to lend a hand in a crisis. "Guests on a normal cruise are pretty needy," she recalled. "The phone calls were going to go insane."

As Amanda reported to the front desk, the phones were already ringing. There was no time to do more than skim the memorandum their supervisors had hastily printed out. It explained how to flag talk of suicide, high fever, or breathing emergencies. Those calls were to be routed immediately to the medical center. A deep sense of panic—and paranoia—engulfed the *Zaandam*. Passengers had little but the phone by their beds. It was a coveted connection to the outside world, and all they had was time to use it. The onslaught of questions was immediate: "Why are we in our cabins?" "What's going on?" "Has anyone died?" "Is it coronavirus?" "Are we safe?"

"They were afraid of the unknown because they didn't know when they were going to get home," said Amanda. "We didn't know if everyone was going to get infected and die. Because the things we were hearing on the news was that COVID was so, so bad."

With passengers locked down, Captain Smit and his crew were engulfed in logistical challenges. The *Zaandam* wasn't built for quarantine, certainly not an indefinite one. Down in the laundry, Wiwit was left to figure out how to handle this radical shift. This was his first cruise running the laundry operation, making it challenge enough under normal routines. He had more than a dozen people working for him, and it took ten- to twelve-hour shifts to keep up with the workload even on a good day. The washers, dryers, and presses were in use 24/7 to keep up with the flow of dirty towels and sheets. Now, with this lockdown, Wiwit had to fend off a scary sense of chaos.

With passengers stuck in their cabins, day and night, and terrified of the deadly virus, they would want even more fresh towels, fresh sheets, fresh blankets. The small wheeled carts to help in the delivery were already lining up outside his laundry. There'd been reports that COVID-19 was transmitted by surface contact. A box of cardboard was said to carry the virus for days, perhaps a week. Wiwit's staff, all Indonesians and Filipinos, had questions about the invisible new dangers—questions no one could answer. Was every sheet a potential source of infection? Could the virus live on a wet towel?

Wiwit wore a mask and gloves when he could, but would that be enough to protect against whatever was on those sheets and pillowcases? There was talk that Wiwit had removed sheets from the bed of a guest so sickened by what they were calling an influenza-like illness that he was unable to walk. Rumors suggested that patient was transported to the medical center in a wheelchair, and Wiwit remained to bundle up the soiled sheets left behind. Word was that the passenger had then died, but no one could be sure.

Wiwit faced more immediate challenges. He was losing staff at an alarming rate to this virus. They kept getting sicker. Their cramped, sweltering work space seemed to amplify the coughs. A couple of housekeeping staff had reported to sick bay.

Indra, a fellow Indonesian who worked under Wiwit, felt the viral bug slowly building inside. Days before the lockdown, he'd felt the subtle aches and then a lingering exhaustion that he couldn't shake. Then he was slammed by a high fever. Indra was determined to soldier through it. He told himself it wasn't COVID-19. "It wasn't just me. There were so many of us getting sick, but we didn't want to tell anyone, especially the doctors, because they would send us to quarantine," he recalled. Quarantine meant days in the windowless cabin with unappetizing food, no sunlight, and, in the end, utter boredom. Usually, the doctor would order bunkmates to be quarantined also, forcing both crew members to stay in their cramped berths for two weeks straight. Working sick was better than that, Indra figured. So, as long as he could make it to the laundry, he planned to work, even if that meant sharing the same air in those small rooms with healthy colleagues. "But at some point, people got too sick and couldn't go on anymore," he said. "So we had to take up the slack, especially Wiwit."

On Lower Promenade Deck, Erin Montgomery sat at her desk in the small office she shared with the food and beverage manager. She felt ill but had slightly recovered, able now to sit up and work but unable to overcome the feeling that she had been run over by a truck. Erin was monitoring the outbreak via the constant stream of emails from medical personnel that detailed a staggering rise in the number of crew members and passengers struck down by this—as yet unidentified—flulike viral outbreak. By March 21,eighty were isolated. And in the last twenty-four hours, another fifty-five had been sent to their cabins.

Some crew had already been confined for days and couldn't come out until completing a ten-day quarantine. These were the CDC's rules, and Holland America had no choice but to comply. Some people started to crack under the strain of it all. They called it isolation, but that was a euphemism for being sequestered in a tiny room for days. The crew cabins weren't just cramped. Almost none had windows. Internet access on the ship was expensive and spotty. The passengers had all been granted free Wi-Fi, so they were online, stuck in their rooms, trying to find out what was going on in the outside world. The crew still had to pay for service, and when they did, it was agonizingly slow. So they were alone, unable to contact friends or family. Despair and then depression set in.

Crews on cruise ships are close-knit. That comes with working together in such enclosed spaces seven days a week for months on end. Soon the healthy crew members began to call friends and acquaintances in lockdown to see what they needed. Were they bored and itching to watch a movie? Could they use Tylenol, or maybe cough syrup? "I'd ring up someone and they'd say, 'Man, I could use a Twix right now,'" one officer recalled. They couldn't have any close contact because of the risk of spreading the virus. So they developed a delivery system: Leave a snack, some medicine, or a pen drive with movies outside the confined coworker's cabin door, knock hard, yell good-bye, and head down the hall. "We'd do a lot of that, 'kick and run.' It was a lifesaver."

Erin's CDC training in late January had honed her skills to identify breeding grounds for disease: spoiled food in the refrigerators, unchecked bacteria in the pools and spas, *Legionella* bacteria festering in a dirty showerhead, norovirus on handrails and elevator buttons, *Salmonella* reproducing in an undercooked chicken breast among the buffet offerings.

The CDC doctors had talked about the dangers of COVID-19, specifically mentioning that the virus was virtually impossible to eliminate from densely populated environments like a movie theater, a prison, or, especially, a cruise ship. Erin walked over to the Lido kitchen and began her investigation. Every knife, fork, and spoon was suspect. What if an infected passenger had touched it? Every dirty plate, every dirty napkin, every used tray might be a vector transporting the virus.

The *Zaandam* was never designed for three-meals-a-day room service to all twelve hundred passengers. But that's exactly what they now faced with the lockdown. Did they have enough delivery carts for such an operation? Mechanics and engineers were pressed into service repairing pushcarts. Fresh water was being constantly produced by a desalination process aboard ship, but no longer could that water be served in a pitcher or dispenser or glass. It needed to be bottled, then delivered to each room to keep out the virus. Long-planned menus and celebrity chef options were swooshed off the table. Instead, the kitchen was reconfigured to mass-produce cafeteria-style dishes and bland food. The kitchen staff churned out an abundance of chicken and overcooked rice. The workload jumped just as more staff members fell sick. They had twice as much work and half as many staff.

One of Erin's tasks was to manage the dishwashers on board, as well as the workers in the garbage rooms on B Deck. Day after day, she had seen the number of healthy staff shrink. Now she faced a logistical nightmare: ten thousand dirty dishes a day and fewer workers than ever. Erin jumped to help.

Back in her cabin, Claudia Osiani surveyed the room. Instead of a crash pad for naps between happy hours and city tours, it was a cell for two. Meals, once a highlight of the cruise, were now cloaked in a whirl of anxiety. Meal schedules were upended, and lunch arrived via a disturbing, invisible operation. Osiani heard the sudden cry *"Foooooooooood!"* followed by the clanking of a delivery cart as it was wheeled down the hall. Then, again, the cry *"Fooooooooood!"* at the next cabin, and the next.

Opening the door, she found a tray on the floor. The tray had flowers, two elegant folded linen napkins, and a full cache of silverware, plus salt and pepper. Pulling it into her room, she crashed into the wall. The tray didn't fit through the narrow opening. She turned it sideways and dragged the food across the rug and into the bathroom. She stared at the crowded tray: plates covered by steel domes, glasses topped with shrink wrap. Had the cook sneezed near it? Was the waiter wearing a mask when he wheeled the food over?

With bath soap, she washed every fork, every knife, every plate. When the soap ran out, she switched to shower gel for the glasses and edges of the tray, which she gingerly brought bedside. Claudia and her husband, Juan, eyed the food with suspicion. "We looked at each other, scared. Who might fall sick next?" They cautiously chewed the food, enjoying not a bite, nor a sip of the complimentary red wine. As they ate, the clanking and clattering continued. She heard the cry—each time more distant—*"Fooooood!"*

The *Zaandam* steamed north, nearing the Atacama Desert city of Antofagasta, in Chile. The navigator was charting multiple options—would they be allowed through the Panama Canal? Were they heading to a U.S. Navy base in San Diego? Diplomatic notes whizzed back and forth as U.S., Dutch, Canadian, British, and French diplomats pressed the government of Peru to allow the *Zaandam* to steam ahead to Lima, rush to port, and unload at least the gravely ill. Holland America was booking charter jets, hoping to swoop into Peru, pick up the passengers, and depart. But the Peruvian authorities weren't budging. They had no stomach for the kind of social uprising that might be provoked by the televised images of over a thousand foreigners—including suspected COVID-19 cases—disembarking and traipsing through Lima on their way home.

"We are battling at very high levels to get plane clearance to move 5000 Amcits," a U.S. State Department officer at the embassy in Lima wrote in a cable. "It is a street fight with the outcome still unclear."

The next possibility was Manta, a port in Ecuador with a military air base appropriated by the Pentagon during the clandestine war fought by the U.S. government against Colombia's FARC guerrillas. The forward operating location (FOL) in Manta boasted a nine-thousand-foot-long runway that could accommodate just about any plane. In 2009, the Ecuadorians tossed out the Americans, banned the clandestine narcotics interdiction flights, and regained control of the base. Perhaps, the U.S. diplomats hoped, there was still some remaining goodwill? But Ecuador had recently been racked by months of civilian unrest; the government was particularly weak.

Ambulance drivers in the port city of Guayaquil were refusing to pick up the corpses of those suspected of dying from COVID-19. Corpses, covered by cardboard or wrapped mummy-style in plastic, were being dumped on the streets next to bags of uncollected garbage. An empty jumbo jet sent to evacuate citizens of the European Union was forced to divert from its approach to the Guayaquil airport when alarmed pilots spotted a phalanx of government pickup trucks and police cars blocking the runway, sirens flashing. The plane had to be diverted to another airport.

Even if the *Zaandam* obtained clearance to let passengers disembark, there was no assurance that Holland America could obtain permission to fly them home. "I'll ask our team in Quito, but early signals are bad, as gov't has shut down movement and borders," wrote a U.S. diplomat in an email. "The governor of Guayaquil has been very active in denying entry."

Few options remained. Emergency medical flights, known as air ambulances, were in short supply everywhere. Wealthy individuals around the world with the means to pay $25,000 or $200,000 for a private escape had already booked jets, helicopters, and yachts for a swift retreat from the virus. Holland America had the cash to book these flights, but what would be the use of that if the plane couldn't land?

Securing a port where busloads of infected people could disembark to catch a flight home was politically untenable. A U.S. diplomatic cable from Quito warned, "As you know, Ecuador (much less Guayaquil) won't take in their own citizens. And they aren't even happy to let (non-infected) tourists take a taxi to the airport TO GET OUT."

The situation was growing more desperate aboard the *Zaandam*. Cylinders of medical oxygen, crucial for patients on life support, were nearly empty. Over the past forty-eight hours, the *Zaandam* had tallied dozens of cases where the patient complained of aches, pains, and other flulike symptoms. Dr. Hall and Dr. Hofmann needed reinforcements, and fast.

Admiral Burke, in Miami, and Keith Taylor, at Holland America's operations center in Seattle, were tasked with finding relief for Captain Smit. Taylor had served for decades in the U.S. Coast Guard and spent his career organizing rescues at sea. He'd coordinated hundreds of search and rescue operations, many in the dangerous frigid waters off the coast of Alaska. The *Zaandam* was near a tipping point. Too many sick people with too little space. If they didn't find a way to spread them out, this virus, probably COVID-19, could rage out of control.

The executives zeroed in on three Holland America ships: the MS *Eurodam*, the MS *Oosterdam*, and the MS *Rotterdam*. They were off Mexico's Pacific coast, closer than any others to the *Zaandam*. They focused on the *Rotterdam*. Like the *Zaandam*, it had been built in 1997 by the esteemed Italian shipbuilding firm Fincantieri. The *Rotterdam* was almost identical to the *Zaandam*, having a similar configuration, length, and weight. More relevant, the *Rotterdam* was empty, its crew awaiting instructions.

*

Corporate issued the orders, and the captains of the other two ships began to recruit volunteers from their crews to join the *Rotterdam*. George Covrig, a Romanian shop manager working for Holland America, was in his cabin aboard the *Oosterdam*, docked off the coast of Mexico near Puerto Vallarta, when his captain's voice dragged him from a dream. "The *Zaandam* is in trouble; people are sick," declared the *Oosterdam*'s captain, Michiel Willems, on the shipwide intercom. Captain Willems asked for volunteers. Still groggy, George began to dress. *Instead of being stuck on this ship, losing my mind, I'm going to go do something,* he told himself. The captain of the *Eurodam* also solicited help from his crew.

Approximately a dozen men and women volunteered, including two physicians, a nurse, and George. The volunteers were transferred to the *Rotterdam*, which was docked in Puerto Vallarta. With a top speed of twenty-three knots, it could reach a rendezvous point with the *Zaandam* near Panama City. But at full speed, it would take another three to four days.

Before embarking on the rescue mission, Captain Bas van Dreumel of the *Rotterdam* was required by ship tradition and maritime law to hold what's known as a ship's council. His crew had signed up for a tourist cruise, and now they suddenly faced a high-risk rescue operation. The crew held the right to approve or reject any major change of mission. The captain made a call of support for the mission, stating that the *Zaandam* needed more doctors, nurses, oxygen, and medicine. The *Rotterdam* would deliver all the medical supplies, and the volunteers from the *Oosterdam* would transfer by tender to the *Zaandam*. Did they agree? A huge wave of applause rolled through the theater. Of course! They would never abandon their fellow crew.

Packed with oxygen tanks, medicine, and the additional medical professionals, the *Rotterdam* sped full speed southeast, while the *Zaandam* headed northwest. Studying the wave charts, navigators aboard the two ships agreed to meet at a small patch of ocean south of Panama City, where waves were predicted to be small, less than six feet. Aligning side by side, they could then use the sheltered lee area between the huge ships to shuttle the medical supplies and the volunteers over to the *Zaandam* with minimal risk of the tenders capsizing.

*

Aboard the *Zaandam*, the officers celebrated the good news. After days of being alone, help was, if not in sight, at least on the way. Captain Smit spoke with confidence as he explained the positive developments in yet another public announcement. Smit sounded encouraging as he shared the news that the *Rotterdam* was rushing to bring a cargo of supplies and medicine to the *Zaandam*. But to the already shell-shocked passengers, the news was anything but comforting. Many were certain they weren't getting the full story. Behind his optimism, was the captain hiding a secret? What about the virus, the stowaway that was rapidly taking control of the ship? The *Zaandam* had recently received supplies in Valparaíso. How could they be needing more?

Dr. Tarling, Carnival's chief medical officer, contacted Dr. Cindy Friedman, the veteran CDC official who led the agency's response to COVID-19 outbreaks on cruise ships. Tarling sounded unnerved as he described how the virus had swept through the ship. Seventy-one people were sick—more than half of them members of the crew. The infirmary was running low on oxygen and needed to evacuate critically ill patients. The cruise line was working on multiple scenarios to get the ship to a port, but none was assured. Tarling confessed to being astounded by how fast the infections had spread.

MARCH 23, 9:10 A.M.
Pacific Ocean, off Iquique, Chile

Working the phone bank, Amanda and Anne Weggeman, the young Dutch woman who had helped translate for patients in the medical center, answered call after call. It was emotionally exhausting and required extreme patience and at times brutal honesty. "One man called and said the air that came into the cabin was recycled air," said Anne. "So he got worried—if everyone had COVID and we got recycled air, of course we were going to get sick. I had to say, 'Yeah, I cannot help it. I'm sorry.'"

Pausing only to disinfect the table, the phones, the keyboards, and the door handles, the volunteers worked until long after dark. Some of the calls were unnerving. One woman was cut short when a man jumped on the line and shouted, "You need to come and get my wife; she's psycho!"

Another call turned into a screaming match. "I could imagine being trapped in a room with someone, but there was literally nothing I could do," said the volunteer. She asked the couple if they needed an outside number. Did they want to dial a mental-health hotline? She was left shaken. "I wasn't trained for this; I wasn't guest services."

Anne was so worn-out that when she finally arrived back at her cabin, she collapsed atop the bed. But beyond the exhaustion, she felt dizzy and nauseous. Her head throbbed and she started to run a fever. Anne tried to distract herself by watching TV, but it was not working. "We had all been working so hard that honestly I was like, Okay, I don't care. It is a bit screwed-up, but at least I can sleep. I couldn't move."

*

Claudia Osiani gave thanks that she had a window in her cabin, a slice of sky and water. Looking into the ocean, Claudia knew she was blessed—it was hard to fathom a room without a view of the sky, the ocean, the air. Her friends, trapped in a windowless cabin, had already called in desperation—with nothing to look at, they were consumed by a growing sense of claustrophobia. As the *Zaandam* sailed north, off the coast of Tacna, Peru, Claudia felt cut off from the world.

In the United States, England, France, and a dozen other nations, family members of those trapped aboard the *Zaandam* launched social media campaigns to save their loved ones. They created a Facebook page, ZAANDAM Cruise: Passengers, Crew, Family & Friends—Latest Updates. In the first hours after quarantine, hundreds joined to share what they knew about the suspected COVID-19 outbreak aboard the ship. Reporters began to interview passengers, and social media was immediately flooded with pleas for help from passengers, crew members, and their families. A newlywed Mexican couple honeymooning on the *Zaandam* created a WhatsApp group. They named it *Zaandam* Prisoners.

As the first full day of lockdown wore on, Amanda began to choreograph workouts that passengers could complete in their tiny rooms. She could touch both walls by stretching out her arms, but she was certain she needed to move—both she and her fellow entertainers were addicted to exercise. It wasn't about just their bodies; it was also about their minds, their lifestyle. Being sedentary was not an option, so they got creative.

With a bed set like an island in the middle of her room, the actual floor space available for Amanda to move was minimal. It was like standing in a phone booth and trying to jump rope. It was impossible. They recorded a *Sit and Be Fit* workout video on a cell phone and then uploaded the routine to the in-room TV channel that all aboard could view. Throughout the video, they smiled and encouraged their invisible audience to make the best of what was clearly a deteriorating situation.

After lunch, a fire broke out on the *Zaandam*. Smoke detectors wailed.

Seven short warning blasts followed by one short blast. The fire alarm was broadcast through every room of the *Zaandam*. Up on the bridge, the first officer was in shock. And now a fire? Claudia Osiani panicked and packed an emergency kit. Were they headed to the lifeboats? Although the fire turned out to be more smoke than flame, the incident heightened tension and a sense of vulnerability aboard the *Zaandam*. Would they make it off alive?

MARCH 24, 8:00 A.M.
Pacific Ocean, Due West of Lima, Peru

Donna Mann and Jorge Hill lay on their bed, trying not to move. Everything hurt too much. Donna was running a fever and was so nauseous she couldn't eat. But mostly she was worn-out. She was so exhausted; it was getting hard to keep things straight in her head. When she called the infirmary, she realized how bad the situation had become. She was told that there were no painkillers, no cough syrup. A doctor promised to come by and check in during the evening.

Donna felt wrecked but was pretty sure she'd find a way through. Jorge was a different story. Even through the haze of her own bout with this virus, Donna was alarmed that Jorge was having difficulty breathing. She knew his history of high blood pressure and asthma. Given what the captain had said in ordering the lockdown, Donna was pretty sure they both had COVID-19. And, though the world didn't know much about this virus, it was clear it preyed on the lungs. Jorge's asthma surely put him at greater risk. When the doctor finally appeared at their door later in the day and measured Jorge's blood oxygen level, she became worried and announced that Jorge needed to be transferred immediately to the medical center.

Several hours later as she fitfully tried to sleep, Donna received an urgent phone call. Could she come to the infirmary? Jorge needed his inhaler and other medicines. Wrapping herself in a long white bathrobe, barely able to stand, Donna stumbled down to the medical center. When she arrived, the door was closed. She knocked. Nobody answered. She knocked again, and no response. Finally, she pounded on the door and a ghostlike figure pulled the door slightly open. The man didn't say a word; he simply pointed to Jorge, who was practically glowing under the bright white lights.

Looking at Jorge, Donna had never felt so sad. She tried to motivate him with words of encouragement and love, but she was unable to focus. Leaving the medical center, Donna wondered if she could make what felt like an epic trek back to her room. She remembered a saying by Samuel Beckett: "in the silence you don't know, you must go on, I can't go on, I'll go on." She repeated those words like a mantra. Arriving back at her cabin, Donna was despondent but also so out of energy that she collapsed into a deep sleep, all the time worrying whether she would ever again see her Jorge alive.

MARCH 25
Miami, Florida

Holland America's logistic teams throughout the United States were working frantically to source supplies for the *Zaandam*. They found COVID-19 tests, N95 masks, disposable gloves, thermometers, and three highly coveted ventilators. They also rounded up medicine that could alleviate the coughing fits and the constant pain felt by so many aboard the *Zaandam*. When the supplies were ready, they were delivered to an airport in Fort Lauderdale. Holland America executive Keith Taylor suggested flying the supplies south, then finding a ship to take the emergency materiel aboard the *Zaandam*. His eyes fell on Peru. The *Zaandam* was near Lima, the capital.

But Orlando Ashford, Holland America's president, Taylor, and the other executives were also monitoring a brewing mutiny aboard the *Rotterdam*. After the initial enthusiasm about delivering supplies to their besieged colleagues, the *Rotterdam* crew heard rumors that ruptured their sense of team spirit. Secrets on a ship are hard to maintain, especially when safety is involved, and the gossip along the decks of the *Rotterdam* was worrisome. Were they being tricked into serving as a floating hospital for the sick patients on the *Zaandam*? Not only would they unload medical personnel and supplies but they would also receive sick passengers from the *Zaandam*. As tension rose on the *Rotterdam,* resentment against their new mission spiked. Delivering oxygen and medicine was one thing, but they didn't feel like they had been treated fairly. Had anyone asked if they were willing to put their lives on the line?

George Covrig, one of the volunteers who had boarded the *Rotterdam* and offered to work on the *Zaandam*, sensed the resentment. It felt like he was being blamed for the sudden change in mission. But what had he done? As he drank a beer with a fellow Romanian crew member who had also volunteered to work on the *Zaandam*, they commented on the ugly stares directed their way. "I felt as if they were saying to us, the volunteers, 'What are you trying to prove?' We stood up and left [the bar]," recalled Covrig. "It was hostile."

As the tension mounted, Captain Bas van Dreumel held a shipwide meeting at the *Rotterdam*'s Mainstage theater. The captain acknowledged the true extent of their mission—the *Rotterdam* would indeed provide cabins to passengers from "the sick ship." Crew members erupted in protest; some threatened to sabotage the mission, hole up in their cabins, and refuse to work.

That evening, they were summoned back to the Mainstage for another meeting, this time via video with Ashford and Dr. Grant Tarling. Angst and anger spread across the room. Tarling tried to downplay the dangers. Crew members, he said, had taken far more risks in recent days by partying without face masks in Puerto Vallarta. The comment angered people so much that Ashford interrupted to ask again, to appeal for help. "I told them that if the tables were turned, they would want the *Zaandam*'s crew to help them," he said. "I gave them a choice to sit it out, stay in their cabins, or help." In the end, the crew did not have much choice. They were stuck on their ships and needed to work, especially if they planned on getting paid or keeping their jobs.

MARCH 25, 12:00 P.M.
UK Ambassador's Residence, Panama City, Panama

Damion Potter, the UK ambassador to Panama, was elated. After a frenetic forty-eight-hour diplomatic push that included the Dutch and Canadian ambassadors and the U.S. Chargé d'Affaires, the Panamanian minister of health finally gave them a bit of good news. The *Rotterdam* would be allowed to use Panamanian waters for a ship-to-ship transfer of medical equipment, including PPE and oxygen, to the desperate medical team aboard the *Zaandam*.

"We knew that getting supplies to the cruise liner was going to be life-and-death," said Potter, "because the oxygen had run out on the *Zaandam*."

They also won a green light for passenger transfers between the two ships. But the ambassador was too exhausted to celebrate. Since March 11, he'd experienced symptoms of COVID-19 and was less than one hundred percent physically. He was also nervous. Panamanian authorities had ordered the Panama Canal shut to cruise ship traffic on March 13. With barely five hundred ICUs in the entire nation, the risks to the Panamanian people were just too great.

"I was pretty breathless," Ambassador Potter explained, describing the post-COVID symptoms, "but I knew this was one of the few times in my career where my job and that of our team was actually life-and-death. We knew that if we could get them across the canal it was going to be two and a half days quicker to get help in Florida rather than the time it would take the ship to dock up the West Coast".

With 229 UK nationals on the *Zaandam* and hundreds more spread from beaches to bungalows, Potter had to retool the entire fifty-five-person staff in the UK embassy in Panama. Diplomats with the UK Border Force, the National Crime Agency, and other areas were pressed into consular duty. Repatriation was the new north.

Potter was relieved that the ship-to-ship transfer was approved. But he continued to brainstorm frantically with fellow diplomats: Was there a way around this logjam? Could they convince the Panamanians to make an exception?

MARCH 25
Pacific Ocean, Aboard the Zaandam

Anne Weggeman lay in her cabin aboard the *Zaandam*, too tired to move. "Maybe I have coronavirus," she told her father, Arthur, who was back home in the Netherlands. But she had no way to know because the *Zaandam* had no COVID-19 tests for passengers, much less for crew members. "I cannot imagine how, given that this virus had already gone around the world by then, they didn't bring COVID tests," stated her father. "But they didn't."

Arthur continued agitating for a way to get his daughter off the *Zaandam*, first from his computer, then on Facebook, and then by phone. He targeted political leaders in the Netherlands, other European Union countries, and the United States, and alerted journalists to his daughter's plight. Anne painted a brave face but she secretly thought, *This is the biggest*

mistake of my life. I don't know how, or if, I will get out of here. I can't smell.
All these thoughts are really scary.

MARCH 25, 12:02 P.M.
Fort Lauderdale, Florida

With ever more desperate reports from the *Zaandam*, Carnival officials could no longer wait two additional days for the *Rotterdam* to link up with the *Zaandam*. The medical center was running short of everything, including latex gloves and face masks. Although they had no clear idea if the plane would be allowed to land at the huge runway in Manta, Ecuador, Carnival officials took a gamble. They chartered a turbo-fan Learjet and packed it with medical supplies. The plane also carried a crew of three: a specialized air paramedic and two pilots. The jet blasted off from Fort Lauderdale international airport at 1:30 p.m. Flight time to Manta was four hours and twenty-five minutes at 422 mph. With a range beyond 2,600 miles, pilot Michael Honeycutt, a veteran of the U.S. Air Force, could double back to Fort Lauderdale without having to refuel, in case permission to land was rescinded en route.

Just before the jet roared off the tarmac, Dr. Tarling sent a short email to John Kutil, director of health policy and analysis for Carnival, seeking urgent approval. "John, We are in critical need of life saving medical supplies to be delivered to *Zaandam* . . . The humanitarian assistance is greatly appreciated."

As the plane roared toward Ecuador, Andrew Sherr, the U.S. consul general in Guayaquil, asked for permission to forgo both border and customs inspections and to allow the plane charter to land, while also designating the medical supplies as *valija diplomática* (diplomatic pouch). This would eliminate nearly all the bureaucracy and permit the jet to land at the Manta airfield. The Ecuadorians seemed willing to go along, but requested the flight to remain secret. Any leaks on social media and the mission might have to be scrubbed. U.S. diplomats were given the green light, and at the last moment they obtained permission for the plane to land in Manta, minutes away from a port where an Ecuadorian navy patrol boat waited to transfer the supplies to the *Zaandam*.

The *Zaandam* neared the rendezvous location off the coast, partially visible from shore. Posts started to appear on social media about a cruise ship approaching. Rumors began to spread. At the port of Manta, Ecuadorian naval commander Romulo Donoso was starting to worry. He'd received orders to run supplies out to a cruise ship in distress, about two miles offshore. He fueled up his coastal patrol boat and briefed his six-person crew. They needed to embark quickly. If coastal residents realized a cruise ship was out there in distress, the mission was off.

CHAPTER 6

SECRET MISSION

MARCH 25

Pacific Ocean, 1 Kilometer off Manta, Ecuador

Romulo Donoso, naval commander of the port of Manta, Ecuador, ordered his lieutenants to lash down the five-foot-tall metal cylinders of oxygen that were so badly needed aboard the *Zaandam*. Donoso knew an explosion of compressed gas aboard his forty-foot patrol boat would ignite a disaster at sea. He inspected the tanks, assuring they wouldn't shake loose during the nighttime resupply mission. These volatile tank cylinders were banned by most airlines after several in-air explosions, including one on a 2008 Qantas flight that blew a hole through the fuselage. The in-flight blasts killed the market for shipping oxygen by air, which explained why tanks had to be sourced locally and delivered to the *Zaandam* by land and then sea.

Even with the badly needed medical oxygen supplies aboard, Donoso couldn't embark. When could he expect the arrival of the masks, the gloves, and the medicine? Pacing the docks of Manta, Donoso made phone calls. The sun was setting, and the emergency airlift had not arrived from the United States. Air traffic control and naval operations reported that the jet was on approach from neighboring Colombia. So he waited. Commander Donoso, a veteran of counternarcotics operations and pursuits of modern-day pirates and smugglers, understood the operation was risky. Fortunately, the seas were calm, but he knew the danger was what he couldn't see.

His team donned gowns, masks, and goggles—all of which would be burned as soon as the mission ended to kill any vestiges of the virus. "Of course we were scared," said Commander Donoso. "We had all the protocols in place, but everyone aboard was worried."

When a small jet tore out of the clouds and angled toward the nearby runway around 5 p.m., Donoso thought it was a military fighter. It was that loud. Donoso instructed the crew to rev up the engines on his Ecuadorian Coast Guard patrol boat. The crew of five sailors stood at attention as Donoso surveyed the craft one last time. He needed to be sure they'd stocked extra gasoline, life rafts, life jackets, fire extinguishers, automatic weapons, and ammunition. They also had a full mechanic's tool kit should either of the boat's 250-horsepower engines run into trouble. An official from Ecuador's Ministry of Health climbed aboard. She would ensure that improvised COVID-19 protocols were followed.

Three pallets of supplies arrived by truck from the jet, and Donoso organized a bucket brigade-style operation to load them on the boat. The boxes held thousands of thermometers, masks, and one hundred COVID-19 test kits. The men carefully loaded boxes holding two lifesaving ventilators inside the patrol boat. Still, Donoso awaited the orders to embark. Diplomatic notes were moving back and forth between U.S. authorities and the highest level of the Ecuadorian government. Final authorization was being negotiated.

Finally, at 7:00 p.m., the diplomats worked it out. "From a life-threatening perspective, we convinced them that we needed this Manta resupply operation, and we reached a consensus to do it at night," explained a senior U.S. diplomat based in South America. At 10:00 p.m., the mission could commence. For three more hours, they waited.

MARCH 25
Seattle, Washington

Back in Seattle, Holland America's senior vice president for marine services, Eric Chamberlain, monitored the operation. There was almost reason to celebrate. The company's emails seeking clearance for the medical supplies to land in Ecuador had worked. The U.S. State Department's pressure and Carnival's lobbying efforts had succeeded.

A bespectacled fifty-six-year-old, Chamberlain was overly qualified to pull off the mission. During his twenty-eight years with the U.S. Coast Guard, he had distinguished himself as a master of logistics, rising in the ranks to become deputy commandant for Operations, among the most complex roles within the organization. With a bachelor's degree in electronic engineering and two master's degrees, including one from Purdue University, Chamberlain had finished his government career with commendations from top brass in the U.S. Coast Guard. Now he was leading Project Gladiator—a COVID-19 crisis team set up at Holland America's offices around the world to track the company's cruise ships still at sea.

Breaking his Incident Analysis Group into teams, Chamberlain instituted a daily log of reports, which he could scan like a military commander receiving battlefield updates. Every ship was required to provide daily updates tallying the number of guests and crew members reporting symptoms that might indicate they had COVID-19. Hundreds of guests on Holland America ships around the world were infected. Those with heavy bouts of coughing, high temperatures, and flulike symptoms were all noted. A week earlier, he'd seen the reports from Australia indicating "the numbers [of those infected] on the *Ruby* [*Princess*] went berserk overnight." Now the virus was spreading quickly on the *Zaandam*.

As the rescue operation unfolded in Ecuador, Chamberlain and the other top executives faced another twist to this military-style operation: They needed to coordinate a secret operation to sneak two passengers off the *Zaandam*. Under the terms of the agreement with the Ecuadorian government, no passengers or crew members were permitted to get off the *Zaandam* and onto the boat from Manta. Thus, few people were to know. There would be no public disclosure as these two passengers were taken ashore, spirited to the Learjet, and flown to the United States. It was a mission that was as covert as it was necessary. Donoso had been briefed: The two passengers showed no signs of COVID-19, but one was suffering from extraordinarily high blood pressure and the other had a case of deteriorating diabetes. They had to get them off the ship and to a hospital, fast.

*

Just after 10:00 p.m., Commander Donoso's boat rocketed out of the harbor. Despite the darkness, Donoso wasn't worried about a collision. Ship traffic was stalled as port closures and COVID-19 panic had—seemingly overnight—left the *Zaandam* and dozens of other cruise ships stuck at sea. Donoso zipped past orphaned ships as he crossed the flat seas toward the *Zaandam*. After ten minutes, he slowed and pulled alongside, aligning his tiny craft with the gargantuan ship. At sixty-two-thousand tons, the *Zaandam* weighed roughly the equivalent of three hundred fully loaded Boeing 747 jumbo jets. Looking up the side of the ship from water level was like staring up the walls of a bobbing steel-encased skyscraper. The Ecuadorian sailors snapped photographs and recorded video. This was a mission to remember. A hatch the size of a garage door opened on the side of the *Zaandam*'s hull and the Coast Guard crew handed box after box of supplies to the anxious team aboard the cruise ship. Despite total secrecy and no announcements to the crew or passengers, word spread aboard the

Zaandam. As the oxygen cylinders were loaded, befuddled passengers who had open-air balconies snapped photographs, recorded videos, then chatted on the in-house phone system. What is going on? they wondered. Did someone die?

Captain Smit and his top officers monitored the operation from the bridge. Smit needed to load the supplies quickly and race away from Manta. He might be forced to abort the mission if protests erupted on shore, or if passengers shared social media posts about the Ecuadorian military assisting a cruise ship infected with COVID-19. But the transfer went off without a hitch. The crew loaded all the supplies onto the *Zaandam*, and the two passengers were taken off the ship. The two sick passengers put on their life jackets as Donoso pulled his boat away from the *Zaandam* and headed back to the port.

On board the *Zaandam*, crew members began to haul the oxygen tanks up to the medical center. Stocks were dangerously low, and the doctors awaited the new supply to keep patients alive. The doctors and nurses needed to boost the blood oxygen levels and help the breathing of their most-compromised patients.

One of their patients was Jorge Hill. He'd been in the infirmary for two days now, and back in her guest room, Donna was growing more alarmed. The doctors seemed to be doing their best, but they were at sea, so they could work only so many miracles. There were too many sick people on this ship. Every medical bed was occupied by someone wearing an oxygen mask. Speaking on the phone, Donna asked one of the doctors what could be done. He said Jorge needed to be in a proper hospital. Donna knew that she had to fight to get him off the ship, somehow. The doctor was sympathetic and would try as hard as he could to make that happen. But his voice betrayed him. For almost two weeks now, the world had refused the *Zaandam*'s pleas for help. There was no sign that was going to change.

Jorge would have to fight this illness where he was lying, at sea, with no port in sight.

The COVID-19 tests posed an ethical and legal nightmare. As a diagnostic tool, the test kits helped identify the raging viral outbreak aboard. Yet those same test results might also complicate Carnival Corporation's harried efforts to allow possibly infected passengers to disembark. Passage through the Panama Canal was contingent on confirmation that there were no COVID-19 cases aboard the *Zaandam*.

The doctors had to be judicious in testing people for COVID-19, if for no other reason than that they had only a few hundred kits to go around after the stop in Manta. Erin, the sanitation officer, asked to be tested, but the doctors said no. "Nothing, even though they had them on board at that point," Erin recalled. COVID was a loaded word, while the designation ILI allowed all sorts of legal cover concerning the disembarkation of passengers suspected of—but not proven to be—harboring the novel coronavirus. Carnival executives had lived through so many outbreaks at sea in the eight weeks since a ship was first infected that they had institutionalized the use of the three-letter acronym ILI in corporate communications to describe the outbreak. In a pandemic, semantics mattered.

One CDC doctor in direct contact with the ship challenged the *Zaandam* medical team. "So, you are telling me that everybody has *influenza-like illness*," the doctor asked rhetorically. "I went through this debate with them on the ship and they were saying 'Well, we don't know that it is COVID.' I was like, 'Are you kidding me? It's COVID. It's COVID until proven otherwise.'"

Carnival's chief medical officer, Dr. Tarling, led the communications campaign. In a series of public relations messages, Tarling signed his letters "Yours in Health," and he wrote to the crew of the *Zaandam*, "What is happening is unprecedented, but it is allowing health experts to learn about the virus and how it spreads. This will help all of you on board, as well as other people around the world."

The *Zaandam* outbreak was just part of a far larger corporate nightmare for Carnival. Executives were battling to simultaneously unload or track down infected passengers from at least six ships on three continents. Intense negotiations were under way in Sydney, Bangkok, Tokyo, San Francisco, and Washington. Although his team had been tracking COVID-19 outbreaks for eight weeks, Dr. Tarling rarely used the C-word in public communications. In one of his five-minute-long videos, he did mention COVID-19. Within days, the video was edited down to three minutes, and all mention of COVID-19 was gone. Some crew aboard the *Zaandam*, especially those with access to medical decision makers, began to question whether the big bosses back in the United States were trying *not* to detect COVID-19.

"We had crew that were deathly ill and none of them got tested. I don't think they were trying to find it. To me it seemed they didn't want this to be a reality," said Erin Montgomery. "But I think the whole world was kind of the same way."

Anne Weggeman could hear ship's officers discussing testing as she lay in her bed, overcome by weakness from an untreated viral illness. "From my cabin, I could hear the meetings of the hotel director," she recalled. "I could hear him because he was talking very loud, and it was always super annoying. But when he had these meetings, it was useful, because I could listen. He said something like 'What's the point of testing? If I take a few tests, and I know it's COVID and everyone has symptoms, what's the use of getting a lot of tests on board?'"

Ecuador's Ministry of Health had little patience for semantics when the two ill passengers disembarked from Donoso's small patrol boat. Officials were waiting on shore to run a health inspection and COVID-19 tests.

Before letting the two departing passengers aboard the waiting jet, they first had to assess the question: Were these guests from that infected ship also infected? The health officials ran rapid COVID-19 tests on the two Americans. The tests provided results in minutes. The passengers tested negative for the virus and were allowed to leave. They were the only ones to escape.

Back at the Learjet, pilot Mike Honeycutt and copilot Paolo Polizzy were ready in the cockpit. Air ambulance attendant Jared Wayt was there to help the two passengers settle in and supervise their medical care during the flight back to Fort Lauderdale. If they encountered any medical crisis en route, Captain Honeycutt could not be sure which nation would authorize an emergency landing. At 11:45 p.m., the jet whooshed off the Manta tarmac, aiming its spearlike nose northeast, racing to a cruising speed of 400 mph. The mission just might succeed.

Aboard the *Zaandam*, the medical staff opened the packages and inspected the masks and gowns. Each box provided a wealth of resources. All those days of rationing oxygen and masks were over, at least for now. The medical professionals had constantly faced infection and death. At last, they had proper protective equipment. This might allow them to launch their first counteroffensive against the virus. But the beleaguered doctors and the nurses inside the medical center never had anything like a full night's sleep. As they monitored the vital signs of half a dozen critically ill patients, they were being summoned constantly to make emergency visits to patients stuck in their rooms. There wasn't enough space in the medical center for all the sick. Doctors and nurses would make brisk runs to a cabin to examine a patient, then rush back to the medical center.

With their restocked supply cabinet, the nurses aboard the *Zaandam* began to distribute packets of Tamiflu flu remedy and bottles of NyQuil cough syrup. These were far from cutting-edge treatment for COVID-19.

But Tamiflu was thought to help curtail the virus's ability to reproduce. And NyQuil thinned out mucus in the lungs and throat, allowing patients to cough up some of the phlegm. It also had powerful additives that provided a deep rest. The sound of coughing, however, still echoed throughout the ship. "You are lying in bed at night, and you hear people coughing outside your door, and a guy in my corridor was coughing for two whole weeks," said one crew member who worked with the medical staff. "It was scary to wake up to the sound of crew members in our corridor coughing. When is someone going to pick them up and give them oxygen? But I didn't hear anyone come."

Hearing news of the successful medical delivery, U.S. diplomats in Washington celebrated. "That mission saved lives and gave the doctors on the ship breathing room to deal with the rest of the sick. We didn't have to say that people died because we couldn't do anything," said one diplomat. But he was unaware of the tragedy unfolding off the coast of Ecuador, inside the *Zaandam*'s increasingly chaotic medical center.

*

A few minutes past 1:00 a.m. on March 26, a blaring announcement startled passengers awake on the *Zaandam*. The message was broadcast exclusively for the crew, but in their heightened state of alert, the passengers listened intently as they sought to decipher the rapid-fire and shocking announcement: *"Medical emergency . . . doctors . . . Deck 7 . . ."*

An emergency medical team rushed to cabin 7007, an upper-deck stateroom with a private balcony, a king-size bed, and a whirlpool bath, where Jeffrey and Jennifer Hagander, from Redmond, Washington, were staying. They found Jeffrey, seventy-five, unconscious on the floor. His wife, Jennifer, was desperate. He'd been feeling ill for the last four days, coughing, and unsteady on his feet. And then, in the middle of the night, he'd walked into the bathroom, and she'd heard a thud. Entering the bathroom, Jennifer found her husband passed out and hanging over the tub. He'd stopped breathing. Jennifer dragged Jeffrey from the bathroom and tried to revive him, but he was limp. The medical team began CPR, and a defibrillator was placed on Hagander's naked chest. The defibrillator found no signs of life and flashed a "No Shock Advised" signal, so they held off. Five minutes later, at 1:20 a.m., they pronounced Hagander dead. The crew sought to console Jennifer and offered her a replacement cabin, a chance to move from the death scene. She refused. It had all happened so fast. She needed to stay in the tiny cabin and digest the unthinkable: She was a widow.

News of the death zipped from person to person, text message to text message, cabin to cabin. All officers on board had access to the Holland America database that kept updated pictures and descriptions of each guest on every cruise. Usually, crew members accessed this as a courtesy, allowing them to greet a familiar person by name or track down a room number. Now it felt morbid. Crew assisted the transfer of the body to the refrigerated room on A Deck used to store flowers. Now the cool, dark room was being put to a more urgent, critical use.

MARCH 26, 7:00 A.M.
Pacific Ocean, off the Southern Coast of Panama

Aboard the *Rotterdam*, George Covrig was battling doubts. His wife in Romania was dumbfounded by his decision to volunteer for front-line duty aboard a cruise ship infected with COVID-19. Hadn't George thought about their three-year-old son waiting for him back home? But George was convinced he would be fine. He was young, strong, and determined. "There are people begging for air!" George argued. His wife wasn't swayed. "What is wrong with you?" she beseeched. They argued on the phone, but George had already committed. "They will give us equipment to protect us," George shot back. "Besides, I'm already here."

In the privacy of his cabin bathroom, George began to talk into the mirror and record videos. These weren't good-bye videos in case he never lived to see his young child turn four. They were more like self-analysis and a private moment to brainstorm aloud. "I had moments where I also asked, What is wrong with you?" George confessed. "But I did it in private."

As the *Rotterdam* approached the emergency rendezvous with the *Zaandam*, several of the volunteers got cold feet. Suddenly, the altruism of helping their fellow seafarers gave way to feelings that the decision they had made was naïve or suicidal. George tried not to succumb to the fear that was spreading among the crew of the *Rotterdam*. One of the volunteers, a nurse, refused to leave her cabin. "What a mistake," she repeated to herself. "What a mistake!" She cried and cried. "She was scared," said Covrig, who tried to ignore his own doubts. The doctors aboard the *Rotterdam* were divided into two teams: One would remain aboard and a second would transfer to the *Zaandam*—which was dubbed "the sick ship." But these volunteers didn't know how deadly the situation had become aboard the *Zaandam*.

Inside the *Zaandam*'s medical center, the condition of Bengt Wernersson—the fit, adventure-seeking seventy-nine-year-old widower from Sweden, Stockholm, traveling alone—was worsening by the hour. He'd been taken from his cabin by wheelchair two days before, gasping for breath. Pneumonia had settled in; his lungs began to fail. "I knew what was going to happen," said his daughter Shanty Dahl, who only days earlier had convinced a local Swedish travel agent to make contact with the ship and inquire about her father's well-being. She dialed the Holland America help line and begged them to relay her message to her stricken father, who was in critical condition. "We miss you. We love you lots. We hope to get you back home soon." Shanty wasn't sure if the message could be delivered, and she knew he was alone. As her father was being helped to a bedside toilet in the medical center, he stopped breathing. His heart had ceased beating. And at 7:45 a.m., Bengt Wernersson was pronounced dead. Shanty never found out if her father had received her final message.

Fifteen minutes after Wernersson's death, Captain Smit took to the ship's intercom. The previous evening, he somberly said, the *Zaandam* had finally received help from the outside world. Off the coast of Ecuador, a daring night resupply operation had been a success. "We are thankful to the Ecuadorian government for its collaboration," he said. The captain left out any mention of the two ill passengers who'd been allowed to be quietly taken ashore. That would only stoke the rumors and controversies already swirling on his ship.

The medical center was thrust from one crisis to another. Dutch passenger Albertus Slagmolen, seventy-two, was slipping away. A jovial retired Peugeot mechanic who enjoyed gourmet food a little too much, Albertus was traveling with his younger brother. After a few days aboard the *Zaandam*, he jokingly told his daughter he was having the time of his life on a floating luxury hotel while the world was hiding in fear of COVID-19. Suddenly, he fell ill in his cabin, suffering from stomach distress, coughing, and labored breathing. Dr. Hofmann had him rushed to the medical center. Once high fever and pneumonia settled in, Albertus said good-bye to his brother. He told the doctors that he didn't want to be resuscitated. Slagmolen understood that he would never again walk on solid ground. The doctors added him to the DNR list.

*

Claudia Osiani was startled when she heard a knocking on her cabin door. She heard an order—*"Temperature check!... Temperature check!"*

She cracked open the door and a gloved hand snaked in. Pinched between gloved fingers she saw a disposable thermometer. It was one of the three thousand brought aboard from Manta. Claudia's mind raced, her heart rate surging. She wondered, *Could a panic attack spike my temperature?*

Both she and Juan were healthy, with no cough or fever, but that hardly made her feel better. Logic was increasingly less important in predicting what would happen aboard the *Zaandam*. When Claudia was honest with herself, she doubted the cruise line would allow her or Juan to transfer to the *Rotterdam*. Dutifully, she filled out the health questionnaire, which asked if she had experienced influenza-like symptoms. *All I want is to get off this boat,* she thought. *Getting on another boat will be a relief. I am on the virus boat.*

It was nearly nightfall when the passengers aboard the *Zaandam* saw the approaching lights of the *Rotterdam* off the port side. George Covrig and the other volunteers prepared for immediate transfer to the stricken ship. The seas were calm, as marine navigators had predicted. This swell-free patch of ocean off the coast of Panama was ideal for the transport tenders, helping assure that none flipped over and dumped its elderly clientele into the water.

The two cruise ships—so identical in length and design that they were called "sister ships"—aligned in a parallel formation, the two massive hulks blocking wind and muting waves. The first tenders were lowered into the water and from *Rotterdam* a convoy of goods was set to be shuttled over to the *Zaandam*. First they prepped the volunteers, including two additional doctors and two nurses. But one of the nurses had rising doubts as she packed her suitcase. She arrived in the waiting area, a cloud of panicked thoughts swarming her mind. As her luggage was loaded onto the transfer boat, she cracked. Sobbing, she apologized. "I can't go, I can't go." Covrig was rattled as he watched stewards escort the broken nurse back to her cabin on the *Rotterdam*.

Sitting in the tender with the others, preparing for the brief crossing to the *Zaandam*, Covrig felt like everything was taking forever. Safety protocols meant he wasn't supposed to touch anything, and the white-suited tender operators looked like they were heading to inspect a contaminated nuclear power plant. Nobody knew if the virus was everywhere or nowhere. Did it live on surfaces for days? Was it safe to touch anything?

The journey across the stretch of water between the two cruise ships took only a few minutes. Stepping aboard the *Zaandam*, Covrig and the others were greeted by a team of security officers and crew, who broke out in spontaneous applause. The clapping felt awkward to Covrig, but it reinforced and amplified the importance of his mission. He and the other volunteers represented a spark of good news. Hope had arrived. As they walked the deserted corridors, dressed completely in white protective gowns, they looked like ghosts.

Covrig and the other volunteers were taken to meet Captain Smit. The scene was disconcerting on many levels. Smit looked scared. He was clearly fatigued by two weeks of nonstop crisis. Despite his fatigue, or perhaps because of it, the captain lavished praise on the volunteers. After a brief pep talk, he sent them off to assume their specific duties. Doctors and nurses went straight to the medical center, where supplies were being stocked. Covrig was sent to the crew mess hall, where the hotel director and several dozen staff members waited. Covrig noted the fatigue, not only on their faces. Bart Groeneveld, the always impeccable hotel director, looked unkempt and disheveled. He explained that room service food delivery was among the most daunting logistical operations aboard the *Zaandam*. Even with a full staff, it would have been nearly impossible. And with their ranks halved by COVID-19 infections and brutal exhaustion, those still working were ragged.

Outside, the crews working the tenders crisscrossing the calm waters between the ships were drenched in sweat. Covered in protective gear, they felt smothered by the tropical Panamanian heat and humidity. As they took the last loads of supplies over to the *Zaandam* in their bright orange boats, anxious passengers watched out their windows and studied the lights of downtown Panama City. It seemed so close, maybe five hundred yards, but also a world away. The busy back-and-forth of the tenders was mildly entertaining, but they mostly awaited news from the captain. With each passing hour, the tension rose. Was there a problem? Had the locks of the Panama Canal been opened?

When the captain's voice crackled across the cabins and decks, it was a disappointing nonannouncement: Their Panama Canal passage authorization was not quite ready. The captain tried to sound reassuring, telling passengers the details were being hashed out. Meanwhile, *Zaandam* passengers received deliveries of fresh water in the form of two-gallon jugs, an unwieldy size but a clear sign that they would not run out of fresh drinking water.

Sleeping in fits, many of the passengers were ill at ease. The passenger transfers they had expected to commence were again delayed. Now the Panama Canal felt more like a bottleneck than a passage, and the lack of any clear movement made their predicament more desperate.

*

In the infirmary, another crisis played out without the passengers' knowledge. At 4:10 a.m., Albertus Slagmolen, from Nieuwegein, a quaint Dutch city outside Utrecht, stopped breathing and died. It was the third death aboard the *Zaandam* in just over twenty-four hours, and another two dozen patients were progressively getting worse. For Slagmolen, the additional doctors, new stocks of oxygen, boxes of cough syrup, and ventilators had not arrived in time. Slagmolen's long-standing quips—about how he loved cruising so much that he would travel the seas until he died—had come true. When his daughter heard the news, she remembered her father saying, "They'll be taking my coffin off a cruise ship."

CHAPTER 7
PARIAH SHIP

MARCH 27, 5:22 A.M.
Pacific Ocean, Anchored off Panama City

At 5:00 a.m., George Covrig walked into the packed kitchen and announced in a booming voice, "What do you need?" It was his first shift as volunteer in the kitchen. He knew the workers had been through hell and were desperate for an extra pair of hands, but he wasn't prepared for the scene in front of him. The staff members looked beyond exhausted, mentally and physically, and long deprived of hope. A woman from housekeeping, starting yet another fourteen-hour shift delivering meals, began to sob. "You're here. I can't believe it. You're here!" she cried, staring at George. She seemed unable to fathom how anyone would volunteer to help them out of this harrowing mess. "I can't believe it," she said again.

From behind a stack of dirty plates, one of the dishwashers peered through a cloud of steam and froze up, expressionless. One man was unable to lift his arm, his entire shoulder blackened by what looked like a dark stain but was actually a series of deep bruises. Cooks crowded around the massive gas stoves, shouting at one another, punch-drunk from producing thousands of take-out meals a day. Some wore face masks, laboring for each breath. Others found the masks impossible to use, given the oppressive heat.

The servers were a haggard mix of waiters and housekeepers, aided by Erin Montgomery, the only officer to volunteer for dish duty. Her long blond hair was matted down from the steamy heat. Tears welled up when she saw George. She was working as hard as everyone else, even though her stripes made it clear she was the boss. Erin normally counted on two dozen men and women to run the dishwashers, clean the kitchen, and take the trash to the big disposals on Deck 4. She was down to eleven. Five days had passed since the captain ordered the lockdown. All passengers were receiving breakfast, lunch, and dinner via this makeshift room service squad. The cavernous buffet-style restaurants designed to feed hundreds were eerily silent. As the kitchen and service personnel worked to keep everyone fed, the virus picked off their coworkers and bunkmates one by one. George counted only fifteen people healthy enough to deliver meals to 716 cabins. The remaining cooks worked double shifts.

The food service and hotel managers gave George and the other volunteers simple orders: "Put on a mask, gloves, and apron, take one of the trolleys, and deliver meals. Knock on the cabin door, leave the tray on the carpet, and move on. Don't speak to the passengers; don't linger."

With supplies beginning to dwindle once again, the menu was heavy on watery eggs, pastries, and cereal for breakfast and a lot of noodles, rice, and chicken for lunch and dinner. Through the chaos, the cooks retained some semblance of Holland America's touches of luxury. When George went to pick up his first trays, he noticed the meals were exquisitely arranged and set atop crisp linen napkins, flanked by weighty silverware. George arranged the trays on his trolley and headed up the "clean" elevator, midships, to make his first deliveries. Later, he'd collect dirty dishes outside the rooms and return via the "dirty" elevator, located near the stern. On each tray, a member of the staff placed a card printed on thick stationery embossed with the *Zaandam* logo and a quote from Mother Teresa: "We shall never know all the good that a simple smile can do."

Down in the laundry, Wiwit Widarto faced an unimaginable workload. He felt driven to serve the passengers trapped aboard the

Zaandam—especially in the cabins with red dots—those with the sick passengers. Wiwit could not know if the virus clung to the soiled linens as he bundled them into the washing machines. But the virus was all he could think of. Wiwit was scared.

Aboard the *Zaandam*, the ship's entertainers were drafted as foot soldiers in the defense against COVID-19. Some worked hand sanitizer duty, refilling dozens of dispensers. Others were in the wipe-down brigade, attacking handrails, elevator buttons, and door handles with antiseptic wipes, all to keep the crew members from spreading the virus among themselves.

Two dancers roamed the halls, tanks of disinfectant strapped to their backs, each holding a spray wand that looked like the weapon from the movie *Ghostbusters*. They jokingly referred to this as the "COVID Buster," on a mission "to blast the COVID from our ship." They walked the silent corridors of the ship for hours each day, leaving a cloud of disinfectant that hit the back of the throat, leaving those aboard with a stinging, burning sensation with every breath.

Unseen dangers were starting to get inside crew members' heads. Anne could hear everything, the walls were so thin—muffled voices, shrieks of anger, and the coughing. Somewhere, maybe next door, someone was coughing. It felt like the man was sitting next to her. She began to worry as the stranger coughed uncontrollably. Was there sufficient Paracetamol or cough syrup to go around—especially for the crew? Anne knew the doctors were crushed. So she tried to put it out of her mind. Inside the room, Anne could feel the dry, stale air rushing in. Was the virus entering via the air vent? She headed to reception, trying to keep her distance when she passed someone in the hall, trying not to touch anything.

At the improvised call center, the task was overwhelming. There were so many calls, and passengers seemed like they were becoming desperate.

The confinement was taking its toll. One grandmotherly-sounding woman began to unravel. "You need to stop this," she pleaded. "You're giving us too much food!" Suddenly, another woman grabbed the phone and started banging it on the table while yelling, "Isn't this annoying?"

The receptionists were not prepared for this, they weren't sure how to ratchet down the stress. One passenger snapped, "Well, can you ask the captain to stop spouting bull, so I can eat my breakfast in peace?" The captain was in the middle of the morning announcement, which was setting her off, triggering a tirade. The woman was so irritated, like everyone, after all these days trapped in a cabin. Who could blame her?

Another call shocked a rookie on the improvised crisis line. It was his first day on 911 duty, and he was clearly out of his league. A more seasoned receptionist—meaning she'd been on the job a few days—took over the call.

"If no one tells me anything," the passenger snapped, agitated, "I'm going to jump overboard! I can't be in this room anymore."

The emergency protocols kicked in. They had to get a doctor up to that cabin. But they couldn't put the woman on hold. The receptionist gestured wildly to a friend across the room, scribbling on a pad, "We need a doctor to this room, now!"

Returning to the guest on the line, she suggested, "How about we take a couple of breaths. Tell me, what are you seeing in your room right now?" She tried to ground the woman's thoughts in her immediate surroundings. "Is this your first time in South America?" She kept the woman on the line until a doctor showed up at her cabin. Had they averted a tragedy?

The next call was equally insane. "The food sucks here!" a woman screamed. Now the receptionist nearly snapped. She wanted to tear into this person. Who complained about food while people were dying? *Calm down,* she told herself, *calm down. We all are dealing with this in our own way.* But deep down, the receptionist was ready to explode in revolt against the petty complaints. They were all battling for the same path to survival; everyone needed to make sacrifices. It had been an intense thirty hours for Captain Ane Smit and his staff. Three guests had died on board. Dozens were sick. Now, Smit had to share the grim news with the entire ship.

The passengers felt Smit had tried to be straight with them, exuding confidence, security, and honesty. Some cruise ship captains rose to power by being brash self-promoters. They basked in the spotlight given a commanding office. But not Smit. He'd shown a genuine humility over the years, which came through in times of crises like this one. When things were normal, he'd go down to the officers' bar occasionally, draw on his wry sense of humor, and crack a few subtle jokes. But Smit was a family man, not one to gad about. He would keep to himself in his stateroom off the bridge, preferring quiet nights to prowling around the ship.

Since everything started to collapse, Captain Smit had come on the intercom several times a day, even when he didn't have much to report. He created a routine, so the passengers could hear his voice, feel as if he were there among them, share a common bond with him and the crew. People were flooding him with requests and petitions from all sides: the panicking port officials, the crew, the higher-ups back at corporate. Smit was handling multiple conference calls with corporate. But when push came to shove on a decision, he made a point of reminding the brass back on shore that *they* weren't on the ship, *he* was. But without their world-class logistics, he would be even more stranded at sea. These were extremely trying times, and everyone on the ship felt they could trust him, that he would be straight with them. Now Smit took a deep breath and activated the public address system: "May I have your attention, please? This is your captain speaking."

Down in the main galley, the dishwashers paused, turning off their roaring machines so they could listen. The loud, expletive-laced kitchen banter dropped away to silence. "I have some news to share, and it is rather sad news," Smit said. The captain's tone of calming confidence seemed to give way on the edges to pain, bordering on anguish. "Unfortunately, three of our fellow guests have passed away."

Someone shrieked. A cook said quietly, "No, no, no."

No one knew what was causing the sickness. Erin had been pretty sure it was COVID-19—she knew enough from her CDC training. But she'd maintained a sliver of hope that this was something less deadly sweeping through the ship, and that had kept her going. Now there was no doubt. The doctors had been putting to use the test kits they'd received from Manta and, later, the *Rotterdam*. "Yesterday a number of patients were tested," Smit said, "and two individuals tested positive for COVID-19."

With those words, a group meltdown spread across the kitchen. One woman balled up on the floor near Erin, sobbing. Tolentino Tamayo, a galley steward from the Philippines, sat down by a dishwasher and began to cry. He'd been working through pain, a worsening cough, and now a low-grade fever. Erin gave him cough syrup and Paracetamol to make it easier. "I'm so scared. I feel like I am dying," he said.

"You could see the last bit of hope people had inside of them deflate," Erin said. She knew where they were coming from. She'd been putting in long days washing dishes, going through the garbage, just like them. She looked at Tamayo, and the others, and knew it wouldn't be long before she, too, would be overwhelmed. "It was the most miserable thing you could imagine," she said. "It was like everybody got punched in the gut. It was horrible."

George, standing next to his trolley outside the kitchen, felt a wave of panic as the captain spoke. He had assumed it might be COVID-19 that was making people sick, but he'd rationalized away those fears and shrugged off the danger. Now it was different. This confirmed that COVID-19 was on board this ship with him, and people were dying. Now, with no way off, George was scared. *Oh my God, what is happening?* he thought. *Why did I come here?*

After the announcement, Erin needed fresh air. She felt the walls closing in. So she walked up to Lido Deck with one of her stewards. They stood on the fantail in the morning sun, a warm breeze blowing across the Pacific. Erin looked around and was shocked. Dozens of ships lay at anchor near the *Zaandam* and the *Rotterdam*. She saw cruise ships, cargo ships, tankers, and container vessels. The shimmering glass skyscrapers of Panama City lined the water. Just beyond, and out of reach, was the entrance to the Panama Canal. The *Zaandam* was stuck in traffic. *This,* Erin thought, *is a graveyard of ships.*

MARCH 27, EARLY MORNING
UK Ambassador's Residence, Panama City, Panama

It's not going to work; The Panamanians simply can't allow the ships to transit the canal, thought Ambassador Potter as he drafted a letter back to the UK Foreign & Commonwealth Office Crisis Team in London. The massive team, overseen by the foreign secretary, government ministers, and senior officials, had been stood up in London to deal with the flood of consular cases caused by pandemic. Daily reports provided a grim tally of the surging number of cases; UK nationals were gravely ill, COVID-19 the suspected culprit. "Everyone was saying 'Great job getting supplies from ship to ship,' and I felt emotionally and physically exhausted," Potter recalled. "We had failed to help passengers either disembark or transit through the canal."

For days, the diplomats had been working every angle they could think of to persuade the Panamanian government to let the cruise ships through the canal. They'd pressed their case via diplomatic WhatsApp chats, phone calls, letters, and video conferences. (Lockdowns and curfews prevented meetings in person.) Ministers spoke with their Panamanian counterparts, but they'd run into a seemingly insurmountable barrier. The cruise line had confirmed COVID was aboard the *Zaandam*, and Panama made it clear that no ship would pass with the virus aboard.

"I was heartbroken that people were dying or seriously ill," Potter recalled. "I felt a responsibility. I felt that there was more that we could do."

CHAPTER 8
DARK THOUGHTS

MARCH 27
Pacific Ocean, off Panama City

Lance Hutton, the retired educator from Missouri, sat inside his cabin on Dolphin Deck, trying not to lose hope. Sharon, his wife, sat nearby. For five days, they'd been trapped in the cramped room—no bigger than a parking spot. The only glimpse of the outside world was the single salt-streaked porthole the size of a windshield. It was sealed shut. Lance and Sharon wondered whether they would live long enough to breathe fresh air again. A few paces down the corridor, an overflow crowd of febrile, coughing passengers filled the medical center and spilled out into the hall.

Lance was a calm and patient man, his voice imbued with a confidence gained from shepherding kids from the farms and small towns of Missouri through the public-school system. Yet anxiety, despair, and regret were creeping in. *I never should have gotten on this ship, never should have taken Sharon aboard,* he repeated to himself.

At the time, the voyage had seemed like a safe bet. The couple had been on Holland America cruises many times and knew the company was careful. *The cruise line wouldn't have let us get on this ship unless it was safe,* he thought, trying to reassure himself. Lance hadn't wanted to sacrifice his dream of a visit to Machu Picchu. Now he was filled with regret as he thought, *I should have just canceled.*

His biggest concerns were more immediate—like the lack of fresh air in the cabin. Some passengers were permitted a brief foray onto the deck for thirty minutes, and Lance and Sharon had been afforded the privilege just once. Staff members wrapped in masks and gloves had chaperoned them, instructing them not to touch anything, not even the handrails, to stay six feet apart, and to keep quiet. They'd moved in unison, a silent column, no talking, no touching, like prisoners being led to the yard. But the short dose of fresh air and the brief warmth of the sun had provoked an amazing therapeutic effect on Lance and Sharon. Then it was over, and they were back in their cabin. And Lance was thinking far more than was healthy.

For weeks, the *Zaandam* had been moving, which at least made it feel like they might reach a port. Now the ship was stopped, the deadly virus thriving and not a single harbor willing to let it dock. Newscasters were singling out the *Zaandam*. They had dubbed it "the Pariah Ship."

Lance looked out his window and studied the blue-hued glass towers of downtown Panama City, so close. But his mind focused on the Canal Zone. Would Panama allow the *Zaandam* to enter the canal? Would any country show compassion rather than fear and allow them to disembark?

After completing the resupply of medicine and medical personnel, Captain Smit announced that the transfer of passengers to the *Rotterdam* would begin. Soon after, Lance heard a knock on his cabin door and squinted to peer through the peephole. All he could distinguish were two people dressed in protective garb. He figured they were from the medical center, and sure enough, they politely asked him to open the door so they could take his temperature. They asked first that he and Sharon don the masks that had been dropped off earlier. Lance strapped one on and cracked open the door, but the crew members stepped back a little. Both were wearing masks, gloves, and protective glasses. "Stay in your cabin, please, right there. We will handle the rest," one of them said, his voice muffled by the mask. They asked Sharon to come to the doorway, and one of them reached inside with a digital thermometer. After it beeped, they called Lance to the doorway, reminding him not to step into the hallway. When they were done, they had the couple fill out a short health questionnaire. Had they been to China? Had they been in contact with anyone with a respiratory illness in the last ten days? Did they have any symptoms of coronavirus infection, including fever, diarrhea, or a cough? Did either of them use a continuous positive airway pressure (CPAP) machine, which aids in breathing while asleep? Lance checked yes. For years, he'd used a CPAP machine to treat his sleep apnea.

The Huttons felt confident. They checked no to all the other questions and were sure their advanced age would give them priority when it was decided who could leave the *Zaandam*. Passing the health screening meant they were fit enough to board the *Rotterdam*. *They're separating the sick from the healthy, spreading us out,* Lance thought as he imagined the relief to come.

Several hours later, a crew member returned to deliver the news: all bad. The CPAP machine might itself be infected and could become a vector, spreading COVID-19 on the *Rotterdam*, the clean ship. The machine that helped Lance breathe had disqualified the Huttons from transferring. The couple—along with 440 other passengers—were forced to remain on the *Zaandam*. As the orange-and-white launches ferried passengers to the *Rotterdam*, anchored just a few hundred feet away, Lance and Sharon were stuck on the *Zaandam*. Stuck on the sick ship. Lance clung to the hope that, isolated in their room, he and Sharon would be shielded from the spreading virus. But now he began to question the company to whom, he realized, he had entrusted their lives.

Lance glanced at Sharon, who was sitting quietly, trying to read something. The couple could only continue what they'd been doing throughout a half century of marriage—trying to take care of each other.

Speaking to a reporter by cell phone, Lance said nervously, "We'd just like to get off this crazy thing and go home."

"Home," Sharon repeated, almost whispering as her husband spoke into the phone.

Isolated inside the cabin, they were left with the one thing cruise ships promised to eliminate: time to dwell on dark thoughts.

*

From his home in Arnhem, the Netherlands, Arthur Weggeman was feeling anxious about his daughter Anne on the *Zaandam*. The last week had been the toughest of her life, both mentally and physically. The sudden lockdown, her new assignment on the help line, the flood of desperate phone calls from passengers asking questions: "When are we going to get off the ship?" "Can we go through the canal?" Anne couldn't answer the queries. No one could. Anne messaged her father to report a bit of good news. She had no cough. Maybe, she suggested hopefully, it was only a mild flu. Then Anne mentioned, almost casually, that she could no longer taste her food. Arthur knew what this meant.

COVID-19 had only sprung into public view a month or so before, and the precise symptoms remained elusive, revealing themselves slowly. Aboard the *Zaandam*, information about typical COVID-19 symptoms took time to get around and then spread from cabin to cabin, one person to the next. Passengers were even less informed than people on shore. Anne hadn't heard the news that losing one's sense of taste or smell was such a clear sign of COVID-19 that data scientists were now tracking Google queries: "Why can't I taste my food?" and "Why can't I smell anything?" These searches were now considered frontline markers of the pandemic's international expansion. But Arthur, on dry land and far from the *Zaandam*, was informed. "I'd just heard an epidemiologist describe lack of taste as one of the symptoms of COVID," he said. "When she told me that she had no taste, at the same time she said that two people had died, it was alarming. It's a horrible thing to hear as a father."

MARCH 27

Pacific Ocean, Anchored off Panama City

Wiwit Widarto was so tired. For nearly three decades, he had stuffed dirty laundry into sacks and rounded up sodden towels, to such an extent that he figured there was nothing that could surprise him. COVID-19 changed everything. Never had so many asked for so much so insistently. And it wasn't only the passengers. The captain had imposed extreme protocols for washing uniforms. The bridge officers' clothes couldn't be mixed with the engineers'. Even the plumbers' clothes had to be washed separately. It was understandable. No one knew how this virus was spreading. But it required more workers, not fewer. And the virus was picking off his people one by one. Wiwit was down to half his staff.

As Wiwit moved from cabin to cabin, he had to do everything, even change dirty towels, like a rookie housekeeper. Yes, he was a staff supervisor, but here he was doing every chore imaginable. Cruise ships were normally buzzing with noise and movement, which made the silence of the last week so strange, so eerie.

The *Zaandam*'s handsome teak decks were empty, the Ocean Bar and Explorer's Lounge vacant. The sprawling buffet-style dining room on Promenade Deck was closed. Wiwit sat with his friend Rendy in the Lido dining hall, fearing what was to come. Other crew members sat apart, silently eating, deep in thought amid the silence of the ship. Wiwit tried to maintain a sense of humor, cracking jokes.

Wiwit lamented that the Bible-study group, which he organized for coworkers every Sunday, was now prohibited. Wiwit had always been at the center of these meetings, and was adept at applying God's teachings to everyday life on the ship, creating parables others could understand. Rendy looked at his new friend. He'd met him on this ship, back in January, and immediately taken a liking to him. Wiwit was so generous, always offering to help. When Rendy's uniform lost a button, Wiwit had the tailor fix it immediately. When they went out, Wiwit always offered to pay. Yet now Wiwit was subdued, worried, and asking Rendy what he'd heard about COVID-19 outbreaks back home in Indonesia. Wiwit feared for the safety of his wife, Anny, and his two sons. Wiwit described his own fears, the cough, the aches, but he told Rendy he would work through the discomfort. Rendy begged him to visit the medical center, but Wiwit refused. He had to assist the passengers, he insisted. There was no time for doctors. But over lunch, Wiwit seemed alarmed, realizing he was becoming very sick. With fear in his eyes, he confessed to Rendy, "I can't taste anything."

*

Juan and Claudia were also feeling the anxiety. Claustrophobia was starting to take a toll on their sanity, testing the strength of their four-decade marriage. The walls seemed to be closing in, psychologically and physically. Claudia kept trying to figure out how to use her psychology training to confront the oppressive confinement. Her lifelong love of yoga and meditation practices helped, but it wasn't enough. She let the subtle rocking of the ocean drift her thoughts to somewhere pleasant, like memorable moments with her children or grandkids. But a wisp of air from the AC vent above her head or a glimpse of the room service tray piled with dishes triggered panic. Was the virus flowing in through the air vent? Might it migrate from a plate and travel across their small room, searching for a way to kill her and Juan? "We prayed to get off the ship," Claudia said. "We didn't know who was sick, who was dying, or where it was. All we wanted was to get off because the virus was there." The room was too small for two grown adults to cohabit day and night. Claudia listened to meditation tunes through her earphones, occasionally breaking away to glance at Juan. He was pressing his back to the bathroom door, speaking on the phone with clients, an effort to keep his business alive and his mind occupied, she figured. Juan caught her looking and flashed a weak smile. *Poor man,* she thought. *He knows he's driving me crazy. Working is his survival strategy, or at least the illusion of working is maintained by his constant phone calls. And the only place where his phone works is over there.* Claudia retreated to her sector, which she defined as the queen-size bed. All hers.

But their stark differences complemented one another. Juan was reserved, pensive, measured, able to keep his cool no matter what. *How does he keep that up?* Claudia wondered, knowing she was the opposite: volatile, opinionated, a nonstop talker, a fighter, none of which surprised anyone, given that she was half Italian, half Lebanese. *I guess I drive him crazy, too,* she thought as she watched him watch her. He listened, made her laugh, understood her. *He's a pillar of strength in my life,* she thought. *He aligns me, gives me absolute security.*

A knock on the cabin door jostled Claudia out of her mental exercise. Medical personnel had already stopped by to take their temperatures many times, the nurse's gloved hand thrusting through the half-opened door, the beep of the thermometer, the collection of yet another medical questionnaire. *By now they must know who is moving to the* Rotterdam, Claudia thought. She had been dreaming, praying that she and Juan would be allowed to transfer. Claudia opened the door and a crew member wearing a gown, gloves, and a face mask delivered the good news. They were among the eight hundred *Zaandam* passengers cleared to leave.

The next day, just after lunch, a crew member appeared at their door. It was time to go. The couple, disoriented after so many days inside the

four walls of their cabin, walked warily down the deserted corridor to the
elevator. The ship was so quiet. They took care not to touch anything along
the way or speak, fearing the virus could be lurking invisibly on any surface,
waiting for the chance to infect and kill. The couple made their way down
several decks to the waterline, to a small marshaling area next to a door in
the *Zaandam*'s thick steel hull. Outside, a little steel staircase led to the
orange-and-white tender, bobbing in the azure waters. The seas were now
rough, dark clouds had rolled in, and water sloshed perilously close to the lip
of the hatchway. Workers dressed in hazmat suits led them to a device that
emitted a cloud of antiseptic, which enveloped their bodies. Their luggage
was also fogged. The tender had capacity for seventy-five passengers, but
to allow maximum distancing, only thirty were allowed on. One of the
crew barked orders not to touch anything or anyone and to sit in their
designated seats, far from anyone else. The sea heaved the tender to and fro,
waves crashing over the gunwale, water pooling on the floor as the rain fell.
A storm had suddenly come up, adding to the tension. Claudia didn't mind.
She was elated to be leaving the *Zaandam*.

Claudia was struck by how the *Rotterdam* was exactly like the *Zaandam*,
almost identical in design. The crew helped them off the tender and onto
the steel floor of the ship, which rocked heavily, hammered by waves and
rain. Crew members, wrapped in protective medical gear, guided them
through a cloud of fumigation mist. Yet Claudia was euphoric. She and
Juan had escaped the *Zaandam*. The couple was led to a cabin on the same
deck as they had occupied on the *Zaandam*, with the same sealed window.
They were told to shower and wash. Claudia scrubbed their clothes in the
bathroom sink far longer than she thought possible.

*

Back on the *Zaandam*, the evacuation of hundreds of passengers eased the pressure on the crew. But the virus continued its silent assault. Alone in her cabin, Donna Mann was worried about her husband, Jorge. It had been three days since Jorge was admitted to the medical center, and the doctors reported he just couldn't shake the virus. At seventy-nine years old, it was difficult to fight an infection once it took hold—particularly a virus as aggressive as COVID-19. And now Jorge was getting worse. He was coughing more, and harder, with more mucus coming up. Given Jorge's asthma, Donna was alarmed. The *Zaandam* had at least one ventilator in the medical center, and she had heard that was how people on shore were surviving COVID-19. The doctors asked her for permission to place Jorge on a ventilator if deemed necessary, and she pleaded with them to do whatever they saw fit, and soon. The doctors listened patiently and promised to consider that option. For now, they'd help Jorge fight this as best he could. It was clear to Donna that he wasn't coming back to their cabin anytime soon.

MARCH 28, 7:30 A.M.
Panama Canal Zone

From his office on the shores of the canal, Rainiero Salas had followed the plight of the *Zaandam* and wanted to cry out in anger. He'd spent his life piloting ships through the canal. So every time another port refused to aid the *Zaandam*, Salas felt betrayed. *In Panama, we would never do that,* he told himself. *Never.*

Salas vowed that should the cruise ship reach the Panama Canal, he would personally volunteer his skills to pilot the *Zaandam* through the complicated set of locks and lakes. He would escort the ship across the isthmus. And as one of the canal's most experienced navigators, he was one of the few mariners who could pull off the challenging operation.

Salas couldn't understand how so many nations could be so cruel. He ran his finger up a map of South America's west coast as he rattled off the names of the ports that had denied shelter to the *Zaandam*—Punta Arenas, Puerto Montt, Valparaíso, Arica, Callao, Guayaquil. This violated his seafarer's moral code.

Salas knew that cruise ships regularly diverted their itinerary to respond to calls for help. Holland America's ships had been among the first to assist the sinking *Titanic* in 1912. The Holland America Line billeted thousands of Allied soldiers aboard its ships during World War II. Modern cruise ships were caricatured by the media as floating bacchanals, but when refugees from Cuba were found bobbing in the Caribbean in 2012, the cruise ship *Oasis of the Seas* diverted course. She rescued, clothed, and brought to Mexico twenty-three Cubans who were about to perish at sea. Now, with the tables turned, the centuries-long code of maritime solidarity felt shattered. Salas told himself that if the *Zaandam* needed help in Panama, he would assume the risk. But would he even get the opportunity? Days before, the Ministry of Health had banned any ship from entering the Panama Canal if there was even a single confirmed COVID-19 case aboard the *Zaandam*. The authorities feared the virus might infect the canal pilots, effectively shutting down one of the world's most critical shipping routes.

Salas, a veteran pilot with twenty-five years' experience working the canal, worried about the people aboard the *Zaandam*. He was no scientist, but he'd heard the reports of flulike symptoms and passengers dying. There was an urgency and moral obligation to assist the stranded ship. "I wanted to show that if Panama could do this, so could the world. We are a small country, but we have a big heart," he cheerily explained, in an echo of a national slogan with the same refrain.

Just after the *Zaandam* had entered Panama's territorial waters several days earlier, a crisis had erupted at the highest level of the Panamanian government. Officials debated not only the question of whether to help the orphaned ship pass through the canal but an even thornier issue: Could they trust the cruise line's executives? They suspected that Holland America had delayed revealing the COVID-19 cases and deaths for hours to keep from upending negotiations to secure passage through the Panama Canal. If Panama had been aware of the COVID-19 outbreak earlier, it could have kept the ships out of Panamanian waters. So, had executives held off confirming the outbreak until Panama agreed to allow the *Zaandam* and the *Rotterdam* into Panamanian waters? The Panamanians huddled to debate their options. Should they force the ships back into international jurisdiction?

The passengers aboard the *Zaandam* were now taking to social media and beseeching the world for help. Many passengers viewed the deaths on board the ship as a sign of the world's neglect. "These people were denied the medical care that might have saved them by all the countries that turned our ship away. The blood of those who died lies upon those who closed their doors to us," said *Zaandam* passenger Laura Gabaroni in a media interview. "We will never know if these people might have been saved if they had received the care they needed. Those who decided to close their doors will have to live with that."

Now it was up to the Panamanian government. Would they take the high moral ground, seizing the opportunity to do the right thing?

MARCH 28, 7:30 A.M.
Panama City

Canada's ambassador to Panama, Lilly Nicholls, broke the logjam by leveraging her relationship with Panama's former president, Aristides Royo.

As both the minister overseeing the canal operation and a much-loved former leader, Royo was among the few Panamanians who had the ear of the current president.

Nicholls spoke to Royo. Potter, the UK ambassador, followed up with a call and WhatsApp messages.

Royo's daughter Natalia was working in London as the Panamanian ambassador to the United Kingdom, so Potter appealed to her on "humanitarian grounds" to work with her father and the government behind the scenes to get permission for the two ships to transit the canal. That argument moved the needle. Royo lobbied the cabinet to let the two cruise ships transit the canal for humanitarian reasons.

*

After reviewing all the options, the Panamanian government announced its decision. The health officials and political leaders approved the expedited passages of the *Zaandam* and the *Rotterdam*, even if such a move would potentially risk infecting the volunteer pilots and the canal itself. The *Zaandam* would go first, followed by the *Rotterdam* close behind. To keep the mission off the media radar until the last moment, they waited as long as possible—until that night—to announce the decision. "It was a tight operation, which was kept confidential and managed by very few people," said Gabriel Alemán, secretary-general of the Panama Canal Pilots' Union. "Media pressure required keeping it all strictly within the group of us who were organizing the operation."

The Panamanians had been provoked into helping the *Zaandam* after hearing about the deaths aboard the ship. Furthermore, they also heard troubling rumors that the port of San Diego had rejected the pleas of the *Zaandam*. If true, that meant that the *Zaandam*, more than ever, needed safe passage to the Atlantic Ocean. The ship's urgent requests for medicine, oxygen, and help for dying patients put further pressure on the Panamanians. They'd already allowed the ships to meet up in Panamanian waters to facilitate the transfer of supplies, including oxygen, from the *Rotterdam* to the *Zaandam*. But the doctors needed more.

To minimize contact between dockworkers and the crew aboard the infected cruise ships, the Panamanian government authorized the ships to skip the traditional older locks system and transport through the faster neo-Panamax locks finished in 2016. Slightly wider, these were deemed spacious enough to dispense with ropes and the land crews who guided and pulled ships through the narrow locks of the canal via a system of mini locomotives. That guidance system employed at least a dozen land laborers (the "tie-down team") and involved ropes that needed to be winched back and forth between land and the ship, potentially touched by workers on both ends, the hull coming within four feet of the canal's banks in some places. The pilots came up with a plan to eliminate as many participants as possible. For the first time in memory, a cruise ship would skip the ropes and land-based assistance.

Panamanian pilot Juan Feliu would run the operation from the bridge of the *Zaandam*, where Captain Smit agreed to clear out all nonessential personnel. But Smit still needed a reduced complement of engineers and navigators to fire up the engines and thrusters to help align the ship's prow as it moved slowly through the first two locks. Then Feliu would guide her along the twisting route across Gatun Lake, an artificial holding lake created by the diversion of rivers and the construction of the canal. Leaving the lake, the *Zaandam* (with the *Rotterdam* close behind) would enter the first of the two locks that would lower the massive ship down to the level of the Atlantic. All told, the operation would take twelve hours for the two ships. With only a single Panamanian pilot aboard each vessel, it would be a daring move. Not only did the canal represent an important slice of national revenue but much of Panama's prestige was also held in the narrow sluices. Should the operation fail, should the canal be infected, blocked, or stalled, it would rain untold political fallout on the nation's president.

Carnival was also facing a huge risk. Given the suspension of normal procedures, the cruise line was asked to sign what in effect was a blank check. If the ship or the canal were damaged, it would fall upon the cruise company to cover the costs.

The Panamanians prepared the *Zaandam* to cross the canal, but they insisted the operation begin late at night. This was necessary for two reasons. First, canal traffic was lighter at night, and second, the sun would be down. After dark, the tropical heat would be more manageable for the volunteer pilots, who were required to wear so much stifling hazardous-duty gear, it looked like they were preparing to inspect a nuclear power plant.

For the passage to be as inconspicuous as possible—hardly a reality given the size and notoriety of the *Zaandam*—all aboard had to follow strict rules. Captain Smit turned on the PA system to instruct the passengers: If there was to be any chance of passing through the Panama Canal, he needed full obedience. All passengers were directed to remain in their cabins. No one was to walk in the hallways or step out on the balconies. No noise. No lights. No stepping out on deck. No peeking through the curtains to see the shore. Captain Smit's precise instructions were tinged with the language of a clandestine operation, which many aboard found deliciously conspiratorial. After so many days of defeat, this was a chance for a group victory.

CHAPTER 9
NIGHT CROSSING

MARCH 29
Panama Canal Zone

Captain Gabriel Alemán was not a man to be bullied. As the leader of the Panama Canal Pilots' Union, he literally controlled the flow between two oceans. The specialized pilots in his union assured that cruise ships, sailboats, and container ships maneuvered through the Panama Canal with neither accident nor delay. These navigators were among the world's most elite mariners. Like magicians, they deftly slipped ships the size of skyscrapers through a man-made canal as narrow as 110 feet in some places. Captain Alemán knew that he held the final word no matter who was pressuring Panama to act. No one could force him to put one of his pilots in danger. If the pilots refused to lead the mission, no one else would be allowed to steer the *Zaandam* through the fifty-mile route of the Panama Canal. No ship passed without one of Alemán's pilots in command.

Privately, Alemán knew he had numerous volunteers willing to pilot the *Zaandam* and the *Rotterdam*. Alemán had never felt so proud of his fellow pilots. Once word circulated that the *Zaandam* and the *Rotterdam* were stuck on the Pacific coast en route to Florida, half a dozen union members offered to navigate the ships to the Atlantic—despite the risk of catching the deadly virus.

To prepare for a COVID-19 mission, the government brought in a rapid-response team, trained to deal with radioactive and toxic spills, to teach the pilots proper protocol. They were dressed in camouflage uniforms and looked like commandos. Over and over, they had the pilots rehearse suiting up and then disrobing. It was the latter that most worried everyone. Whatever protective clothing being worn during the mission would collect viral material over the course of hours. It would be among the most COVID-exposed material in all of Panama. Any slipup or safety lapse might jeopardize not only the ongoing operation of the canal but the health and welfare of the nation. Alemán had no doubts. "We told the health ministry and gave them the assurance that we had the capacity to do this, and that it would be done by volunteers."

The Panama Canal Authority and the Ministry of Health were convinced that what Alemán proposed was feasible, both from a health perspective and operationally. "That's when the wheels started to turn," said Alemán. "We told the Panamanian authorities when we presented the volunteer candidates that this was a historic opportunity for the Panama Canal to show that the humanitarian sentiment in this country could be put above ourselves. And that's what motivated this operation."

One after another, the pilots stepped forward. Alemán had so many volunteers that officials from the Ministry of Health were brought in to complete a deadly estimation: If COVID-19 invaded each and every one of these bodies—despite promises of layer after layer of protective gear, including diapers so they wouldn't have to undress if they needed to go—who among the volunteers was best suited to weather this viral storm?

The officials at the Ministry of Health chose four men who were, if not fit for the mission, less weighed down by comorbidities, like obesity or breathing ailments. Two men were designated as pilots for the *Zaandam*. Another two were assigned to the *Rotterdam*. As contingency plans advanced, however, those risks were calculated to be unreasonably high.

The administrators of the Panama Canal then made an unprecedented and dangerous gamble: Each cruise ship would take just one pilot. Rainiero Salas would command the bridge of the *Rotterdam*, while his colleague Juan Feliu would lead the *Zaandam*. "I had a feeling of helplessness," said Salas, describing the long wait until the mission was finally approved. "I did what I did as an act for humanity."

MARCH 29, 7:30 P.M.
Panama Bay, Outside Panama Canal Zone

Back on the *Zaandam*, Wiwit Widarto was trying to find the strength to call his wife, Anny, at their home in Batam. He was almost twelve hours into his workday, hoisting load after load of dirty sheets, pillowcases, towels, and linen napkins into the big machines. Many of his men remained too sick to work in the stifling heat. Then there were the guests. They called and called, asking for new sheets, or just needing to talk. Wiwit felt like he had to come to their aid. It was his job, his calling, and it always had been. The guests always came first.

Wiwit had walked up and down these corridors a thousand times. But now, wearing his uncomfortable face mask, it was increasingly difficult to keep his energy and spirits up. Wiwit was scared but was convinced he had to tough it out, especially now that it was time to call home. He had to put on the best face he could for Anny as he called via WhatsApp, audio only enabled. They exchanged hellos, and Wiwit tried to calm Anny down, set her at ease, but failed. "Please don't be sad," Wiwit said. "You need to be a strong mom. For the kids."

Anny was taken aback. "Why would you say that?" she asked. It was like he was saying good-bye, she thought. Anny switched the WhatsApp call to video, wanting to study his face. She was shocked. Her husband looked gaunt and drained. But what worried her more was that she could tell that he was frightened. Wiwit must have noticed her concern, as he quickly switched the call back to audio and mumbled something about the ship's Wi-Fi being too weak for video. Anny knew that was an excuse. Maybe he didn't want her to see him that way, didn't want her to worry. "I'll take a photo of myself later and send it to you," he promised.

Anny pressed him, trying to find out what was wrong. Finally, Wiwit confessed that his fever was rising and the coughing was worse than ever. He had lost all sense of taste and smell. Wiwit knew he'd caught something that wouldn't go away. In the medical center, the staff had told him that medicine was in short supply. Wiwit told his wife that those limited stocks were being rationed for the most seriously ill passengers. Wiwit was relying on home remedies, like hot tea with lemon. He had to cough it out, get better, then work some more. "As long as our passengers are healthy, I'm okay with that," he told Anny. Then he interrupted the conversation. He had to go. A passenger had called, requesting a fresh blanket.

Anny was shocked. Why was Wiwit insisting on working as he fell ever more ill? Before he hung up, she asked her husband, "How can they save all the medicine for the passengers?"

Wiwit seemed distant, taking his time before answering.

"Please, please rest," Anny pleaded. "Please. Don't work while you're feeling unwell."

"I can't. I can't afford to do that," Wiwit finally responded. His voice trailed off. "Lots of my staff are falling ill. Someone's got to work."

"Please, stay strong," Anny said; now she was crying.

Wiwit said he had to go, had to hang up. "Please, pray for me."

MARCH 29, 9:00 P.M.
Pacific Ocean, Entering the Panama Canal

With the cruise ship darkened, the passengers and all but essential crew were confined to their staterooms, bunks, or positions aboard the vessel. Salas and Feliu boarded the two cruise ships, each donning blue plastic gloves, baggy gray booties, and a white jumpsuit (complete with baggy hoodie). The suits were sweltering, sealing in heat and humidity. The cheap plastic goggles and face mask made the various members of their support team so homogeneous that they had to write one another's names on the back of one another's shoulders with a marker—just to be sure who was who.

Before Feliu entered the bridge to take control of the *Zaandam*, a colleague strapped on an orange backpack with a four-gallon tank filled with chemicals, which he blasted across the floor and walls. No one knew if it would work—or even what noxious chemical formula was being used. Later, when entire cities fogged their streets, critics mocked the advent of "theatrical hygiene." But in these early days, desperate guesses were about the only possibility to stave off this mysterious virus.

When the chemical mist settled, Feliu entered the bridge of the *Zaandam* and was shocked by what he saw. Captain Smit and his key aides looked crestfallen and worn out. Usually, the transfer of power from the presiding captain of a cruise ship to the temporary Panamanian pilot was rife with lighthearted jokes or even showmanship. This time, it felt like a deadly serious passing of the torch. No longer able to keep up their morale or their faith in finding a port, the officers of the *Zaandam* looked defeated. As Feliu took command of the ship, he felt not only their desperation but also their appreciation for what he and, in fact, the nation of Panama were doing.

Feliu knew that nearly every country in South America had refused port, denied medical emergency evacuations, and even refused the requests to bring aboard medicines. At a most crucial moment, Panama had broken the boycott.

Instead of seven days to San Diego, a port where it was unclear if they were to be given shelter, they now could be within striking distance of Florida in four days. Port Everglades was the home port to much of Carnival Corporation's fleet. That precious time—three fewer days of transit—might be the difference between life and death for the sicker passengers. Captain Smit looked grateful as he welcomed aboard Feliu, who ascended to the bridge and temporarily became captain of the *Zaandam*.

As the mission got under way, Feliu guided the *Zaandam* into the first stretch of the canal. Captain Smit stayed by Feliu's side to respond immediately to any navigational orders. Together, they needed precise control to maintain the alignment of the seven-hundred-foot-long ship. Weather and wind were favorable, but in the canal the margin for error was measured in seconds and feet.

*

The lore of the Panama Canal celebrates the immense engineering prowess of the project, and rightfully so. But it's easy for mariners and passengers to miss the overarching role that disease played in its construction. The channel is more than sluice gates, controlled flooding mechanisms, and technologically sophisticated monitoring stations. Its shores also contain a series of mass graves. To build the Panama Canal, engineers not only had to dig, blast, and haul away mountains of material; they also had to defeat a triad of deadly enemies: malaria, yellow fever, and their uncontrollable method of transmission, the mosquito.

At least twenty thousand workers—nearly all from the West Indies— died during the early years of canal construction. The massive construction project was led by Ferdinand de Lesseps and a bevy of fellow French investors, including many politicians, who would later rue their involvement. Having spearheaded the creation of the Suez Canal in 1869, de Lesseps basked in his success. He coolly estimated that if he could dig through the sands of Egypt in ten years, he'd be able to rip through the rocks of Central America in six.

Convinced that yellow fever and malaria were caused by "bad air" and invisible particles, which they called "fomites," that infected bedding and linens, de Lesseps and his French colleagues could not have devised a more lethal work environment had they tried. To dissuade ants from climbing the tables inside the French-run hospital, small ceramic dishes filled with water were placed around each table leg. This standing water created a plethora of fertile mosquito breeding grounds near the workers. Believing that infected air was the cause of yellow fever, hospital windows were left wide open, allowing swarms of *Aedes aegypti* mosquitoes to buzz toward their prone victims.

While malaria was a common ailment, it was far less fatal than yellow fever, which caused jaundice and left victims with skin that took on a deathly pallor. While many victims never felt symptoms, a small subset fell into a cycle of spiking fevers, headaches, extreme thirst, and finally the "black vomit"—a result of intense internal bleeding.

An estimated 85 percent of workers involved in the early French attempts to construct the railroad and canal were infected with yellow fever. The death toll between 1881 and 1889 averaged between three hundred and six hundred workers every month, depending on who was counting and who was deemed worthy of a tally. Afro-Caribbean workers hauled away dead colleagues in wheelbarrows, then dumped them into mass graves. Many of the workers dashed away at the first signs of these outbreaks, the dreaded arrival of "yellow jack." In 1889, de Lesseps and the French went bankrupt and abandoned the colossal effort.

In 1903, the United States took control of what remained of the project, supporting rebels in slicing off the westernmost horn of Colombia to create the republic of Panama. Besides redesigning the canal and moving its course to a route above sea level, the revised canal design became feasible after Dr. Walter Reed and his Yellow Fever Commission proved that mosquitoes were spreading the disease. William Gorgas, the sanitary officer for the project, finally got the disease under control in the whole country of Panama by leading a campaign to eliminate mosquito-breeding sites, mitigating the transmission vector.

Panama only recovered full control of the canal (along with 400,000 acres of land and 7,000 buildings) on December 31, 1999. After nearly a century of foreign domination, the small country now controlled access between two of the world's most heavily traveled oceans. As a result, Panama is a maritime powerhouse, and the nation's leaders understand the economic importance of shipping. In 2020, more than 9,600 vessels worldwide flew the Panamanian flag, roughly one of every five registered globally. In March 2020, with the eyes of the world following the plight of the *Zaandam*, the Panamanian government understood the symbolism at stake. "Nobody wanted to receive them, not even the United States government. It was incredible," said Captain Alemán, the pilot union chief. "This was a way to help those people. Thank God, we could get it done here. If we could do it, how can they not do it there in the United States?"

In the storied history of the canal, few passages would be as widely watched—or as nerve-racking—as the transit of the *Zaandam* and the *Rotterdam*.

*

As the *Zaandam* slipped into the Miraflores Locks, the first stretch of the Panama Canal, at 9:21 p.m., passengers and crew were united in cautious optimism. Crossing the canal brought them close to home port—if U.S. authorities would allow them to dock.

Despite the orders for silence, in the bowels of the *Zaandam* the dishwashing operation continued at a pace as frenetic and noisy as ever. As he stacked dishes, sorted silverware, and tended to famished fellow workers, George Covrig was struck by the sound of a song. Who was singing? Covrig was mesmerized as he listened—a pitch-perfect voice cut through the clanging plates and the rhythmic thump as the dishwashing machines clacked and whirred along their endless loop. The singer, a Thai waitress, serenaded the room with an aria in her native language. George could not understand a single phrase, yet he started to cry. He was certain she was singing to save herself, to save them all. Might she also be blessing their collective dream to cross the canal?

In her cabin many decks above the dish room, Donna Mann felt trapped. Her husband, Jorge, remained in the infirmary, in critical condition, fighting to breathe. Had he been put on a ventilator? Was he still alive? Donna had reason to doubt the information related to her by the *Zaandam*'s medical staff. They'd shifted their story so many times, she was unsure what to believe. One day the doctors announced that her husband was better, and then they told her he was about to be intubated, with medevac flight details being finalized. But after a flurry of questions about her medevac insurance (and lack thereof), Jorge was not evacuated. Her only certainty was that each additional day at sea increased the chances that once again she would be a widow, losing her second husband on a trip meant to celebrate their wedding anniversary.

*

As the *Zaandam* entered the first lock of the canal, hydraulic pumps flooded the chamber, and within minutes the massive ship was raised forty feet. Officials in half a dozen embassies, at Carnival HQ in Miami, and at

Holland America's offices in Seattle, as well as the top administrators for the canal, were watching. Most of their concerns focused on the health and welfare of the canal pilots. Should either Feliu or Salas have a medical emergency, the entire plan would be placed in jeopardy. To allow for a more expedient transit, Panama Canal authorities cleared out all other ships. For this night, and until dawn, the Panama Canal was an exclusive route, just for the *Zaandam* and the *Rotterdam*. Captain Alvaro Moreno of the Panama Canal Pilots' Union repeatedly checked in with the pilots to assure that everything was fully operational. Extensive abort plans had been worked out by the Panamanians. But once a ship entered, there was no reversing. They were committed to bringing the ship through the canal and into the Atlantic.

Halfway through the canal, the *Zaandam* was making rapid progress. In just three hours they were already in Gatun Lake, where the *Zaandam* was allowed to advance at such a brisk pace that canal officials monitoring the vessel's progress realized that they were on track to set a record. Never before had a cruise liner passed through the canal in under ten hours. This crossing was tracking closer to eight. For passengers, the progress through the canal—made mysterious by the darkness and hushed voices—felt like a huge step toward reaching the United States. After days of delays, they began to celebrate as the journey continued. Home port might be in sight. They awoke the next morning to the welcome sensation of the ship pitching and rolling. The passage had been a success. The *Zaandam* was now in the rough waters of the Atlantic Ocean.

MARCH 30
UK Ambassador's Residence, Panama City

Inside the UK ambassador's residence in Panama City, Damion Potter had been bracing for the worst. "Until one a.m., until I had confirmation,

I assumed that anything could derail the plans. Who knows: A new strain? More people dying? Not enough equipment? The world was in chaos," explained Potter.

Then, he got word from the foreign minister: "It's done." Potter felt a surge of euphoric adrenaline. "I couldn't really sleep and then had to get up early to prepare my children for school, so I didn't get much rest." But there was little downtime for the diplomat or his team. That day, the final commercial flight in what would prove to be six months was set to take twenty-four Brits to London, and even that flight was not certain. Furthermore, the U.S. government was sending conflicting signals about accepting the passengers of the notorious cruise ships.

UK diplomats fanned out across the United States, and teams were assembled near Holland America headquarters in Seattle and near Carnival Cruise offices in Florida. An intense campaign was launched to follow the course, not only of the beleaguered ship, but the workings of the Trump White House. "We needed to have a position where they wouldn't just let the U.S. citizens get off. That was a risk. At one point it was, 'Nobody is coming in.' Then it was, 'Possibly only U.S. citizens.'" The diplomats lobbied hard to include British and other nationals in the disembarkation. "There were a lot of things in the air," Potter said. "Which is why the UK diplomatic networks in the United States were so critical."

*

After the exhausting journey, pilots Salas and Feliu went ashore and carefully changed clothes, dumping their soiled gear into a pile that health officials told them would be incinerated. Driven to their respective homes, each man was placed under a fourteen-day quarantine. Their valiant mission was over, and the world had been shown an example of solidarity. "Soon after that, the attitude around the world toward cruise ships changed," said

Captain Alemán. "There were still a lot of other ships sailing around the world with passengers who were sick. The *Zaandam* crossing the canal helped people understand that the risk is low, so you've got to help." He paused, then concluded, "If we hadn't allowed them to cross, it is likely that no other port in the world would have let them in."

CHAPTER 10

DESPERATE PLEA

MARCH 30, 2:30 A.M.

Caribbean Sea, Anchored off Colón, Panama

As the *Zaandam* emerged from the Panama Canal well before dawn, Captain Smit still faced a grim journey ahead. Beating the odds, his ship had made a record quick passage through the Panama Canal. But the virus was spreading with exponential zeal. At least two hundred people aboard had gotten sick, and cases were also being logged aboard the *Rotterdam*—supposedly the healthy ship.

Smit ordered the officers to drop anchor just off the port of Colón. He needed to wait for the *Rotterdam*, which was two hours behind, in the *Zaandam*'s wake.

Over the past few days, the *Zaandam* had secured several dozen tanks of medical oxygen—some from the *Rotterdam*, some while waiting off the coast of Panama, and a few tanks from the Ecuadorians during the Manta operation. But that supply was dwindling. Patients in sick bay were consuming oxygen faster than the stock could be replenished. They crowded into the infirmary, gasping for breath. The doctors were worried about two passengers from the United States who were in critical condition and getting worse.

The *Rotterdam* cleared Gatun Locks, the last stretch of the canal, at 4:20 a.m., two hours after the *Zaandam*, and approached her sister ship. As the temperature rose over the Gulf of Mexico, the intense tropical sun bounced off the thick, wraparound windows on the bridge. Smit raised anchor and headed deeper into the Caribbean Sea, the *Rotterdam* close behind. They now had an open pathway to Florida. But docking authorization—even in their home port—was still far from certain.

*

Every breath for Wiwit Widarto was now a struggle. His cabin on B Deck had barely enough room for either him or his roommate to slide past the bunk bed. Despite decades with Holland America, Wiwit hadn't yet earned the privilege of sleeping in his own cabin or having a private bathroom. His bunkmate was the head tailor, who worked for him in the housekeeping department. They, in turn, shared a bathroom with two other crew members from the adjacent cabin.

The virus had invaded Wiwit's lungs, and his fever was raging. His chest had tightened, the coughing worsened, and his sense of taste and smell were gone. But still, Wiwit continued to labor on the front lines. He wore a face mask as he moved through the corridors, knocking on passengers' doors. But no one could wear a mask in the laundry room, where it was so hot.

*

Erin Montgomery walked down the narrow corridor on B Deck, unnerved by all the additional red dots stuck to the cabin doors. *They are spreading everywhere,* she thought as she returned to the noisy dishwashing room. As sanitation officer, Erin had documented the spread, alerting her boss that the ILI, or whatever they wanted to call this viral surge, seemed to be turning into a shipwide outbreak. Passengers and crew alike were being struck down with terrifying speed.

Erin put all that second-guessing aside. With more than half her staff knocked out by COVID-19, she was fighting a losing battle to maintain any sense of team unity. Many of the staff who showed up were so worn-out, they could barely lift a tray of food, crack a joke, or maintain the rousing camaraderie that was a hallmark of all Holland America ships. With three-meals-a-day room service, the dish team had to deal with a tsunami of dirty utensils, plates, and bowls. Trays were piled upon trays. Soiled glasses were balanced on shelves. The task was complicated by the heightened protocols to protect the officers. Holland America executives didn't know if the virus lived on dirty dishes. Could it spread the infection to vital ship's control centers, including the engine room and the bridge? Erin had to order her people to separate plates and silverware for each operational group. They washed the officers' dishes separately from those of the engineers in the engine room. It was maddening, and scary. But it was now part of the job. Erin was too knocked out, physically and mentally, to question the orders she received.

Looking around the room, Erin paused for a moment, taking it all in. For nearly two weeks, they'd washed roughly nine thousand plates a day. Tolentino Tamayo, a dishwasher from the Philippines who'd signed up for the dishwashing job to save money for his husband's kidney transplant, was still working—even after he had collapsed at one point from exhaustion, then curled into a ball under a washing station. Erin knew Tolentino was too sick to even stand. "Please, go down to your cabin and stay there," she urged him. "You've done enough." Tolentino stared back at her, barely able to respond, his eyes wide with fear. "Yes, madame." Finally, he left.

MARCH 30
State Department, Washington, D.C.

As the *Zaandam* headed into the Caribbean, Keith Taylor, the no-nonsense former Coast Guard commander who ran Holland America's marine operations, was pressing State Department diplomats for more help. For days, Ramon "Chico" Negron, the veteran diplomat, was running point on this and other cruise ship outbreaks. He had been hearing a lot from Taylor. Negron oversaw a group that the State Department had created to deal with crises like these: the Coronavirus Global Response Coordination Unit. Negron's mission was to bring the cruise ships home before COVID-19 killed even more passengers and crew, especially Americans. Negron's efforts had been the difference between life and death for the passengers on the stricken ship. Starting with the diplomatic push on countries along the Pacific coast of South America—Chile, Peru, Ecuador, Colombia, and, finally, Panama—State scored key victories for Holland America that undoubtedly saved lives on the *Zaandam*. The ship simply wouldn't have received medical aid in Manta or in Ecuador or, more crucially, passage through the Panama Canal had it not been for the diplomats. Now Taylor was back, asking for help.

There were two gravely ill American citizens on the *Zaandam*, he explained, and time was running out. They needed to be airlifted to a hospital. They could die at any moment. Holland America had two ideas. They could send the *Zaandam* to Cozumel, some one thousand nautical miles north. The other option was a lot better. The *Zaandam* was scheduled to track close by San Andrés, a tiny island in the Caribbean, off the coast of Nicaragua, that is a territory of Colombia. The *Zaandam* would barely have to veer from its northeasterly route to reach San Andrés, half the distance and time it would take to get to Cozumel.

U.S. diplomats in Colombia received the first calls just before 6:00 a.m. They started working all the embassy's contacts inside the Colombian government, asking, pleading, negotiating permission for the *Zaandam* to dock at the tiny island. It was a simple plan. The *Zaandam* could drop anchor two miles offshore and use a tender to transport the passengers to an ambulance waiting at the dock, where the two sick Americans could then be rapidly taken to the island's airfield, a few minutes away. Holland America was already arranging for a chartered jet with medical personnel aboard to fly from Fort Lauderdale to pick up the two gravely ill passengers. Within three hours, they could be flown back to a hospital in Fort Lauderdale.

The diplomats were counting on Colombia, a long-standing ally and recipient of billions in military aid, to accommodate U.S. demands. But as the pandemic advanced, it was proving difficult for the U.S. government to sway anyone, even those controlling an island just eight miles long and two miles wide. Half a dozen officials at the U.S. embassy got to work, but approval proved elusive.

On San Andrés, local officials, including the harbormaster and a representative of the Ministry of Health, didn't have the authority to approve anything. Colombia's president, Iván Duque, had banned flights and ships to and from the country, so he would have to approve the rescue plan. But the news from Bogotá was maddeningly slow. Diplomatic notes had to be delivered but also translated and moved through the bureaucracy to land on the desk of the one man who could actually authorize an emergency rescue operation, President Duque. Not only would the Colombians need to okay the unloading of the passengers but they would also have to lift a flight ban and allow for the flying ambulance to touch down, then return home.

Officials from the U.S. embassy in Bogotá scrambled to outline the arguments to the Colombian leader. Not only was this an emergency evacuation but the incoming flight would be stuffed with medical supplies, including PPE gear and badly needed medicine. Even the basics were in short supply on the *Zaandam*. And people were dying.

San Andrés island is a cruise ship magnet during normal tourist seasons. Dozens of ships stop every year, each carrying thousands of passengers, who disembark to spend their money while visiting beaches flanked by coconut plantations. More than one million people visited San Andrés in 2019, supercharging the local economy. But now the sight of a cruise ship was synonymous with a deadly pandemic. San Andrés was COVID-free; not a single case had been reported. By midmorning, Governor Everth Hawkins Sjogreen could sense that islanders feared the *Zaandam* would sow death and sickness if allowed to dock. The island's population of seventy thousand wasn't happy about taking that gamble. Locals argued that it was a question of cultural survival. Should the pandemic tear through the islands, what was left of the fragile Afro-Caribbean Raizal communities would be at risk of getting wiped out. Roughly half the archipelago's residents are Creole-speaking Raizal, descendants of Africans who were enslaved by English and Spanish colonizers. During the past two centuries, Spain and England traded rule of the island until it became part of independent Colombia in 1822. Then, nations across the region, including Nicaragua, joined the fight. The Raizals were often caught in the middle, engendering an innate suspicion of outsiders that endures until this day.

MARCH 30, 10:00 A.M.
Caribbean Sea, 150 Miles Southeast of San Andrés, Colombia

On the bridge of the *Zaandam*, orders came from corporate HQ. The ship was to make a run toward San Andrés, to be in position to dock if the diplomatic push succeeded. Around 10:00 a.m., Smit executed a sharp turn to port, setting the *Zaandam* on a direct course to San Andrés. Within a few hours, Captain Smit could have the *Zaandam* moored just off San Andrés's tiny harbor.

*

In her cabin, Donna Mann was boosted by the captain's announcement detailing the medical mission to San Andrés. Her husband, Jorge, was one of several patients who might die without the assistance. Donna allowed herself a small dose of optimism. Perhaps her husband finally could be transferred to a hospital, where his odds of survival would be far better. She received no firm confirmation, but the constant queries from the medical personnel indicated that Jorge was likely to be one of the lucky two passengers they planned to evacuate.

*

As the *Zaandam* approached San Andrés, the ship loomed so large that even from five miles away, islanders could see it from shore. Governor Hawkins, a stocky forty-three-year-old San Andrés native of Afro-Caribbean descent, had been elected governor six months earlier, in October 2019. Hawkins cut an imposing figure: He had a gleaming smile, clean-shaven head, and an affinity for yellow polo shirts. A lawyer by trade, the governor had myriad reasons to worry about the *Zaandam*'s docking in San Andrés. Two weeks earlier, media reported that the first COVID-19 death to hit the nearby Cayman Islands was that of a sixty-eight-year-old Italian passenger from the Carnival-owned ship the *Costa Luminosa*. Puerto Rico's first two COVID-19 cases were an elderly couple who'd also become infected on the *Costa Luminosa* and were evacuated to one of the island's hospitals. Governor Hawkins knew his people. They feared this latest foreign invader would bring death and illness to this remote and exposed population.

President Duque had prohibited foreign cruise ships from docking in the country. But behind the scenes, the U.S. State Department was pulling all kinds of levers. This was a matter of life and death; American citizens needed to get off the ship, onto a small transfer boat, then into a jet, and they'd be gone. The chance of anyone on shore being infected would be minimal, they argued. The Colombian officials were supportive, predicting the president would approve. But this took time to move up the chain of command.

Before noon, Keith Taylor warned the diplomats that he'd set a 3:00 p.m. deadline. If President Duque didn't sign the executive order allowing the patient transfer by that time, the whole mission would be scrapped. The jet prepared to fly from Florida couldn't take off any later, as nighttime landings were not an option at San Andrés. The diplomats, however, were charged up. They'd made huge strides since the 6:00 a.m. alert that the cruise line needed a hand, and by 2:45, the odds were improving. All signs indicated it wouldn't be long before the paperwork would be ready and the president would sign.

But Taylor was sure of his schedule. As a decorated rescue coordinator for decades, he knew his timetable was fixed. At 3:15, with no diplomatic authorization, Taylor pulled the plug. The rescue mission was off, and Captain Smit received orders to fire up the engines and head north.

MARCH 30, 3:30 P.M.
Caribbean Sea, 3 Miles West of San Andrés Island

On the bridge of the *Zaandam*, Captain Smit had no choice but to continue his search for a safe harbor. Despite stark evidence that a growing number of his crew and passengers were near death, the logistics of landing had been overwhelming. Once again fear of COVID-19 and the unknown consequences of bringing this wily virus back to shore had conspired to keep him at sea.

Captain Smit told the navigators to redirect the *Zaandam*'s course northeast and join up again with the *Rotterdam* farther out to sea. In the late afternoon, the captain broke the latest dose of bad news to the passengers: "Plans to have emergency medical supplies for the *Zaandam* airlifted at San Andrés fell apart," he admitted. "Both ships are proceeding north to the East Coast of the United States."

The *Zaandam* and her sister ship motored toward the western tip of Cuba, where they would turn hard to starboard, then make a beeline to Port Everglades. They could be back at home port within three days. But troubling rumors were now whirring back and forth between Carnival and the State Department. The diplomats could hardly believe what they were hearing: The White House was waffling, unsure of what to do with the ship. It now seemed possible that the United States might leave its own citizens stranded in the Caribbean. Carnival Corporation and the cadre of diplomats who were opening a way for the *Zaandam* were forced to consider a drastic plan B. If the United States rejected the *Zaandam*, could they return to Panama? Was there a chance that once again Panama would be their solution, the only nation with a heart?

Yet again, the *Zaandam* was abandoned at sea.

CHAPTER 11
RACE TO SHORE

MARCH 31, 5:04 A.M.
Caribbean Sea, 760 Miles Southeast of Miami

As the *Zaandam* headed northeast in the Caribbean, George Covrig, the shop manager turned volunteer turned room service waiter, tried to get some sleep, or at least rest. He could do neither. The strangest thing had gotten on his nerves, almost grown terrifying. It was the spraying sound outside his door. Someone was walking the hallway with disinfectant, spraying, spraying, spraying. George tried to block out the hissing sound. He flipped on the map channel, hoping to be distracted by television images of the *Zaandam*'s progress set to a soft-rock sound track. But the spraying sound came through, breaking the eerie quiet of the locked-down cruise ship.

George decided to return to work. Delivering meals was better than this torture. As he made his way to the kitchen, cabin after cabin was marked by those gut-wrenching little red stickers. They were discreet, he thought. Perhaps the passengers might never know, given that they were prohibited from going outside their rooms. But George saw them, and he knew.

For close to a week, he'd been trying to keep his spirits up, trying to motivate the others. As George walked down the narrow hallway, he saw a ghost—a man, or maybe a woman, dressed from head to toe in white garb. The face was half-covered by a mask, a plastic shield distorting the eyes. The figure was walking silently toward him. Only the doctors and nurses dressed like that. They had no choice. They touched the sick, the dying. The ghost crossed his path and walked on.

In the kitchen, George heard metal plate covers crashing on the floor, the sound of water sloshing around, and the hiss as clouds of steam escaped from the dishwashing machines. The squeak and scream of off-kilter trolley wheels added to the jarring cacophony. One battered room service cart after another went by, while shouts, orders, and jokes in Tagalog, Spanish, and Indonesian filled the air.

George headed over to the line. Two men were arguing over command of an increasingly rare find: a functioning trolley. Many were falling apart, their wheels missing and welding cracked. George doubted he'd be lucky to score even a semifunctional cart. He assumed he would again be stuck pushing, dragging, and hauling the unwieldy contraption from room to room. A flawed wheel, he now understood, meant the difference between a fourteen-hour shift that was draining and a fourteen-hour shift that was devastating. The simple pleasures, George told himself: a trolley without broken wheels. George examined the selection before him, then rushed to a cart he knew was in relatively good working condition. Reduced to defending a four-wheeled cart like a treasure as the shifts stretched longer, George, too, began to wear out.

The breakfast shift commenced at 5:30 a.m., when George and eighteen others began delivering meals to the hundreds of guests bunking throughout the *Zaandam*'s decks. The breakfast shift lasted until nearly noon, with all the back-and-forth of orders, missing items, and the return of the soiled trays. For ten minutes, they took a break, if they were lucky, and then headed into lunch prep and delivery service, which lasted another five hours. The second break was a full thirty minutes, which allowed them to prepare—like an Ironman competition—for the third leg. Five hours of delivering food, then an hour more cleaning up the dinner plates.

When George and the galley crew finished at 9:00 p.m., they had spent roughly fourteen hours on their feet. Many could barely talk.

No one could push, drag, and coax a loaded trolley that many hours. The fatigued deliverymen would sometimes slip away for a brief escape, hoping to find a quiet place to stash their carts, then slump onto the floor to rest for a moment. Some would hide out in an attempt to recover their energy. When George came upon his huddled colleagues, he smiled compassionately as he passed. They'd been in this hell longer than he, some as many as eight days. George tried to lift their spirits when he saw them resting behind parked trolleys. But it wasn't enough. All he felt in return were stares of defeat. The *Zaandam*'s normally cheerful crew members were past smiling.

*

Lance and Sharon Hutton finished another round of Arizona rummy. Each player began with three cards, then four, five, six, all the way to thirteen, discarding sets and runs when they got them. The low scorer won. The winner took the pot. Before lockdown, they'd liked this game, which they'd learned years before from friends in Florida. Sharon had enjoyed a bit of gambling at the *Zaandam* casino. She liked playing quarter slots, or poker. But after almost nine days in their room, Lance was beyond bored with rummy. They'd fallen into a sort of routine. Sharon would slide to her side of the bed, pick up the Sudoku puzzles she'd fortuitously brought along, and dive in. She'd glance at Lance and he'd look back at her, each trying to smile. They were all talked out after all this time here, doing nothing, stuck in the cramped room. It was hard to make the hours pass, sitting all day, no place to go, nothing to see, barely any room to walk around. There was a window, but the sea view outside rarely changed. Lance looked over by the door, at the breakfast tray with the dirty dishes, another forgettable meal done, another to come in a couple of hours. Gourmet food, dinner shows, and fancy dress had been highlights of his previous cruises. He'd enjoyed the pageantry that made each meal a high point of the day. Now he suspected each plate was making him sicker.

Initially during the lockdown, Lance had been handling the meals fine, feeling grateful to the kitchen staff for finding a way to bring them any food, not to mention hot food (or at least warm) three times a day. During this unprecedented crisis, he understood the massive efforts to keep him and Sharon and hundreds others fed. But now something was amiss. Why had he lost his appetite? The food didn't taste right. His stomach was acting up, steadily getting worse. The pains, the sudden discomfort, were unfamiliar. Like many an eighty-year-old, he had lots of health issues, but not stomach trouble.

Lance knew Sharon was worried, as always. He also knew she was feeling strange. Her stomach was not right. But this infection—whatever it was—had attacked him harder. Stomach bugs were commonplace on ships. Norovirus outbreaks spread from person to person on a cruise ship and led to acute abdominal pain and nausea. Maybe that was it. With all the varieties of meats and chicken and seafood dished up by room service, *E. coli* bacteria was another possibility. Whatever infection he had, Lance was not overly worried. He imagined safety standards might be lower, given the emergency and the challenges of so many deliveries. He tried to ignore his discomfort, but both he and Sharon knew something wasn't right.

Lance began to hunt down the connections between his room and the outside world, where the virus lived. He approached the peephole. He studied the crack beneath the door. Was the virus this close? Now that passengers had died, and so many were sick, everything felt suspect.

Lance became obsessive as he listened to the whoosh of air filling their cabin. Hour after hour he couldn't stop focusing on that single ominous sound. Was he slowly being infected? Would the virus find a way into their cabin via the air duct? When Sharon's nephew, an engineer, investigated the ship's ventilation systems after some online sleuthing, he reassured them there was little to worry about in that department. Their air was pumped in from an external source. If the virus was entering, it wasn't through the vent, he told them. The arrival of food also made them nervous. First the rap on the door, then the muffled voices, and the quiet footsteps of an unseen server fading away until he reached the next cabin and repeated, "Food!" Lance feared these trays were a vector for the virus.

Being locked up this long in a room ten feet by twelve feet tested the limits of his patience. "All day in the same place that I slept. There's no place to go, nothing to see. No activity in my life," Lance said. He needed movement, even at his age. Back home, in Missouri, he lived on a golf course and played several rounds a week with friends. Or he'd find chores around the house, or out in the yard. Sharon was seventy-nine, but she liked to be active, too. It could be reading in the backyard, or walking the winding streets where they lived, at her own pace. She'd been an active woman all her life. Her father had taught her to fish when she was a child, and at school she'd played softball and been a cheerleader. After they married, she'd joined a league and played field hockey. Now she, too, was feeling claustrophobic in the tiny cabin.

Lance's mind kept returning to his regrets. It was his fault they were aboard the *Zaandam*. He had gambled that it wasn't so dangerous, hoping too much that they could salvage their long-anticipated trip. He was angry at himself and angry at the Holland America Line for allowing the *Zaandam* to leave Buenos Aires in the first place. The *Zaandam* left port even after Holland America had seen three of its cruise ships overwhelmed by COVID-19 infections in the weeks before. These decisions were all about money, he thought. The Holland America Line had been too cheap to cancel. He mulled it over as he lay back on the bed, time passing, slipping by, slowly, without purpose. Only one thought was comforting: *At least we don't have COVID-19.*

But as Sharon looked at her husband, she realized his health was declining rapidly. Three hours earlier, she had alerted the medical staff, asking for a check-in. But the word back was disconcerting. The medical center was swamped, the empathetic receptionist explained. There were so many sick people aboard. Sharon knew that Lance needed more medicine. But the receptionist was doubtful any doctor could be spared, so Sharon dug Imodium pills from her toiletries bag. Lance swallowed a pill and lay down, but it seemed to Sharon more like he'd collapsed. Although they were on the same deck as the medical center and only a few doors down the corridor from it, their pleas for help from the ship's medical staff went unanswered. Sharon and Lance were alone and getting sicker.

MARCH 31
Washington, D.C.

On land, a wall of political opposition seemed to coalesce in unison against the *Zaandam*. From the White House, word filtered out that certain cabinet members were incensed that the cruise lines paid no taxes in the United States and were based in tax havens, including the Cayman Islands and Panama. The word from President Trump was hard to fathom, as well. One day, the president defended cruising as an industry in need of saving, and the next he countered that he didn't want the infection numbers to rise in the United States. Letting infected cruise ships enter U.S. ports—even with sick U.S. citizens on board—might alter public perception about the spread of what he had mocked as a weak virus. President Trump dodged many of the crucial decisions regarding the nation's response to coronavirus, and he decided to pass the cruise ship issue to Vice President Mike Pence, who, in turn, pushed the critical issues to his trusted White House homeland security advisor, Olivia Troye.

As Olivia read the latest situation reports regarding the *Zaandam* inside her West Wing office, she felt sickened. It was heartbreaking to watch from afar as the virus took such a toll. All those older people getting sick, dying, as port after port turned its back in fear. *They could be my grandparents,* she was thinking.

From the earliest days of the cruise ship outbreaks, in January, when Olivia was assigned to the White House Coronavirus Task Force, the virus had haunted her dreams. *Maybe I have post-traumatic stress,* she thought. Olivia had followed several infected cruise ships, but this was different. She was starting to have nightmares about the *Zaandam*.

As the ship navigated north, Olivia couldn't believe the confusion. Florida governor Ron DeSantis declared he had no interest in allowing the ships to dock in Fort Lauderdale or anywhere in his state. Olivia was stunned, so she called Dr. Deborah Birx, one of her mentors, really more of a personal hero. Birx, sixty-three, was a badass. A retired army doctor and brilliant virologist, Birx rose rapidly in the infection-fighting world at a time when few women reached the highest ranks. She went from the National Institutes of Health to the Walter Reed Army Medical Center and became a leader in the fight to control AIDS. In 2014, President Obama named her the nation's Global AIDS Coordinator. Birx was tough and unflappable, and Pence designated her the coronavirus coordinator in February.

"What can we do to help these people?" Olivia asked Birx, hoping for an ally. It was an appalling scenario, Birx told Olivia, but there was little they could do. Cruise ships were a rabbit hole, and the White House didn't need a cruise ship crisis to further drain resources and brainpower. Olivia was stunned, but she understood the clear message: Let the locals handle it.

Several weeks earlier, the federal government had deployed massive resources to coordinate the docking of Carnival's *Grand Princess* at the Port of Oakland, California. It had been a logistical nightmare. The overlapping jurisdictions, regulations, and teamwork required were huge, so the White House had simply passed the problem down the line, forcing every state to invent its own protocols.

They were all exhausted by the ceaseless outbreaks on cruise ships. Dr. Martin Cetron, director of the CDC's Division of Global Migration and Quarantine, was also at his wits' end. COVID-19 crises on ships consumed thousands of hours and countless other resources that were badly needed on land. The cruise lines assumed that the world, especially the U.S. government, would bail them out wherever they arrived with a shipload of sick people.

Orlando Ashford, president of Holland America, penned an op-ed for the *South Florida Sun-Sentinel* in which he ignored any responsibility on the part of the company and instead chastised the world for the plight of the *Zaandam*. "The international community, consistently generous and helpful in the face of human suffering, shut itself off to *Zaandam* leaving her to fend for herself," he wrote. The ship was the victim of circumstances no one could have predicted, he said. "The coronavirus has run rampant through neighborhoods, businesses and nations, catching us all off guard." Holland America was betting that the world would come to the stricken ship's aid, like it had every time COVID-19 struck its other cruise ships at sea. "That ship couldn't sit off the coast of any of those countries indefinitely," Ashford said later. "We had to end up someplace. So, it was just a function of who was going to go and step up."

Leading U.S. politicians railed back at the arrogance. "Let's get something straight," wrote Congressman Hakeem Jeffries, chairman of the House Democratic Caucus. "The major cruise lines sail under foreign flags to avoid paying the U.S. corporate tax rate. . . . And now some want the American taxpayer to bail them out? Get. Lost."

Despite the whirling political ploys and plays, Olivia realized the verdict was clear: The White House was not going to run point on this crisis. They were punting the problems and logistics back to the locals with a clear message: Deal with it.

MARCH 31, 10:20 A.M.
Fort Lauderdale, Florida

"We've talked to the Coast Guard, and I don't think it wants them to come in. I talked to the White House about it. And we don't want it to come in," declared Governor DeSantis, a rising star in Trump's Republican Party who knew how to play to his conservative base. Florida was suffering one of the deadliest surges of COVID-19 cases in the country. Schools had closed. The economy was shutting down. The civilian populace was terrified. It was a no-brainer, DeSantis said. "Having a cruise ship come in? It creates problems. And we want to focus on Floridians."

But Carnival had one last card to play. Port Everglades was their home base and received millions in docking fees and services every month from the company. If any port might be sympathetic to the economic impact of cruising, perhaps it was Port Everglades, in Broward County. Carnival executives hoped local officials could be swayed to let a massive corporate benefactor bring their COVID-laced ships home to port.

Meanwhile in Broward County, lawyers were scrambling for legal justification to block the ship from entering U.S. waters and docking at their port facility—even though it was filled with hundreds of Americans. For more than a week, the county's approach to the humanitarian crisis aboard the *Zaandam* was to search for a legal strategy to prohibit the ship from docking, internal emails and documents show. A tidal wave of public opinion supported these efforts as local citizens flooded the county commissioners, the mayor, and other officials with emails demanding the ship be rejected. "You have most of Broward County under 'house arrest' to alleviate the strain on our hospitals and hospital workers and yet Florida is going to allow a disease-filled ship to dock here in Broward," one woman wrote. "Get real, stop it now."

Dozens of passengers aboard the *Zaandam* ratcheted up their own social media campaigns as the dueling narratives escalated the rhetoric and tension. But in Broward County, the pleas of the passengers were drowned out by angry and scared residents. One by one, the commissioners came out with their verdicts. No permission was to be given for the *Zaandam* to dock. Broward County lawyers drafted an official resolution saying as much.

Regardless of the wishes of local county administrators, State Department diplomats and Coast Guard commanders knew it was untenable to keep the *Zaandam* at sea. The diplomats believed that repatriation was the undeniable right of every U.S. citizen. It was clear to them that letting Americans die off the coast of Florida was unacceptable. The diplomats and other government officials involved were not going to abandon fellow citizens at sea, no matter the inaction of a sitting U.S. president. Quietly, the diplomats began building bridges, negotiating a way to bring the *Zaandam* home.

Recognizing the forces arrayed against them, Broward County officials ceded turf and deferred to what was called the "unified command." Instead of denying entry to the cruise ship, they flipped the table and said, yes, the cruise ship would be welcome—then required the cruise line executives to sketch out every possible evacuation scenario, down to the details on how they planned to disinfect hundreds of suitcases.

The unified command included top administrators from the port authority, the CDC, the U.S. Coast Guard, and even the county sheriff's office. From the beginning, they played hardball with Carnival, Holland America's owner. They demanded to know how Carnival planned to evacuate passengers from the infected ship without sowing COVID-19 throughout the state. And they made it clear that the cruise line would foot all the bills. Carnival had been experiencing COVID-19 outbreaks on its ships since late January. But now, company executives seemed unsure of how to proceed. Broward County demanded that the cruise line find the solutions, which is how Dale Holness, the county commissioner, ended up in a near-empty public hearing room in the middle of the COVID-19 lockdown, calling for testimony from a former nuclear submarine commander.

Carnival Corporation could not have cast a stronger advocate for their cause than their chief maritime officer, William Burke. Dressed in a navy suit and lilac tie, Burke cut an impressive figure when Holness summoned him to the podium just before the lunch break. Burke had a bravado that rubbed some people the wrong way. He was a military commander, not a social worker. But in his testimony and body language before Commissioner Holness, he starred in both roles. When speaking, Burke bowed his head, his hands clasped deferentially in front of him. When he asked, politely, for help, he sounded humbled. Burke described the *Zaandam* as an orphan abandoned by the world. He ticked off country after country—eight in all—that had rejected the *Zaandam*'s urgent requests to dock. From southern Chile to northern Mexico, from Martinique to Miami, not one port had let them come in. When Burke mentioned that the cruise line had failed to evacuate passengers on their deathbeds in Colombia, he paused to remove his reading glasses—was a tear about to fall? Burke recounted how Carnival had reinforced the ship's medical center with additional doctors, nurses, and ventilators. But fourteen passengers were seriously ill, and many more had recovered from what the company assumed was COVID-19. They'd done some testing, he admitted, but complained that there weren't enough kits to go around. As for the crew, it was even worse. "So, we are coming to the place of last resort," he declared. "I hope that the two people that we would like to medevac today will survive the couple-day transit."

It was a powerful moment, one that drove home the desperation and crisis the world faced with this ship. People were dead; others were dying. Burke's warning was clear: The ship needed to find a port before the situation spiraled out of control. For fifty-eight minutes, the politicians grilled Burke. He fielded the questions and drilled back his dire warning to such effect that by late afternoon the political tide began to shift. Encouraging words from President Trump helped. "They're dying on the ship," the president commented during a White House briefing. "I'm going to do what's right, not only for us but for humanity." Trump promised to call Governor DeSantis. A few hours later, DeSantis obeyed. The *Zaandam*, he proudly stated, was now welcome, though he sought to portray the decision as a pro-Florida move. "Clearly, we're going to be willing to accept any Floridians who are on board," DeSantis crowed.

APRIL 1, 7:45 A.M.
Caribbean Sea, South of Cuba's Westernmost Tip

As the politicians wrangled on land, Captain Smit had yet another crisis in the *Zaandam* medical center. Doctors aboard the *Zaandam* were barely able to sleep. Work shifts never ended, never started anew. Even with the reinforcements, they were in survival mode. Separated from the rest of the crew for sanitary reasons, they were even more isolated. There was no downtime, especially with patients agonizing on ventilators.

The medical team needed to transfer the most critically ill from the ship to a fully equipped intensive care unit. They'd wanted to evacuate them even before they'd crossed the Panama Canal. Their hopes had soared when the *Zaandam* approached the island of San Andrés; then the disappointment was followed by the battle to pump oxygen into the patients' ever weakening bodies. Sick passengers now filled the beds in the infirmary, and dozens more were suffering throughout the ship's multiple decks.

The doctors and nurses visited passengers in their cabins, saving space in the infirmary for the worst cases. They didn't have nearly the staff to attend to all the passenger calls. Crew treatment could be more sporadic. Hundreds of passengers and crew members had fallen ill on the *Zaandam* and the *Rotterdam,* though limited COVID-19 testing made it impossible to know exactly how many had the virus.

Hospital beds on land were also scarce—and ignorance reigned even in the medical community. Protocols for this brazen new outbreak were written on the fly. Given the lack of any proven medical strategy, COVID-19 treatments were being improvised week by week, and they were sometimes haphazard. Even the world's best hospitals were struggling to discover the most effective remedies to slow the advance of a virus that was suspected not only of destroying lung tissue but also clouding brain functions. Bizarre psychedelic dreams were widely reported as a symptom of COVID-19's storming of body tissue. At sea, there were even fewer options for the doctors. For most patients, all they could provide was cough syrup or Tylenol, and even those medicines were being rationed for the most serious cases.

While a shortage of cough syrup was problematic, the ongoing shortage of oxygen was more severe. On A Deck, Erin Montgomery had watched as a stock of thirteen metal cylinders filled with medical oxygen—lashed to the corridor wall just outside her cabin—shrank rapidly, seemingly by the hour.

Every morning, there were fewer. Now just four remained. This lifesaving gas was nearly gone—yet again.

Smit crafted a plan, and at 7:45 a.m., he put it into action. First, he ordered the *Zaandam* to pause briefly. The *Rotterdam*, trailing close behind, did the same. Smit's crew headed over to the *Rotterdam* in an orange tender. When they came back, they had commandeered several tanks of medical oxygen. A nurse also climbed out of the tender and joined the *Zaandam*'s medical team. In less than an hour, they were again headed northeast, making an end run around Cuba and on toward international waters off the coast of Florida.

*

Wiwit's friend Rendy walked into the medical center and was stunned by the disturbing scene. Weakened passengers and exhausted crew crowded into the chairs along the hall outside Dr. Hall's office, waiting to be treated. The harried doctors and nurses ducked in and out of the rooms, tending to patients laid up on hospital beds, IVs dripping in their arms, beeping machines monitoring their vitals, tubes rhythmically pumping oxygen into their lungs. Dr. Hall summoned Rendy inside. Through the glass wall of one of the rooms he could see Wiwit in the bed, lying on his back. Tubes ran into his nose; an oxygen mask covered his face. Dr. Hall explained the dire situation. Wiwit was severely ill, he said. Rendy had already noted with worry his friend's labored breathing. Dr. Hall asked Rendy to contact Wiwit's family and let them know the seriousness of the situation. Dr. Hall didn't speak Indonesian, so Rendy would be the one to break the news, to prepare them.

Dr. Hall said he was sure Wiwit had COVID-19, and there were spots on his lungs that were worrisome. The doctors on board were not pulmonary specialists. They didn't have the equipment to diagnose

Wiwit's multiple symptoms properly or come anywhere close to providing full treatment. They had twice tested Wiwit for COVID-19, and both tests came back negative. But were these false negatives? Rendy asked. It didn't really matter. The doctors, here and on shore, assumed all those with respiratory ailments had COVID-19. Rendy took it all in, looking at his friend, who was so ill. Just a couple of days earlier, they'd eaten lunch together. Wiwit had looked bad, but this was disquieting. Dr. Hall wouldn't ask him to notify next of kin like Anny Doko unless they feared for his life.

Rendy assured Dr. Hall he'd call Wiwit's wife, and he quickly left the infirmary to allow the medical staff to continue their quest to save patients. A short time later, Rendy received new orders: "Please don't call Anny." The cruise line's HR department would handle the delicate task. Rendy took this as yet another bad omen. All he could do was hope they could save his friend Wiwit.

APRIL 1
Batam, Indonesia

Anny Doko was at work when the phone rang, and she missed the first call. The Holland America rep called Wiwit's sister that evening, speaking to her in English, although she barely understood the language. Wiwit's sister had trouble understanding but knew it must be important if someone had taken the trouble to track her down. It sounded to her like the person was saying Wiwit was sick, but she couldn't be sure. She asked Anny's brother Hans, who spoke fluent English, to call the cruise line to find out what was happening. The cruise representative told Hans that Wiwit was suffering from shortness of breath and had been admitted to the medical center. He was gravely ill. Anny was distraught when Hans relayed the news. For days, she'd been praying for her husband, praying he didn't have COVID-19, praying for him to recover and return home. No one from the cruise line had even called to confirm her husband was sick, until now.

APRIL 1, 7:48 P.M.
Fort Lauderdale, Florida

For three days, the Broward County unified command battled with the cruise line. Time and time again, they'd gone back to Admiral Burke with requests, demanding the company take care of the most minute details. Who would be in charge of disinfecting the vans? What wording would they use for the medical questionnaire? One sticking point was confirmation that Carnival must pay to transport every passenger home on charters and not book them on commercial flights. This single line item would cost the company heavily, and Burke was slow to respond to questions from Dr. Cindy Friedman at the CDC. In a series of emails, Friedman asked how the cruise line would get passengers home. No one, she insisted, should fly commercial. This was a complex, expensive demand. There were residents of many countries on the ship, and flying them all home would be difficult. Many countries had shut down their national airspaces, so it would take time to negotiate entry.

Burke came up with a plan to charter jets for the U.S. citizens and for the citizens of those nations that agreed to receive emergency flights. For the remainder, he sought to stash the foreign travelers on the East Coast and the West Coast of the United States, placing them in hotels in Georgia and California until their respective governments allowed them to return home. These details, however, were not clearly stated, and officials at the CDC felt that Burke was trying to unload his problem onto local governments.

It felt like a tricky maneuver, and officials at the CDC were angry. "What? Do they think they're just going to off-load people?" Marty Cetron asked one colleague, incredulous.

Eventually, Burke agreed to the government's terms. By nightfall, the unified command approved the twenty-page agreement that would authorize both of the notorious cruise ships, the *Zaandam* and the *Rotterdam*, to dock at Port Everglades. The cruise lines agreed to a byzantine accord that outlined the precise movements for over a thousand healthy passengers. They would board sealed buses, which would bypass airport terminals and deliver the passengers straight to the tarmac at the Fort Lauderdale airport. Charter flights would then fly them out of Florida to Atlanta, San Francisco, Toronto, London, and Paris. Another flight was being arranged to repatriate the two hundred Australians aboard.

APRIL 1, 11:50 P.M.
Caribbean Sea, 20 Miles off the Coast of Miami

Just before midnight, Leo Lindsay was awakened by a shocking sound. Carl Zehner, his husband, was breathing irregularly. It sounded like he was gasping, maybe hyperventilating. For days, Carl had felt unwell, and Leo had done what he could, using all the tricks learned during his career in nursing. At first, when the fever set in, one of the ship's nurses provided Tamiflu. But those stocks were soon exhausted. Carl's fever kept surging back, especially in the afternoon. The fever was accompanied by pervasive chills. Carl shook so hard, it seemed he was having convulsions. The nurse advised Leo to remove the covers when Carl felt the chills. But Carl begged Leo to get into bed to warm him up.

Carl was now so weak, he couldn't stand up. Taking the few steps to the bathroom or moving from the bed to sit on a chair was nearly impossible. "How much longer do I have to stay up?" Carl pleaded.

Leo looked at him, knowing he had to get him the few steps to the bathroom.

"I can't do it," Carl said. "I can't."

Leo knew Carl better than anyone; they had just celebrated their fortieth anniversary, which is why they were on this voyage to begin with. Carl was tough. But this virus was stripping away his strength. As his husband's breathing became more irregular, Leo rang reception. A nurse arrived within minutes and was alarmed when she measured Carl's blood oxygen level. "We have to take him to the doctor," she said to Leo. "Now."

Port Everglades was so close—on the TV map channel, it looked to be just twenty miles away. The captain had suggested they would soon dock, perhaps in a matter of hours. But Carl was declining precipitously, and Leo was certain they had no time to spare.

APRIL 2, 8:02 A.M.
Caribbean Sea, 11 Miles East of Miami

After breakfast, passengers were told to place all their luggage in the hallways and await instructions for a medical check prior to disembarking. After twenty-six days at sea, they were finally going to get off the ship and onto dry land. The cruise had begun as a fantastic voyage to the exotic ends of the earth, only to be suddenly and shockingly transformed into a desperate flight from an invisible, deadly stowaway. The *Zaandam* had become a floating prison of sorts during the lockdown. Its passengers were left to their own devices, alone in cabins as the virus sickened and killed around them. Now relief was close. But many people were so stunned that joy was hard to come by—especially for the sick and dying. Many people were fighting for their lives. Salvation was in doubt.

As the *Zaandam* steamed toward Florida, the crew delivered to each cabin an envelope that contained luggage tags and yet another health questionnaire. The number of sick people was rising, and the *Zaandam* had yet to receive approval to dock. At least 107 passengers and 143 crew members had been diagnosed with the virus, far more than the night before. And, more worrisome, ten people were now considered critically ill and were gasping away the last of the ship's oxygen. On the *Rotterdam*, passengers and crew were also falling sick. It was a grim scenario, but it didn't even tell the full story.

Many crew members and passengers like Lance and Sharon Hutton were suffering alone, inside their cabins. For at least five days, the couple had been unable to receive medical attention. All food was now starting to look revolting to Lance. What he did manage to eat led to urgent trips to the toilet. Sharon, too, was having bouts of severe intestinal distress, which at seventy-nine years of age could be life-threatening. She also developed a hacking cough, which was worrisome, given her bronchiectasis. For years, when she had a chest cold, it often worsened and led to pneumonia. She and Lance both feared that she was particularly vulnerable to coronavirus settling in her lungs.

Sharon and Lance scanned the instructions for disembarking. It was a rather simple questionnaire, but they both agreed they were too sick to walk to reception for the required temperature check. Sharon picked up the phone and dialed for help. Three times she called, but no one came to their aid. No doctor or nurse called back or visited their room.

Holland America was eager to execute the protocols they'd developed in exchange for permission to dock. The passengers would be called down in groups; then the doctors and nurses on board would conduct a medical screening. Each passenger would be checked for fever and asked three questions: Had he or she experienced a fever, a cough, or shortness of breath in the past twenty-four hours? Every passenger who passed would get a disembarkation clearance card, a ticket off the ship.

Lance and Sharon gave up on seeking medical help in their cabin. They both felt awful, but they made it down to reception for the medical checkup. A doctor took their temperatures three times, and they were normal. Both were designated fit to travel. The next day, they'd be headed home, the doctors confirmed. Holland America's plan was to bus them to the Fort Lauderdale airport, where they'd catch a charter flight to Atlanta, along with nearly two hundred other passengers. Then they would transfer to a regularly scheduled commercial flight to St. Louis. But Lance and Sharon were drained and feeling sicker than ever when they returned to the cabin. Boarding a plane the following morning felt impossible.

Captain Smit maneuvered the *Zaandam* east of Port Everglades, just outside U.S. waters. But on shore, there was a glitch. The docking agreement lacked final approval and final signatures. The lawyers were battling. Inside the medical center, patients were agonizing. Fourteen had been deemed sick enough to be taken off the ship and straight to waiting ambulances. But on shore, the lawyers weren't budging. The *Zaandam* would have to wait. Smit put his ship into a holding pattern, moving in a series of circles, waiting for the harbormaster to provide final clearance to dock.

APRIL 2, 3:45 P.M.
Sea Buoy, 2 Miles East of Port Everglades Channel

Captain Todd Cooper's gray-hulled fifty-two-foot pilot boat pulled alongside the *Zaandam*, two miles east of the Port Everglades sea buoy, around 3:45 p.m. For nearly a decade, Cooper had been guiding huge ships into the sprawling port. But this had to be among the most delicate missions of his career. He was one of eighteen harbor pilots certified to take ships through the tricky currents and narrow channel leading to Port Everglades. Like everyone else, he worked twenty-eight days on, twenty-eight days off, day and night. Today, Cooper was supposed to be off duty, but he was determined to guide the *Zaandam* to port, COVID-19 be damned. So, Cooper volunteered to work on his day off. If he was exposed to the virus on the *Zaandam* and had to go into quarantine, he'd have been off anyway, so the port wouldn't be losing a pilot in the end.

Cooper, a slim man with short gray hair, had followed the news of the *Zaandam* as port after port in South America denied the ship's pleas for help. When Cooper heard the *Zaandam* was passing through the Panama Canal, he figured the ship was headed home. "I just felt it," he said. Standing inside the hatchway, he imagined the fate of those aboard. *Man, these people started out on a dream vacation and now they're prisoners at sea,* he thought. *I'm bringing this ship in.*

But Cooper immediately noticed a problem as his boat approached the *Zaandam*, three miles offshore. The ship was moving at bare steerage, the nautical equivalent of coasting, which is standard practice to assure a ship maintains enough headway to enter the port channel and counter the swift currents. But the harbormaster still hadn't given the green light, so technically the *Zaandam* didn't have authorization to enter U.S. waters, much less the port. The captain of Cooper's launch, Ben Orgain, picked up his VHF radio and called Captain Smit on the bridge of the *Zaandam*. "Captain, you're not authorized to come in. We're waiting for the final approval," he said. "Please, don't go any closer."

Smit had been holding short of the buoy for three hours, circling, pausing, circling some more, waiting for clearance to dock while the politicians and lawyers were haggling on shore. It was all coming down to the terms for full indemnification provisions, sovereign immunity clauses, that sort of thing. But Cooper couldn't guide the *Zaandam* to port until the harbormaster received approval from the county and the port management. Heading in early would surely spark an uproar—further roiling the waters. Smit's answer shocked Cooper: "We have to dock now," the captain replied, his professional calm giving way to nervous urgency. "We are running out of oxygen."

Cooper knew what that meant. He called the harbormaster on his cell phone. "Call your supervisor right now," Cooper said. "Someone has to make a decision, or people are going to die."

A few minutes later, the harbormaster gave the go-ahead over the radio. "Bring it in."

This moment had been a long time coming for Cooper. He'd volunteered for the job and had already talked it over with his wife and three grown kids. They were all behind him. Cooper gave himself a crash course on COVID-19, as best he could, given how little anyone knew about the outbreak. The biggest challenge was procuring N95 masks and the gloves, goggles, and a full-body Tyvek protective suit. Nobody had any to share, not the port, not the pilots' association, not the county. But Cooper knew about an environmental-services company near the port that had stock. When Cooper called, he was told that he was welcome to come over and take whatever he needed. He'd been trained in hazmat duty, how to put on and remove the protective layers properly. He knew what he needed. "Help yourself," someone said when he got to the warehouse. So he did. Now Cooper was covered in the PPE gear as he prepared to board the *Zaandam*. He'd already told Holland America what he needed: "Clear my path of everyone; then have one mate take me up a dedicated elevator, and then to the bridge. No checking IDs, no asking to sign the pilot's forms. If I see any passenger, I am going to turn around and leave."

Cooper climbed into the shell door cut into the ship's dark blue hull, pausing for a moment in the marshaling area inside to get his bearings. He made his way to the dedicated elevator and went up into the ship. He walked onto the bridge and felt a sense of relief fan out across the room. Captain Smit had clearly become unnerved. He'd guided the *Zaandam* back from the ends of the earth, traveling halfway around the world, ports slamming shut along the way, countries denying humanitarian help, passengers sickening by the dozens, some dying, while his crew was ever more decimated. Even the United States seemed determined to deny docking permission. Hit by one crisis after another for the last three weeks, Smit was stretched to the limit and in need of reinforcements—even if only for a few minutes.

"Captain, we are clear to proceed," Cooper told Smit. "Increase engines to full ahead to make at least ten knots." They briefly discussed weather and ship conditions; plans to dock on the starboard side, in Berth 21; and a standard procedure known as the master pilot exchange. Cooper explained that the port had been cleared of traffic for the *Zaandam*. "The pilot has the con," Cooper announced, meaning he had command of the ship. The officers, helmsman, and lookout on the bridge called back, following nautical norms. "Pilot has the con," each said.

As a harbor pilot, Cooper wouldn't actually steer the great ship. His job was to give the officers the verbal commands they needed for heading and speed. Cooper paused, scanned the waters with his binoculars, and spotted the guide lights high atop poles, one red, closer, and one green, farther away. Line up those two, Cooper knew, and he was navigating the center of the channel.

"Steady on course two six eight," Cooper told the helmsman, beginning to align for docking. The port was in sight. "Two six eight," the helmsman responded, bringing the ship around. Cooper ordered the captain to reduce speed to eight knots as the *Zaandam* passed the channel jetties, ideal speed for countering the currents.

The channel into Port Everglades is roughly two miles long and narrow; just a hundred feet of water lay on either side of the *Zaandam*. Entering the channel was a battle against crosscurrents caused by the pull of the Gulf Stream. Before the *Zaandam* entered, Coast Guard and police patrol boats cleared all craft out of the way. As Berth 21 came into view, Cooper moved from the center of the bridge to the glass-enclosed wing on the starboard side so he could see the dock far below. The helmsman followed, transferring control of the ship to an identical ship steering system on the wing. Cooper ordered the ship's engines stopped, and told the helmsman to activate the thrusters to ease the *Zaandam* into berth.

Just after 4:30 p.m., the *Zaandam* was finally home. But along the dock there was a stark reminder that the crisis was far from over. Thirteen ambulances were lined up, drivers off to one side, dressed in full-body protection.

APRIL 2, 7:00 P.M.
Port Everglades, Berth 21

One of the first people scheduled for medevac from the *Zaandam* was Wiwit Widarto, who was fighting for his life. Dr. Hall had done what he could, but Wiwit's condition had deteriorated, the virus relentlessly destroying his lungs. Wiwit needed the care of an ICU.

Carl Zehner also needed urgent care. Throughout the previous day, he'd lain in a semiconscious state in the infirmary. Leo was distraught. They'd X-rayed Carl's chest and discovered he had pneumonia, and immediately put him on oxygen. And the COVID-19 test had come back positive. Leo had been waiting alone in the cabin for word. Every time he called, the frazzled nurse cut him off. She was too busy dealing with patients in front of her. Leo needed to see his husband, and it was clear they were not going to permit him to do so. Determined to see Carl, Leo walked to the medical center. *I'm going to go visit,* he said to himself, emboldened by two glasses of wine.

Leo walked right into the medical center—the door was unlocked. The receptionist, sitting behind the counter opposite the door, stared, surprised by this unannounced visitor. "Which room is Carl in?" he asked. She motioned to the hallway on the left. Carl's room was on the right, opposite the little pharmacy and next to the medical staff's offices.

Carl called out, "Is that Leo?"

Leo knew this world; he had been in similar places a thousand times as a nurse.

They had Carl hooked up to an EKG, which beeped with his heartbeat. Medical telemetry recorded the other vitals. Oxygen flowed into his nose through a tube. An IV line snaked out of his right forearm, but fortunately, he hadn't been intubated. He was in bad shape but was receiving far better care than Leo thought possible aboard a ship.

By the time Dr. Hall was alerted that an intruder had entered their sanctum, Leo had been sitting next to Carl for a good while, just watching him zone out on TV. He spoke to his husband, even though it was clear Carl wasn't registering much. Dr. Hall watched respectfully, not wanting to intrude, but needing to take charge. "Well, you scared my staff half to death by coming down here like this, and you have broken all the protocols we have," Dr. Hall said politely, smiling. Leo could tell from the accent that Hall was South African, and his bedside manner seemed excellent. "Well, I'm sorry," Leo replied. "But this is my husband, and I wanted to see him. And there was no provision for me to come down here and see him. So I just did it."

Hall left, allowing Leo to sit a little longer. Later, the doctor brought Leo a gown and mask and invited him to return whenever he liked. With Carl half asleep, Leo decided to take a look around, making his way down the narrow hallway. In the room across from Carl's, the doctors and nurses were caring for one sick patient. Next door, a man was moaning in the dark. Leo could barely make out the silhouette of someone. The man was hooked up to the machines, his breath labored, just like Carl's. "Help me. . . . Help me," the man cried, desperation palpable in his weak voice.

Past two other rooms, the hallway branched to the left and right, with a series of locked doors. Leo wondered if the morgue lay behind one of the doors, filled with the bodies of those who'd succumbed to this terrible virus. "It was horrible," Leo said later, still affected. "It was like something out of a horror novel." Leo walked back to his cabin, shaken by it all. The *Zaandam* may have docked, but Leo knew it would be a while before they made it to dry land.

Down on the dock, the stevedores maneuvered a gangway into place to roll the patients out on gurneys and wheelchairs and into the ambulances. Each ambulance had been assigned one severely ill patient. Within minutes, they moved Wiwit down the gangway and into an ambulance. The ambulance sped off. A medical team at Broward Health Medical Center was waiting for him. A dozen more seriously ill passengers were to follow. On land, they'd get the best care possible. Florida had some of the finest hospitals in the country. But for some, it was simply too late.

CHAPTER 12

TRAPPED ON DRY LAND

APRIL 2, 6:32 P.M.

COVID-19 Ward, Broward Health Medical Center

The awaiting ambulance rushed Wiwit Widarto straight from Berth 21 to Broward Health Medical Center in seven minutes. Broward Health was prepared for grave COVID-19 cases like Wiwit. An entire floor had been isolated and reserved exclusively for patients suspected of having the virus.

Wiwit was sealed off from the world, on land, isolated yet again in a cabin-size space. Alone in the sterile room, he was treated by doctors and nurses in protective clothing. They'd quickly adapted protocols written years earlier during fears of an Ebola outbreak in the United States. Those hypothetical procedures were being upgraded from day to day during this raging pandemic.

Wiwit was not allowed any visitors, ever. COVID-19 patients had to fight, suffer, and—far too often—die alone. Wiwit lay in the ICU bed, an EKG machine beeping, an IV in his arm, oxygen flowing into his damaged lungs. His other vitals—pulse, blood oxygen level, and blood pressure—flowed across a screen above his head. The doctors knew Wiwit had entered the ship's infirmary days earlier, complaining of a cough and shortness of breath. The ship's doctors did what they could. They'd tested him for COVID-19 twice, but the results were negative. But false negatives were common in these early rapid-testing kits. Now the doctors at Broward

Health had him tested in the hospital, this time with the more reliable PCR method. The result was no surprise: Wiwit had COVID-19.

Wiwit remained awake, his oxygen level dangerously low. The doctor needed to sedate him in order to treat this disease. The doctor did what he had to do, slowly adding a sedative to Wiwit's IV until he was unconscious. Now the doctor could work in peace. He needed Wiwit's body to slow down. The doctor fought to increase the oxygen level in Wiwit's bloodstream. But like so many people fighting COVID-19 on this floor, Wiwit would have to remain in a medically induced coma while his breathing was regulated by a ventilator. This was his only chance for survival.

*

The video streaming across her phone screen shocked Anny Doko. There was her husband, unconscious, lying so still. She could see a tube disappearing into his throat. The machine was doing its work. Staring at the image on her phone in Batam, eleven thousand miles away from the hospital, Anny sat at her dining room table, distraught. The nurse could only get so close on the other side of the glass window of the isolated ICU room. But Anny could see Wiwit clearly. He looked so distinct, and so far away. She felt racked by the pain of not being there with him.

It was a miracle of sorts that Anny had even tracked down her comatose husband. The cruise line hadn't updated her since a missed call, two days earlier, when Wiwit was still in the ship's infirmary. When Anny saw a story someone had posted on Facebook about a sick *Zaandam* crew member who'd been rushed to a hospital, she told her brother Hans, "That must be my husband."

Hans spoke English and was a clever investigator, and it didn't take long for him to locate Wiwit at the hospital, call the ICU unit, and speak with a doctor. Anny had a cousin in Seattle who also spoke fluent English, and he helped, as well. Wiwit, the doctor told the family, was very, very ill. The nurses agreed to keep Anny abreast of Wiwit's condition. The family created a WhatsApp chat group with the nurses; the group included Anny, her two sons, and other close relatives. Now they had a link to Wiwit, the closest they would ever get to visiting privileges.

Anny asked the nurse for a favor. Could he hold the phone close to Wiwit so that she could talk to him? Anny understood that Wiwit couldn't respond. But maybe he could hear; maybe it would help him feel accompanied, not so alone. The medical team explained that Wiwit was in a medically induced coma so the ventilator could do its work. But Anny was sure Wiwit would hear her, somewhere deep inside. She spoke calmly, serenely, telling Wiwit that they were waiting for him at home in Batam.

"Hold on," she whispered. "We still have so many plans."

APRIL 3, 8:45 A.M.
Port Everglades, Berth 19, Aboard the Rotterdam

Back on the *Rotterdam*, Claudia and her husband, Juan, watched passengers laboriously shuffling off the ship from the window of their cabin on Deck 2. They had a unique vantage point, with a sweeping view of the gangway leading to land. A fleet of buses lined up on the dock, the drivers dressed in face masks and full-body protective suits. Police motorcycles were waiting, red lights flashing. This was all part of the protocol to escort the buses, clear traffic, and deliver these unwanted visitors to the airport. Claudia felt overwhelmed by the anticipation, the giddiness of knowing they, too, were on the verge of escaping. Physically, they felt fine, confident they'd escaped infection. But Claudia felt the walls creeping in, and Juan was anxious. They needed to walk on land.

After weeks at sea, looking at the world through a sealed window, the empty feeling of isolation had become a form of low-grade torture. Claudia couldn't take the sensation of floating on water out of her mind. She was sick of washing and disinfecting everything that entered their room. She was sick of those little bars of soap. Sick of the plates, the utensils, the bottled water. This was supposed to have been a journey to relax, to reflect on their forty-two years together. Instead, it had mutated into a series of nightmares, testing their marriage and their sanity like nothing before. Juan and Claudia passed yet another temperature check and completed the medical questionnaire. The previous day, they had docked and immediately filed into the customs center, socially distanced, masks on, not touching anything, like they'd been told, waiting to have their passports stamped. Then they returned to their cabins, awaiting their turn to go ashore, jealously guarding the cards that read "Cleared to Debark."

Claudia and Juan felt lucky. They were supposed to leave within hours. A bus would deliver them to the airport, skipping the terminal and pulling alongside the chartered flight on the tarmac. The cruise line had arranged a flight to Atlanta and then all the way to Argentina. They were headed home.

Claudia and Juan placed their suitcases outside the cabin door. Occasionally, they peered through the peephole to observe the movements in the hallway as passengers made their way down. They'd been warned it could take a long time to get everyone off the ship. All they could do now was watch and wait.

APRIL 3, 9 A.M.
UK Ambassador's Residence, Panama City, Panama

Ambassador Potter was hardly able to believe what he was seeing on the TV screen: the ambulances lined up, the *Zaandam* passengers disembarking, and what felt like a fantasy come true. With so many ways the journey to

Florida could have gone wrong, Potter had checked his enthusiasm. His twenty years in the Foreign and Commonwealth Office had taught him never to assume the mission was complete. But here, finally, was the proof. "Watching the BBC and seeing those passengers get off was a moment of genuine joy and relief," he said. "What was the big picture? To get people medical care as soon as possible. And to help British nationals get home. I was relieved. Pleased.

"Diplomacy is often serendipity and always about people," mused Ambassador Potter. "We held the queen's birthday party early in February 2020, a month before the first COVID-19 cases in Panama. We were the only [Commonwealth] country to do a 'national day' because we had moved it forward. That is where we met all these ministers again, only four weeks ahead of a lockdown. So, we had fresh interactions with all these contacts."

APRIL 3, 9:45 A.M.
Port Everglades, Berth 19

When Rick de Pinho, a patent lawyer from New Jersey, and his wife, Wendy, left the *Rotterdam* and headed down the gangway, they squinted in the sunlight. They both wore face masks and took care not to touch any surface, not to crowd the people ahead of them in line, just as they'd been instructed.

They walked off the ship in a daze. The scene was surreal. Crew members and port workers were covered in full-body protective gear, masks, and gloves. It was hard to make out facial expressions under all that, but they were clearly terrified of the plague this flock of elderly people was hauling ashore. Rick looked up at the *Rotterdam,* relieved that they were finally leaving it all behind. Someone guided them to a bus, driven by a man dressed in a hazmat suit. Rick felt people were treating them like they carried the

Black Death, even though he felt fine and had never even been tested for COVID-19. But he had been on the death ship, the *Zaandam*, then the *Rotterdam*. Around all those sick people, near the dead.

Police cars and motorcycles surrounded their bus. It seemed like overkill to Rick. Were they worried that passengers might duck out of line, make a run for it? As the couple boarded the bus, county sheriff's officers on motorcycles assembled in front and behind the bus, their lights flashing. Each passenger received a bag with a bottle of water and a bag of pretzels. Then they waited and waited—sitting for nearly two hours inside a bus packed with passengers, all wearing masks and surgical gloves, all bunched together. Rick was starting to wonder if this was the best idea, all crammed in the bus. He could hear a cough here and there, which was unnerving.

Finally, the buses left the docks and headed toward the airport. The police cleared the route, allowing them to run red lights, as if even the briefest of stops—at a traffic signal—would unleash COVID-19 on the world.

The caravan drove past the terminal at Fort Lauderdale international airport and veered through a gate that was clearly not for regular passengers. The bus drove straight onto the tarmac, within feet of a waiting chartered jet. Customs and immigrations officials sat at a folding table in the blazing sun, wearing masks and gloves, waiting for them. They searched all the passengers' bags, scrutinized their IDs, and told them to climb the stairs to the aircraft. The plane lifted off more than an hour late, around 1:30 p.m., and the flight to Atlanta was as surreal as the cruise. Passengers sat spaced apart and wearing masks, trying their best to keep their hands to themselves. Many were giddy, taking selfies, calling family, euphoric to be headed home. Others stared ahead, catatonic, as if they could not believe where they were.

When the charter landed in Atlanta, there was no sealed bus, no police guards making sure passengers didn't stray, nobody to verify their temperatures. The plane taxied to the far end of the airport and they boarded a crowded bus, which took them to the busy terminal. From there, they walked to the baggage claim, acting as if nothing out of the ordinary had ever happened aboard the *Zaandam* and the *Rotterdam*.

The crowds were lighter than usual, but still bustling. Rick felt like he carried a dark secret. All those people, going about their lives, unaware that he had just spent weeks aboard the plague ship. Rick and Wendy missed their connecting flight to New York and had to wait in line at the counter to rebook. They were hungry—there had been no food on the flight from Florida—and they had hours to kill before their connecting flight to New York's JFK airport, so they looked around, wondering. Could they go to a restaurant? In a daze, wearing their face masks and surgical gloves, they found a bar and ordered bacon cheeseburgers. *We're in the general population; no one's wearing a mask,* Rick told himself. He looked around, worried someone would call them out for coming from a cruise ship where COVID-19 raged. No one seemed to notice or understand. *It's as if we somehow got cleansed of the virus when we were up in the air,* Rick thought. The cruise line had made them someone else's problem. For Rick, it felt jarring and irresponsible. "In the morning they were treating us with hazmat suits," he said. "And now we're sitting at a bar eating burgers?"

APRIL 3, 11:03 A.M.
Port Everglades, Berth 21, Aboard the Zaandam

Sharon Hutton remained on the *Zaandam*, so sick that she couldn't rise out of bed. Lance, beside her, was worried. A week of battling a pervasive stomach virus had sapped his strength to such a degree that he found it hard to find the will to do anything. He could barely call reception and ask for help. People were streaming off the *Zaandam*. And the Huttons had their disembarkation cards and two seats reserved on the 12:30 charter to Atlanta, with two hundred other passengers. Then they would face a four-hour layover and another flight, this one to St. Louis. But how could they disembark if they couldn't walk? And what about the public safety concerns? Hadn't the cruise company spent endless hours negotiating clear step-by-step disembarkation procedures with the government and agreeing that passengers with COVID-19-like symptoms would be prohibited from boarding a commercial flight?

Lance couldn't believe they'd been cleared to fly, given how sick they were. But the folks downstairs didn't seem to understand when Lance explained how bad they felt. All the doctors saw was that they had no fever and no obvious COVID-19 symptoms. It was time to unload the boat, and anyone who could walk off was encouraged to do so. Problem was, Lance and Sharon knew they were too weak to move. Lance sought to explain to the receptionist that they were physically unable to get off the *Zaandam* on their own. "Could you send someone to help?"

The operator seemed perplexed: "Why do you need help to get off the ship?" she asked.

"We're sick," he said.

Minutes later, a nurse appeared at their door, shielded by face mask, face shield, full gown, and booties. The nurse examined Sharon and grew visibly alarmed. "Why haven't you called us to tell us you were sick?" Lance was incredulous. For days, they had asked for help, but no one would come. A day earlier, Lance had called three times, requesting a doctor, but no one had come. Lance answered the nurse in a weak voice: "We've been trying."

The nurse took Sharon to the medical center. Lance stayed in the cabin. Sharon had been sick for the better part of a week, but now her vital signs were alarming. She was feverish. She was coughing and wheezing, her lungs working harder but pumping less air. In the medical center, a doctor administered medication to ease the bronchial inflammation and ordered nurses to bump up the oxygen flow to her weakening lungs. For the doctors, there was little doubt. A lab test later would only confirm their suspicions. They had suspected within minutes of observing her that COVID-19 had taken hold of Sharon Hutton.

As Sharon was consumed by coughing fits, her blood oxygen fell to a dangerously low level. Lance was in their cabin, just down the hall from the medical center, getting sicker. He was now alone, coughing and fighting off the infection that was spreading throughout his body.

To his surprise, Lance once again was cleared to disembark. He should go home, the *Zaandam* staff instructed. Sharon would be staying, but only long enough to get her to a nearby hospital for proper care. Lance wanted to leave the *Zaandam* more than anything. After weeks trapped in his cabin, he wanted to fly home. But Lance was not leaving his wife there on that ship. He stayed put.

APRIL 4, 8:45 A.M.
Port Everglades, Berth 19, Aboard the Rotterdam

Starting at breakfast time, the exodus from the two ships continued on April 4. More buses departed. Claudia and Juan heard there were charter flights to the far corners of the world; it was understandable that this logistical nightmare would include delays. They heard about passengers booked on flights to Atlanta, San Francisco, London, and Paris. But they'd begun to worry the night before, when the flow of passengers getting off the *Rotterdam* slowed, then ceased. Was their flight running behind schedule? Claudia wondered. Maybe arranging a flight for them to Argentina just took more time. Speaking to her husband, Claudia proclaimed with confidence, "I guess our turn will come tomorrow." They just had to be patient.

By the afternoon, Claudia and Juan began to worry. The flow of passengers had stopped again. The buses had departed. "I'm going to find out what is going on," Claudia declared. She called reception. The woman who answered was nice enough. It took a moment to unravel what was happening. "Oh, we're so, so sorry, but you will not be disembarking today," the receptionist announced cheerfully.

"What do you mean?" Claudia asked.

"There was a problem with your flight to Argentina. We need you to stay on the ship a little while longer, while we work out a solution."

Claudia's mood swung from elation to despair in seconds. She grilled the woman on the other end of the line, but there was little information to unearth. The receptionist didn't know the details. All that was certain was they were not flying home, not today. Then there was a knock on the door. When Juan peeked outside, he found their luggage at their door. It had been sent back.

Then, suddenly, the captain's voice jolted loudly over the shipwide intercom. He offered no calming words, no explanation, no instructions about what was to come. He appeared to be giving orders to the remaining crew members on the *Rotterdam*.

"It was like we didn't exist," Claudia said. "We were like ghosts on a ghost ship."

"Personnel will now move to Deck 2," the captain declared. Or that's what Claudia thought he had said. "Deck 2, Juan? That's us, right?"

Juan nodded. The captain appeared to have authorized the crew to commence some sort of procedure on their deck. Soon, a powerful chemical smell wafted into their cabin. A pungent disinfectant stench burned the back of Claudia's throat, causing her to wince. She heard movement in the hallway, and then it was gone. "They're gassing us!" she exclaimed.

Claudia was allergic to disinfectants. They made her feel as if she were suffocating. Engulfed in a toxic cloud, Claudia grabbed a face mask and burst out of the cabin, desperate to breathe fresh air. With Juan, she ran to an exit and they dashed outside. The sun blinded them momentarily. The warmth and humidity felt foreign after being cooped up for so long. Claudia fell to the deck, gasping for air. She felt as if she were dying. *After all we have been through,* she thought, *and now they want to kill us?*

Claudia spotted a surveillance camera and ran toward the tiny lens, screaming in Spanish for someone to help. Soon, one of the ship's officers arrived, looking for this woman he'd seen on the security feed. Claudia screamed at him, scolding him for trying to poison them. The officer didn't understand her machine-gun Spanish, so Juan sought to explain in English. The officer apologized but insisted they return to their cabin. Politely but forcefully, he said, "You cannot stay out here."

"I am not going back into that cabin," Claudia shouted, again in Spanish. As Juan translated, the officer asked them to wait. He'd find a solution. Minutes later, he returned with good news. They were being transferred to a new room on the nearly deserted *Rotterdam*. Not just a room, he explained, but a cabin on an upper deck with a private balcony. They had been given an upgrade. But they felt like orphans, forgotten on an empty cruise ship, with no sign of liberation. Their lockdown at sea continued. Yet another port had turned its back on Claudia and Juan.

APRIL 4, 9:45 A.M.
Port Everglades, Berth 21, Aboard the Zaandam

Lance felt even worse by morning. He couldn't get ahead of this malady, whatever it was. When the phone rang, he was startled to hear Sharon's voice. She needed to tell him herself, she said. They'd tested her for COVID-19, and it was bad. She had the virus. Lance could tell that his wife was more than just upset. She was also very afraid. COVID-19 preyed on old people like them, they had heard. After Sharon hung up the internal line, Lance's cell phone rang. It was their only daughter, Amy Williams Hutton, calling from her home in Missouri. As Lance described how bad he felt, Amy grew alarmed. Her dad was clearly getting sicker, alone in that cabin, and no one was coming to his aid. Amy tried to encourage him, talking about new treatments, new drug cocktails that were promising, that were saving people from this virus. But Lance knew that at his age, COVID-19 usually meant the end.

Amy started making calls. She needed to locate medical personnel on the *Zaandam* or on shore to help her father. "I called Holland America's emergency passenger hotline, and they finally got a doctor to check on my dad," she recalled. The doctor was immediately concerned. Lance needed to go to the medical center at once. Before long, Lance was lying in a bed near Sharon. He was ill and getting sicker. The doctor ran a test, and soon the results came in. Lance was also infected with COVID-19.

*

By the next morning, April 5, Sharon's condition had become critical. The virus had done so much damage that the doctors were concerned she was developing pneumonia. But the medical center was no hospital. They didn't have what they needed to treat her. Sharon was far from the only person stuck on either the *Zaandam* or the *Rotterdam* and in desperate need of hospital care. Over the last two days, the cruise line had already taken nineteen passengers and one crew member—Wiwit—to hospitals because they were so sick. But there were still twenty-three people too ill to get on a flight home, and now many of them urgently needed hospital care. Getting COVID-19 patients off the ship required laborious negotiations with port officials, and complicated protocols. Soon, the talks took on an urgent tone. One Carnival medical case manager, Dr. Jae-Hong Min, urged the port director by email to approve plans to take five critically ill people off the two ships. They all required oxygen, and without a hospital, they might not survive. One of those patients was Sharon Hutton.

Air ambulances were standing by to fly the patients to AdventHealth Orlando, one of the best-equipped hospitals in Florida for COVID-19 treatment. At midday, port officials approved Dr. Min's request, clearing the way for Sharon Hutton and four others to be flown to Orlando.

The next day, Lance Hutton would follow Sharon on another air ambulance flight to Orlando. Within a day after getting off the *Zaandam*, the couple would be together again, but this time in the same COVID-19 ward, one languishing across the hall from the other, breathing only with the aid of ventilators. After all they'd been through, the Huttons would finally be off the *Zaandam*. But now they'd have to face the challenge of surviving on land.

APRIL 5, 10:23 A.M.
Port Everglades, Berth 21, Aboard the Zaandam

Carl Zehner lay in the medical center, his breathing strained. A test confirmed what Leo had suspected: His seventy-four-year-old husband had COVID-19. The ship's doctors were pumping as much oxygen as they could into Carl's lungs, but his breathing capacity had declined precipitously. The IV was keeping him hydrated, and his vitals were being monitored. There were limits to what they could do for him on the ship. Leo knew Carl needed a fully equipped hospital. But like the two dozen other people who required care on shore, Carl was up against strict controls on who could disembark. The unified command had to approve transport to a hospital, and that took time. And the hospital had to agree to take him, which was complicated due to the soaring demand for beds to accommodate critical-care patients. As a retired nurse, Leo, sixty-nine, knew the only way to get his husband off the ship sooner than later was to agitate. Leo laid siege to the medical center, calling night and day, demanding detailed updates on Carl's deteriorating condition. He also took up Dr. Hall on his open invitation to visit Carl. He'd review Carl's medical chart, ask Dr. Hall and the nurses about treatment plans, or just sit there, hypnotized as he studied the lines of his beloved's vital signs flowing across the telemetry machines.

Once they told him Carl was infected, Leo asked Dr. Hall if he could get a COVID-19 test. Leo was taken aback by the response: "Well, you know, if your test is positive, we can't let you disembark," Hall said. Protocol was that anyone with COVID-19 would have to be isolated on the *Zaandam*, unless they were so sick that they needed hospital care. "And we're going to be going back out to sea." Leo had no interest in being stuck on the *Zaandam*, for who knew how long, so he left it at that. Luckily, he felt as healthy as ever.

Lobbying for his husband allowed Leo to keep his focus for a week. His mission was to save Carl, to fight for the best medical care possible. Leo paced the medical center, wearing a mask and gown to make Dr. Hall happy, peering into the rooms, which were still filled with patients, even though they had been in port for three days. He imagined what was behind the closed doors: There were offices for Dr. Hall and the other medical officers, where they could escape all this, just for a moment; a couple of storage areas; some examination rooms up front; and the line of three well-equipped hospital rooms along the hallway, including Carl's room. For Leo, this caretaker role was part of the marriage vow: "in sickness and in health." *This is my duty, and this is what I need to do for him,* Leo told himself.

Now Leo fought to send his husband to a hospital. He sat in the cabin, finishing up another email to one of his allies in this campaign, the mayor of Fort Lauderdale. For a couple of days, they'd been going back and forth. "I kept saying to him, 'Why won't my husband be able to get off?'" Leo said.

"And I asked, 'What would you do if your husband was critically ill and unable to get off a ship?' " The mayor listened compassionately and promised to help. A moment later, the phone rang. Leo couldn't believe what he was hearing. Carl had been cleared to be taken off the ship and would be flown to AdventHealth Orlando. Leo, however, wasn't going anywhere. With all the charter flights for healthy passengers long gone, Holland America would have to find a way to get Leo back home safely to Nashville, and get the county to approve the plan. So Leo settled back in the cabin to wait.

Doctors and a medical team awaited Carl in the emergency room when he arrived in Orlando. His breathing was so compromised that doctors decided to place him on a ventilator immediately. When they told Leo by phone, he was shocked. He knew a respirator was a doctor's last resort. The procedure was fraught with risks, starting with the complex process known as intubation, which included threading a thick tube into the patient's trachea. The intervention heightened the risk of infection, could damage the larynx, and might even lead to internal puncture wounds. Roughly one-third of patients put on ventilators died. Leo knew the risks and the odds; his initial instinct was to reject the suggestion. "No, I do not want that," he told the nurse.

The response was succinct. "We have to," the nurse replied.

Leo spoke to the doctor and attempted to make the case against using the ventilator. The doctor explained that Carl's lungs weren't expelling enough carbon dioxide from his body. His blood oxygen level was falling. Without a ventilator, Carl would not last much longer. Leo reluctantly agreed. But he wanted to break it to Carl. As someone from the medical team held a phone to Carl's ear, Leo, back on the *Zaandam*, spoke. "Carl," he said. "I'm sorry. I don't want this. I didn't want this to happen, but they're going to have to put you on a respirator."

"Well, anything you say is okay," Carl responded. Once they'd intubated

Carl and turned on the ventilator, they took him to the COVID-19 ICU, where he would fight for his life.

Back on the *Zaandam*, Leo was determined to find his way to the hospital to be with Carl. But the hospital was closed to visitors, without exception. Then Leo received a call from reception. The *Zaandam* was set to leave Port Everglades. They were moving Leo to the *Rotterdam*, which had been granted permission to remain at Port Everglades several days longer. Leo was pleasantly surprised. He was given a cabin with a balcony. He opened the sliding door and took in the humid breeze, the smell of the ocean, the tropical warmth. After more than two weeks inside a stuffy room, the only view of the outside world through a sealed window, Leo was finally free to breathe fresh air. It was a bizarre sensation. His husband was facing a killer virus, alone, so far away. For three days, Leo waited inside his luxurious digs, alone, fearing the worst about Carl. Then the phone next to his bed rang. Holland America had finally found a way for him to return to Nashville on a chartered jet with a few other stranded passengers and crew members. Within hours, he was on a bus, then on the jet, flying to the northwest. He'd be home by dinner.

APRIL 6, 5:00 P.M.
Port Everglades, Berth 21, Aboard the Zaandam

After watching one socially distanced passenger after another shuffle down the sloped gangway, leaving the *Zaandam* and disappearing into the labyrinth of security protocols in Port Everglades, Amanda Bogen, the twenty-seven-year-old entertainment host, felt relieved. Her panic level ratcheted down. Most of her guests, as she'd learned to call them after four years at sea, were safe and headed home. The most critically ill passengers were in hospitals, getting the best care possible. These last weeks had been nothing but angst and worry, bordering on despair. Amanda had felt helpless to do something, anything, to help all those people under her care, to protect them somehow from this horrific virus. So many of her friends on board had gotten sick, and some of her guests were dying, or dead. But most were safe and gone. Finally, Amanda felt she could relax. All she wanted to do was go home to Washington State, where her family awaited.

The mood on the *Zaandam* was fraternal—after two weeks of chaotic lockdown, officers were now allowed to gather on deck, to slow down for a moment and take stock of what was left of their sanity. Several singers and theatrical cast members were allowed to disembark in Port Everglades. They were deemed nonessential for the operation of the *Zaandam* and sent home. Amanda wandered the *Zaandam*'s open-air terraces and decks with the other officers. For the first time in weeks, she and her exhausted mates enjoyed a moment of peace and quiet. It didn't last long.

Amanda was extremely well connected on the *Zaandam*. She knew who was who, from the engine room to housekeeping. Now she began asking around, wondering when she and the other entertainment staff would be sent to shore. Amanda figured she and her team were practically next in line to disembark. Why on earth would the *Zaandam* need an entertainment coordinator aboard? If anyone should be deemed nonessential, it was someone like her.

Amanda packed her bag, finally ready to head home. Then a casual comment from a ranking officer shocked her. "Better get some sleep," he noted casually. "Before we leave tomorrow."

"What? We're leaving?" Amanda was confused, and now suddenly nervous. Was she going to be trapped again at sea? The more she asked about this, the more she felt like crying. Word from the bridge was clear: No more crew would be allowed to leave the *Zaandam*. The CDC had drawn the line: Passengers could disembark but not crew. In essence, Amanda was

banned from entering her own country. Rejected by authorities on shore, the *Zaandam* was now preparing to leave the cruise terminal and return to sea, again forced to combat the COVID-19 outbreak as best she could. With thousands of cases ravaging Florida hospitals, few advocates for the cruise ship crew were to be found. Passengers—those who had been so vocal on social media—were repatriated. Problem solved. Thousands of cruise ship crew—unable to protest unless they wanted to risk unemployment, and many being charged exorbitant rates for internet connections—were effectively silenced. They could be sent back to international waters and essentially ignored. "We found out the day before," said Amanda. "No one knew. The corporate office didn't know. Our captain didn't know. The world was changing. It's not like anyone planned this to mess with our minds; it was an ever-changing situation and we got completely forgotten."

APRIL 6, 7:04 P.M.
COVID-19 Ward, Broward Health Medical Center

After four days in the COVID-19 Ward, Wiwit's hold on life was slipping away. The doctors and nurses tried everything. They showed Anny how they placed Wiwit on his stomach, to make it easier for his lungs to inflate, and for the ventilator to keep him breathing. Anny watched the video feed of Wiwit on his belly, still in a coma, his breathing controlled by the machine. But it wasn't working, the doctor was saying. Wiwit's blood oxygen level was dropping. Few could survive this, the doctor explained, so Anny Doko needed to prepare for her husband's death.

Anny was distraught. She'd thought this might happen but had tried to put it out of her mind, to keep away those negative thoughts. Wiwit needed her to be positive, believing he would beat this, she thought. She must remain strong.

But now the doctor was telling her that the end was near, that she had to make a harrowing decision. Wiwit's lungs were filling with fluid and nothing they had done was stopping that deadly process. The stress on his body was surging, and there wasn't enough oxygen in his bloodstream. He was drowning in his own fluids. When that time came, the doctors could only revive him with the defibrillator, gambling they could shock life back into his body. But that procedure could have devastating consequences, the doctor warned. Anny had to make a choice: Did she want him resuscitated? Or would she prefer to let him die? Anny felt her husband was already gone. She felt certain that he would never fully recover, never lead a normal life. She talked it over with her family and they agreed. "I decided to not allow the doctors and the nurses to resuscitate him. If he flatlines, let him die in peace," she said. "That's what God would want to happen. If God wanted him alive, he would be alive."

The doctors needed her to confirm her decision in writing. Anny stared at the emailed document, suffering over the idea of signing it. "I was afraid," she admitted. "I was afraid because he was the breadwinner of the family." Anny's youngest son, Matthew, brought her to her senses. Sitting nearby as his mom agonized, Matthew said quietly, "No matter what, we need to bring Papa home."

Anny knew what she needed to do. "I love my husband, but I realized I couldn't be selfish," she said. Anny looked at her son. She asked him to pray for God to help them, and to allow them to bring Wiwit home. Then she signed the release form.

CHAPTER 13

PRISONERS IN PARADISE

APRIL 7, 1:15 P.M.
Port Everglades Channel, Headed to the Caribbean Sea

As the *Zaandam* pulled away from Port Everglades, Amanda watched the skyline of the city grow smaller. Unsure of what lay ahead, and with no outlet for her despair, she started to jog, then to sprint. For an hour, she tore around and around Promenade Deck. "I was trying not to cry while I was running," she confessed. "I was just praying."

Despite her grief, Amanda recognized that she was one of the privileged few aboard the *Zaandam*. Just one deck below, the misery stacked up. The vast majority of those left on board—hundreds of fellow crew members—were headed back into lockdown. The CDC ordered corporate to quarantine everyone to assure COVID-19 was no longer spreading aboard the *Zaandam*, or any other cruise ship that wanted to return to a U.S. port. Amanda, a ship's officer, still maintained a few meaningful little privileges—fresh air when needed, access to the library, and free internet communications with friends and family. But most of the crew without an essential job would have to quarantine for two weeks. These support systems provided the strands from which Amanda wove a lifeline.

*

Overall, the prognosis for the crew was bleak. The world was locking down by the day. Nonemergency air travel was banned. Borders were sealed.

As hospital rooms filled to capacity, no nation would allow cruise ship workers to disembark, much less let them board planes to fly halfway around the world to their distant homes. Dozens of Carnival ships, the *Zaandam* and *Rotterdam* among them, were blocked from getting home by a web of ever-changing restrictions wrought by the pandemic. Tens of thousands of crew members were idle, with no passengers to serve. They were stuck on their ships, many still confined to their cabins day and night, banned from going outside. Facing uncertainty and locked away from their family and friends, at least four cruise ship crew members ended their lives by jumping overboard as cruise lines searched for a way to get them home in the weeks and months that lay ahead. Others organized protests to fight for the right for free internet, so they could at least stay in touch with their loved ones.

APRIL 8, 2:03 P.M.
COVID-19 Ward, Broward Health Medical Center

By early afternoon on April 8, the doctors at Fort Lauderdale's Broward Health Medical Center knew there was nothing more they could do for Wiwit. Destructive inflammation, a hallmark of the coronavirus, had sapped his lungs' ability to deliver life-critical oxygen to his bloodstream. Wiwit had only a few hours, at best, until death. It was time to prepare the family.

Anny was startled awake by the WhatsApp video call. She could see on her phone that it was the hospital in Florida. It was just past 2:00 a.m. in Batam. For days now, she had been speaking with the nurse, or maybe the doctor, around 10:00 a.m. her time. The family would gather around the phone, listening to the latest report on Wiwit's condition, watching the video feed of him unconscious in the hospital bed. Anny knew this call meant awful news. The doctor didn't mince his words. Wiwit's condition was getting worse, fast. "If his condition weakens further," the doctor said, "we believe that he will pass soon."

Anny, her youngest son, Matthew, and her brother Hans were shocked. Anny began to weep. The doctor started to explain what he meant, but Anny already knew. She'd signed the release form. There was no turning back. Wiwit would soon be gone. She thanked the doctor but made a final request: Could they dial her once they knew Wiwit was dying? "Please call me," Anny pleaded. "I want to be able to see my husband, be with my husband for the last seconds of his life." The doctor paused before answering, then said, "Yes, we'll call you if we see that situation happening."

"We just waited," Anny said. "And I prayed. I still believed a miracle could happen." As the sun came up in Batam, Anny's phone rang. The doctor was there on the fuzzy video image. Wiwit had died thirty minutes earlier, around 6:30 p.m. local time, he said. Anny broke down, blindsided and angered. "Why didn't you call? I asked you to call," she repeated over and over. "I wanted to see him. I wanted to see him."

The doctor apologized. But Wiwit's condition had worsened so fast, there was no time. "We were trying our best to save him; we really tried," he said, clearly saddened by losing this patient. "It was a chaotic situation. We forgot to call you."

As Anny cried, the nurse came on the line. He'd been so kind all along, always there for the family's questions, his phone ready to show them Wiwit. Anny had one more request. She and the family needed to see Wiwit.

So he turned the phone to Wiwit, who was lying on the bed, tubes still attached. Anny asked the nurse to take Wiwit's hand. And on the other side of the world, in Anny and Wiwit's living room, the family began to pray. The prayers for salvation rang out as the family watched the video image of Wiwit's inert body, halfway around the world, in Fort Lauderdale. After days of agony, on sea and now on land, COVID-19 had finally taken him.

Having the nurse hold Wiwit's hand allowed Anny to feel as if she were closer, with her husband one last time. She needed to help his spirit get to where it needed to go.

APRIL 9, 9:00 A.M.
Port Everglades, Berth 19, Aboard the Rotterdam

On the *Rotterdam*, Claudia, Juan, and five other South Americans were the last of the passengers still on board. For a confusing and infuriating week, they had waited, confined to their cabins, until finally at 9:00 a.m. on April 9, they were given clearance to walk off the ship. A chartered jet waited to commence the long flight home to Argentina, they were told. But it took hours for the bus to get to the airport, including a long wait in a cramped room at the port for the arrival of stranded passengers from another Carnival ship that had docked in Miami. The bus finally pulled into Miami–Opa Locka Executive Airport, driving right onto the tarmac, where two private jets were fueled up and ready to go. It appeared as though the long nightmare journey was finally coming to an end. One by one, people's names were called, those from Chile, Mexico, and elsewhere. But not Claudia, Juan, or the other Argentines. Finally, a woman boarded the bus and curtly announced that no Argentines would be able to leave. "Your government has refused to authorize your return flight," she said tersely. Argentina had closed all airports weeks earlier because of the COVID-19 pandemic, and every flight into Argentina required full approval from the government. According to the cruise line, government red tape was getting in the way.

With nowhere to go, Claudia and Juan, a pair of Uruguayans, and the three other Argentines on the bus were taken back to the port and brought alongside the *Rotterdam*. Broward County Sheriff's Department officers were waiting on the dock, the lights on their squad cars flashing. They had orders to keep the group there by the ship until someone figured out what to do with them. Claudia was exhausted, despondent, on the verge of tears. *They clearly don't know what to do with us,* she thought. It was a grotesque turn of events, from the euphoria of surviving this god-awful odyssey and the real prospect of heading home to this—forced by armed police to wait inside the bus until someone decided their fate. After yet another excruciating delay, word finally came down from the cruise line. The seven passengers would have to reboard the *Rotterdam*, destination unknown. There was nothing any of them could do.

The following morning, well before dawn, the *Rotterdam* headed out to sea to link up with the *Zaandam* once again. The Argentines and the couple from Uruguay were the only passengers from the *Zaandam* still at sea. The United States was now turning its back on the two ships, and everyone aboard. They were all in limbo again, facing the prospects of sailing to nowhere in giant circles in the Caribbean, searching for a way home.

APRIL 10

Caribbean Sea, Between Freeport and Nassau, the Bahamas

Inside her cabin on the crew deck of the *Zaandam*, Erin Montgomery doubted she had the strength to walk ashore even in the unlikely case she was given that option. Erin, like Amanda, was stuck on the ship in a sort of uncharted limbo, blocked by the cruise line from getting off in Florida even though she, too, was a U.S. citizen. While the ships were in port, the government was refusing to allow anyone off unless the cruise lines had arranged private transport home—car, private jet, anything that would assure the person would not come into contact with others. So, for the moment, they were stuck at sea.

Erin had nearly recovered from the initial infection that had attacked her lungs, but now something else had zeroed in on her intestines. Waves of painful cramps kept her waylaid in bed. "As it moved through my body, I had a lot of weird things happen. Every one of my toes peeled. Every day a different toe, and then my whole foot peeled."

Erin called down to the medical center, pleading for help. Dr. Sonja Hofmann arrived, sat near Erin, and took her temperature. Dr. Hofmann noted that Erin hadn't improved since the previous visit. There wasn't much she could do for her. She'd already prescribed a drug for the nausea and another for the diarrhea. Erin needed to rest in her cabin for a few more days, Dr. Hofmann explained before leaving.

Erin was worried she had COVID-19 a second time. But she'd never know, because she was not tested for the virus. As Erin battled the bizarre symptoms, she imagined her team. With the passengers off-loaded, they'd gotten a break. Now they needed to wash only the dishes for the crew. That was still fifteen hundred or so meals a day. Erin wondered how they would pull it off. After the intense shifts that she'd shared with them, she thought about when and how they would ever get home. But now she didn't have the strength to think much about it anymore. She needed to sleep.

APRIL 10

Caribbean Sea, West of Freeport, Aboard the Rotterdam

Claudia Osiani walked out to the balcony, furious. She'd packed her suitcase three times, disembarked, even arrived at an airport—where she was banned from boarding a charter jet, which flew off without taking her home. Claudia blamed the Argentine government for her plight, describing the consul in Miami as "less than useless." Why, if all the other passengers had gone home, was she still aboard a cruise ship? Why wasn't she on a flight to Argentina?

Claudia was sure the captain was navigating a repetitive circular route in the Caribbean, awaiting instructions, killing time. With no chance to escape, she returned to a familiar role: caretaking. Every morning, she rang up her Argentine friends on board and cheerfully chatted about the sun, the sea, and the wind. She dubbed it "weather therapy." Claudia's top priority was a cute elderly couple who had succumbed to the nightmare of lockdown by taking their sleeping pills. She knew that in situations like this, of extreme, prolonged stress or trauma, people tended to self-medicate with whatever was at hand—booze or, in this case, sedatives. Claudia worried her friends might be dead when they didn't pick up the phone, but luckily that didn't happen. Claudia was able to help put their minds at ease by calling over the ship's phone, giving them soothing, detailed descriptions of scenes outside the cabin window.

Claudia and her husband, Juan, used humor to break up the day. They pretended they were interior decorators, and they set out to design an imaginary upgrade to their entire suite—all two hundred square feet. Wine bar or cappuccino machine? Modern Jacuzzi or classic bidet? Laughing at their captivity, Claudia and Juan video-chatted for hours with their grandchildren. Learning Snapchat cartoon features, they giggled their way through megabytes of whiskers and floating heart photos.

Juan and Claudia watched so many hours of *Animal Planet* that they felt they'd gone on safari with every animal on Earth. And they laughed at Holland America for never pausing the looped cruise ship promotional video on the in-house TV channel. The promo reel highlighted the *Zaandam* with all of its amenities, depicting never-ending activities.

The camera flowed among buffets, bars, and restaurants, and highlighted group activities ranging from lectures to line dancing. Under lockdown, the snazzy video felt like a satirical slap in the face. In just weeks, the promise of a flight to fantasy on a cruise ship was replaced by orders to avoid all others. To hide from a predator.

Another TV channel featured a live camera shot from the bow of the *Zaandam*, displaying the open ocean in a wide-angle panorama. Rather than bringing calm and tranquility, the live feed further emphasized to Claudia that they were plowing the seas in useless circles. It was oppressive. She felt as if she were incarcerated in some kind of surreal, vaguely luxurious floating prison.

Claudia knew that her years as a psychologist provided exactly the emotional tool kit she would need to endure yet another stage of this voyage to nowhere. "I thought to myself, *Well, I'm here; I can't cry and throw a tantrum like a child. What am I going to do with this?*" What surprised her, however, was the difficulty in applying her survival skills to a new patient: herself.

Help came in the form of her eighty-year-old neighbor, a man named Tito from Uruguay, who, like clockwork, every morning strode out to his balcony, adjacent to Claudia's, and bellowed to the ocean, *"Toooooooday . . . can be a gooooooooood daaaaaaay! Let's nail it!"*

"It gave me goose bumps," said Claudia. "Despite us all feeling awful, Tito's attitude—every day—was our wake-up call. Sometimes I screamed with him. . . . Between the three balconies, none of us got depressed. We may have cried in our cabins, but when we talked, our spirits picked up, even without being able to see each other."

Claudia found a secret treasure during the new lockdown—a coffeemaker. After weeks of brewing in the bathroom using recycled tea bags stuffed with coffee grounds, she now had the ability to make a proper cup of fresh coffee. "Seeing a coffeemaker was something incredible. That really made me happy."

APRIL 11

COVID-19 Ward, AdventHealth Orlando

For more than a week, Lance and Sharon lay across the hall from each other in the Orlando hospital, both on ventilators and sedated. "I never imagined that my parents would be fighting for their lives at the same time, but that is my reality right now," their daughter, Amy, back in Missouri, posted on Facebook. As Lance improved, Sharon's body began to shut down. She was particularly susceptible to respiratory ailments. Colds were always hard for her to shake. She often had a nagging cough. The coronavirus was devastating.

By Easter weekend, though, she seemed to improve. They eased her off the ventilator. The nurses arranged a video call with Amy, who was at her home near St. Louis. Sharon was lucid enough to listen as Amy broke down, trying to express just how much she loved her mother. "I love everyone," Sharon replied softly. Three hours later, Sharon went into shock. Amy called, pleading for a final moment with her mom, and a nurse placed the cell phone to Sharon's ear. "I was at least able to tell her good-bye," Amy said, "and tell her it was okay to go, even though it wasn't." At 11:01 p.m. on April 11, Sharon Hutton died of acute respiratory failure caused by COVID-19-related pneumonia.

For another three days, Lance lay a few beds away on a ventilator as doctors prepared to wean him off the breathing machine. He was unconscious, unaware that his wife had died a few feet away. As soon as he came to, doctors planned the delicate maneuver of removing the tube that snaked down his trachea and into his lungs. Done wrong, the tube removal could damage his throat or even lacerate his vocal cords. But when Lance awoke in a groggy haze, he reached up and ripped the tube out of his own throat, shocking the doctors. As he lay recovering in the ICU, drifting in and out of consciousness, doctors urged Amy to hold off telling him that his wife was dead. "They didn't want him to get agitated," Amy said.

Lance rapidly improved, his blood oxygen level returned to normal, the fever subsided, and the coughing eased. Then Amy called her father in Orlando for what she described as "the hardest conversation I've had in my life." Lance was never a very expressive man, and he tried his best to keep his emotions to himself. It was hard for him to fathom the depths of this loss, the woman he'd shared his life with for so long. It was unimaginable. But Lance decided one thing as he took in the loss of his wife, lying there in the hospital. He was going to live, no matter what.

As Lance grew more alert, he was moved out of the ICU to a normal room, then to a long-term care and rehabilitation center as he nursed his body back from the brink. Against all odds, Lance Hutton seemed to be beating COVID-19.

APRIL 11, 8:20 P.M.
Caribbean Sea, Northwest of the Bahamas

Circling around the Bahamas, the *Zaandam* crew faced further disappointing news. Disembarking in Florida was off the table. Unloading the passengers had been a logistical nightmare for local and federal governments. Now that the ships were in the relative calm of the Bahamas, the *Zaandam* and *Rotterdam* crews were out of the media spotlight. Rapidly, they became a low-priority problem.

Carnival Corp. and the Holland America Line had been swamped by multiple shipboard outbreaks. Captain Smit's crew members were battered by stress and exhaustion, and now he needed to ask them to lock down yet again. Smit took to the ship's intercom and began by explaining that they were still in full crisis mode. He also stressed that when an emergency hits at sea, there is no plan B. "We are all on the same team," he declared, "and we deal with crises here and now."

To stamp out the COVID-19 outbreak aboard the *Zaandam*, Smit announced another fourteen days of confinement. The crew members were now living in guest cabins, and while visiting was prohibited, they were allowed fresh air. In addition, meals in the dining room allowed for supervised encounters.

The ship was divided into a Red Zone for those who were ill or suspected of being sick, and a Green Zone for those who had already been through the COVID-19 cycle—roughly a third of the crew at that point. Every person in the Red Zone was placed under lockdown. Anyone found wandering, crossing through, or sneaking into that part of the ship—however briefly— would be quarantined.

APRIL 14

Caribbean Sea, the Bahamas

Anne Weggeman, who worked aboard the *Zaandam* as a receptionist and then on the emergency medical line, was shocked by the captain's announcement of another two weeks of lockdown. She called friends in London to vent her frustration. But the situation was getting worse everywhere. Instead of expressing sympathy, Anne's friends told her to stop crying and complaining. They gave her clear instructions, and a direct order: "You are going to look at the little lights of optimism that are there. Look at the friends you have. Look at the sun. It is shining."

"It was a slap in the face," she said. "They woke me up."

Weggeman had nearly recovered from COVID-19 when her second quarantine began. Physically, she had improved so much that every day she was strumming a guitar and composing songs. Music was her therapy. Fear was sliding away and in its place a transformation had taken root. "For me a game changer was to accept my situation," she said. "All the time I was struggling, all the time I was fighting and not accepting the situation made it the biggest Hell for me. Once I accepted that we went back to sea for two weeks, it was, wow. Not actually so bad here. Look what you can do. But it has to do with surrender and acceptance of your situation and that's a choice you can make no matter where you're at. That's what changed everything for me."

Weggeman was anxious to return to the Netherlands to be with her family, but a deep loyalty had developed among the crew members—not unlike the unwavering bonds that firefighters on the front lines develop. Weggeman saw her colleagues not as fellow workers, but as brothers, sisters, aunts, and uncles. The range of age and nationalities was staggering. "We helped each other in a way that I never experienced with my friends or family. We had to take care of each other; I never felt alone. I always felt supported by the people around me on the ship in a way that I didn't know was possible."

Despite the captain's dire warnings about moving around the ship and transgressing by entering the Red Zone, the antsy crew members were determined to socialize after such a stressful and restrictive number of weeks. Relieved to be free of the torturous schedule that involved delivering meals, towels, and advice to the passengers, the crew of the *Zaandam* decided to do something for themselves. Romantic interludes exploded as a pent-up fury of hormones turned the ship into a sexually charged tinderbox. "At first it was really hard to break the rules," said a *Zaandam* officer who worked on the bridge. "But later, yeah, it got easier, and people would look for each other. It was like a game."

Earlier rounds of these same games led to another problem for Holland

America, one that was kept particularly quiet. So many weeks of lockdown, so many intense moments of near death had led to a rash of flash sexual encounters that were now being tallied in the number of female crew wondering what to do about their surprise pregnancies. Trained as an obstetrician and gynecologist, the *Zaandam*'s lead medical officer, Dr. Warren Hall, was now called to tend to the many cruise ships anchored around the Bahamas, people with direct knowledge of the pregnancies said. He now spent his hours zipping in a lifeboat as he visited one cruise ship after another, attending to pregnancies, including a life-threatening ectopic one (when the fertilized egg remains outside the ovary, often in a fallopian tube). "Poor Warren," one friend of the beleaguered doctor recounted. "There must have been forty girls pregnant."

APRIL 23, 7:31 P.M.
Murrieta, California

Donna Mann was in the bathroom of her Southern California home when the lights suddenly conked out. Running into the attached bedroom, Donna was confused as the lights clicked back on. Next to her bed, she saw her husband's alarm clock flashing the time of the outage: 7:31. What was going on? It had been days since she had left the *Zaandam* at port and her husband, Jorge Hill, in the ICU back in Florida. While he fought COVID-19 and was unable to receive visitors, Donna tried to piece together their life back home. The momentary power outage was something she would always remember. "Jorge must have been telling me good-bye," said Donna when she later learned that Jorge had died at 10:31 eastern standard time, exactly the moment when her lights blinked off in California. She was left devastated. "I am a widow twice. I had been married for forty-one years to my first husband. And to find Jorge, at this late stage of my life, was such a bonus. He had also lost his wife. And to have that snatched away after only eight years! I wish I could say there was something positive. But now it is déjà vu and I am going through widowhood again."

APRIL 24, 5:13 P.M.
Caribbean Sea

Claudia Osiani was losing hope. For more than two weeks, they'd been near the Bahamas, circling, running east, then west. Now they were anchored. She sat on the balcony, as there was nothing else to do. Staring at the same blue-green sea, the same beautiful waning light at the end of the day, the same cruise ships all around, moving slowly around their anchor points, just like the *Rotterdam*.

Claudia had just ended another WhatsApp call with a contact at the Argentine Ministry of Defense. He genuinely wanted to help but couldn't do much for them. Before that, she'd berated the consul general in Miami, demanding help to get home. For days, this had gone on, she and Juan agitating over their plight. "We have been shaking things up. We've done what we could. The government has reached out, but nothing," she said, leaving a voice message for a *Bloomberg Businessweek* journalist. "Everyone blames each other."

The truth was, no one seemed to know how to negotiate a journey from the Caribbean to Argentina. Claudia sat in her prison of a deluxe suite, recognizing she needed to find acceptance. But acquiescence was not her style. She would keep fighting until someone found a route off this ship. Claudia and Juan were utterly exhausted, physically and mentally. "We don't know if we are human beings, fish, things, tissue? We've lost reference to who we are," she said. "Nothing has changed. It's all very, very difficult."

Suddenly, the *Rotterdam* was moving. It eased close to another huge cruise ship, the name *Caribbean Princess* splashed across a white hull, its nineteen decks dwarfing the *Rotterdam*. A great maneuver was afoot all around them. Tenders sped among the ships, transferring crew according to nationality. There were thousands of stranded crews on the dozen or so ships around them, and the cruise lines had come up with a plan. The Filipinos, Indonesians, and South Africans were massing on the *Rotterdam*. U.S. citizens were headed to the *Emerald Princess*. The *Zaandam* was headed to the Netherlands, with crew members from Europe aboard. The phone rang, and Claudia was taken aback by what she heard. They were transferring to the *Caribbean Princess*, the cruise line's representative said. They were to be ready first thing in the morning.

Overnight, dark thunderheads stretched to the horizon, jagged lightning strikes illuminating the sky. By dawn, the winds had picked up. Violent waves pitched the *Rotterdam* up and down, jerked it from port to starboard. Claudia and Juan were supposed to head to the tender's hatchway, but the seas were too rough. With waves crashing into the small craft with alarming force, for now they had no choice but to wait.

By 1:00 p.m., the storm had passed. They were ready to move. Claudia settled into the tender, the seas remarkably smooth. She watched the *Rotterdam* fade into the distance, happy to finally leave. She'd felt abandoned there. Not once did the captain check in; not once did he offer those soothing words he'd been trained to deliver. They'd been forgotten from the moment they were forced to board that ship. Leaving was a joy.

There were seven of them in the tender, five Argentines and two Uruguayans. They were the last passengers from the *Zaandam*'s pariah cruise still at sea, and now they were headed toward their third ship. For six weeks they'd been adrift, and no one seemed to know how much longer this would last. As they stepped off the tender, the sailors began to disinfect them. First their luggage; then they sprayed some kind of mist in Claudia's path. She prayed that it wouldn't be too bad and feared another allergic reaction. Then an officer called them over. "We're sorry, but protocols require us to put each of you in a separate cabin," he announced.

Claudia couldn't believe what she was hearing. They were a couple. For weeks and weeks, they'd cared for each other. It was how they'd survived all this. *And now they want to separate us,* she thought, incredulous. "I am not going anywhere without my husband," she declared. The others said the same. Juan translated, and a standoff ensued. The officer slipped away to consult with his superiors. Moments later, the officer relented. Couples would be able to bunk together.

As they made their way to their cabin, Claudia and Juan were shocked at the surreal scenes before them. The vast ship looked like it was hosting a party. Crew members lounged here and there, winding down after everything they'd been through. Clearly, they were not expecting any passengers. They gawked at Claudia and Juan, and the couple gawked back. Their escorts explained that this ship was for crew members from Latin America. They'd been arriving for days, gathering from multiple ships. The plan was to head south, slowly dropping crew members in Brazil, Uruguay, Argentina. With flights shut down worldwide, there was no other way to repatriate cruise ship crews. They could fly home on private charter flights, but that would cost a fortune, even if the cruise lines were able arrange it. What the cruise lines did have were ships, and they were all empty. The trip south would take weeks, but at least everyone would be headed in the right direction.

As they settled into their cabin, Claudia and Juan were stunned. Once again, they were the misfits on board, the only passengers surrounded by a desperate ship's crew, probably in danger of being forgotten. They talked to their friend in the Ministry of Defense, and even he was taken aback by this latest development. "Don't worry," he said, trying to cheer them up. "We're ninety-nine percent there in terms of getting you home."

All Claudia heard was that there was a 1 percent chance it would all fall apart. They'd be adrift once more, destination unknown. Looking at Juan, she said bitterly, "No one wants us."

CHAPTER 14
FINAL GOOD-BYE

APRIL 27, 2:03 P.M.
Caribbean Sea, Between Freeport, the Bahamas, and Miami

The *Zaandam* lay at anchor roughly fifty miles southwest of Freeport, the Bahamas, under a brilliant blue sky. The aimless circling in the Caribbean had ceased, at least for now. Captain Smit asked the men and women under his command to assemble in order to honor Wiwit Widarto. Many of the original crew members were still aboard the *Zaandam*. Later, most would be moved to other ships for the long journey home to Asia, Africa, or Europe. Now scores of *Zaandam* crew members made their way through the Mainstage theater and then outside to the open swath of Promenade Deck at the bow. They found places along the deck, leaving space for the captain, who would lead the ceremony. He would stand near the flagpole and next to the seaman's bell.

On the starboard side, the officers and engineers lined up, smartly dressed in their dark Holland America uniforms, white hats clutched in their hands. On the port side, stewards, bosun's mates, dancers, singers, cooks, dishwashers, plumbers, mechanics, and laundry workers quietly waited for the captain to begin. The crew represented many nations, but mainly the Philippines, Indonesia, Thailand, South Africa, the UK, and the Netherlands, plus a smattering from the United States and South America. The ceremony for Wiwit was the first time the crew had been permitted to gather since the virus attacked. Honoring Wiwit fit the maritime code, but the crew members also needed a collective catharsis, a moment to take stock of all they had been through.

Captain Smit's crew had reached their limit, and even come close to the breaking point. For weeks, they'd dedicated all their collective energy to protecting the passengers, working themselves to the limit. One thing they could all be proud of was they'd never given up, even as the virus picked them off.

Even the most composed officers donned their sunglasses, trying to hide the tears that welled up. This was especially hard for the officers, starting with Captain Smit. They were responsible for every soul on the ship, and Wiwit had died on their watch. These men and women of the crew shared a remarkable camaraderie forged from the intensity of living and working together seven days a week, for months at a time. Funerals on a ship cut deep. Social distancing, isolation, and the dark weeks-long lockdown had deepened those bonds. They had been to hell and back since the virus struck the *Zaandam*. Many were just coming out of long isolation periods as the cruise line fought to halt the pandemic's spread on board. Losing one of their own was devastating.

The captain introduced one of Wiwit's closest friends, an administrative clerk from Indonesia named Vicky. He spoke eloquently about Wiwit, reminding everyone that Wiwit was a deeply religious man. Wiwit's family wanted Vicky to pass along a special message for the crew. "They are gracious for all that we've done here," he said. "And I also want to say that to all those who took care of us, especially those of us who got sick." Vicky paused, looking at the assembled crew. "We all have a new perspective. Maybe the world will not be the same again after this," he said. "But as we say at Holland America Line, *Zaandam*, with love, with respect. *Zaandam* stronger."

Several hundred yards across the sparkling azure water, Amanda Bogen came out on her cabin balcony on the *Emerald Princess* to watch. She'd been transferred along with the other U.S. citizens who were members of the crew to the ship, which was now anchored close to the *Zaandam*. Many ships were in this staging area at sea, all forced out of ports by the pandemic. The *Rotterdam* was nearby. Like dozens of ships, it had lain at anchor or sailed around in tight circles or erratic zigzag patterns for weeks now, killing time as the cruise lines searched for a way home.

Amanda wanted—needed—to be with her friends on the *Zaandam* for the service. She held great memories of Wiwit. When she'd guided passengers on a behind-the-scenes tour of the *Zaandam*, she'd always taken them by the laundry. Wiwit would come out, smiling, dressed in a freshly washed uniform, and invite them inside, then proudly show them around.

Amanda saw the crew lined up on the bow of the *Zaandam* as Captain Smit called for a minute of silence. Then two bosun's mates raised the Dutch flag, then lowered it to half-mast. One of the bosun's mates stepped up to the seaman's bell and rang it eight times, slowly, symbolizing the end of a fallen sailor's last watch. Amanda could hear the bell breaking the silence, all the way over on the *Emerald Princess*. Could it provide closure for the hellish voyage she'd endured? As the toll of the bell faded, the crew members dispersed to their posts or their cabins. They had honored Wiwit, but there was work to be done to prepare the *Zaandam* and the crew to return to Europe. Soon, the ship would resume circling the Caribbean again.

Modern cruise ships need movement to function: Their engines provide electricity for light and ventilation, and waste-treatment systems work best when a ship is under way. So, periodically, they must pull up anchor and move, killing time until a port opens up. A route home for the hundreds of crew members still on board the *Zaandam* remained elusive. For now, their only home was the ship.

APRIL 27, 2:11 P.M.
Aboard the Caribbean Princess,
13 Miles East of Port Everglades

Aboard the *Caribbean Princess*, Claudia and Juan couldn't complain about the new accommodations. They had a luxury suite with a balcony, and the food was superb. The *Caribbean Princess* was far more modern than the *Zaandam* and, with a capacity for 3,600 passengers, three times the size. The ship had multiple pools, a huge casino, more shops, more bars, more restaurants. More of everything, compared with the *Zaandam* and the *Rotterdam*. But in this surreal situation, none of that mattered. Juan and Claudia were still confined to their cabin. An officer had warned them of the restrictions, speaking through a mask, while keeping his distance. Claudia quickly read his emotions. She could tell he was nervous, probably terrified they were bringing the virus into his world. Claudia understood his anxieties, but she was beyond trying to empathize. They'd been in quarantine for more than a month. Doctors had checked them six times. In each instance, after every exam, they were deemed COVID-free. But here they were, on another ship, waiting, forced to stay inside another cabin, unable to fly home.

Claudia stepped out on the balcony, phone to her ear, trying to concentrate on what the man from the Argentine Ministry of Defense was explaining. She could hear the music below, or maybe aft. The crew was turning it up. Was there a party at one of the bars? Or maybe by the pool? The crew and staff were now free, young people letting off steam. The only passengers to worry about were a few Argentines and a couple from Uruguay, also confined to their quarters. Who could blame them for partying?

After two full days aboard the *Caribbean Princess*, no one from Holland

America could yet tell them what was ahead. Claudia listened, but the man on the phone was repeating the same message as before: The foreign ministry was negotiating with the Americans, but it was tough. The Americans were up against presidential decrees that banned foreign visitors from setting foot on U.S. soil. Claudia thanked him and hung up, even more frustrated. The ship was preparing for a thirty-day journey to South America, then would head to Africa to repatriate the stranded crew. More than once, she and Juan imagined the worst-case scenario. "What if they leave us on this ship, make us return home by sea?" Claudia could think of no worse nightmare, and now it was looking like a possibility.

That night, everything suddenly changed. An executive from Holland America called to report a breakthrough. The Argentines had been granted permission to fly home. The *Caribbean Princess* was headed for Port Everglades, where Claudia, Juan, and the five other passengers on board would be taken to the airport for their long-awaited and long-delayed flight to Buenos Aires. The prospect had been dangled before them once before, but this time she had renewed hope.

*

A few hours later, just after dawn, Fort Lauderdale spread out before them. Wearing face masks and full-body gowns, Claudia and Juan walked, with the others, single file down the gangway, straight onto a bus. Every person they neared—customs agents, cruise line workers, the bus driver—was dressed in protective gear. Claudia felt as if she were toxic, sowing terror inside the soul of everyone nearby. For a moment, it irked her. She and Juan had been tested for COVID-19 half a dozen times, and the result was always the same: negative. Any shred of public health logic would show there was no reason to worry that they were infected. Still, the world was treating them like medical pariahs. But she put all that out of her mind.

She was off the ship, headed to the airport, boarding the bus, free, and finally off the ocean.

The bus sped toward the airport and drove straight onto the tarmac, same as before. Claudia could see a chartered aircraft with the faded logo for Eastern Airlines peeling off the fuselage. The bus stopped a few feet from the tired-looking airplane, near two U.S. immigration agents dressed in masks and sitting in the blinding sun at a folding table. The agents checked all the passports, opened every piece of luggage, and waved them off up the stairs leading to the rear door of the aircraft. Claudia still couldn't believe they were leaving. Any second she expected they were going to be yanked off the plane, like the last time. She and Juan made their way up the stairs, taking one final look around. The flight attendant caught her attention, motioning her to take a seat in the last row. Claudia felt numb. Was she in shock? She had fantasized about this moment many times, "but now that we were there, on the plane, we couldn't believe it was happening."

As they tried to make sense of it all, a group of athletic young Argentines filed into the plane from the front entrance, giddy at the prospect of going home. An entire polo team from Argentina had been caught by the COVID-19 shutdown in Florida. They had also waited weeks to board this flight. They took their seats, calmly, deliberately. Some laughed, as if this had all been a slight inconvenience in their lives. *Clearly, their forced stay in the United States was far less torturous than ours,* Claudia thought.

A few minutes later, the doors were sealed, and the plane began to taxi across the airport. It was now fifty days since the *Zaandam* had departed Buenos Aires for what Claudia had expected would be a two-week dream vacation. It looked like their escape was becoming a reality. The plane finally turned onto a long runway, the jet engines revved, and moments later they were airborne. After twenty minutes in the air, headed south to Argentina, Claudia and Juan allowed themselves a moment to relax. They would land in ten hours. *This time,* Claudia thought, *we really are going home.*

APRIL 28, 1:03 P.M.
Caribbean Sea, Southwest of Freeport, the Bahamas

The phone rang while Erin Montgomery, the sanitation officer, was asleep in her cabin on the *Zaandam*. The voice delivered an urgent message. "Pack your bags," she was told. "You're leaving tomorrow." Erin hung up, despondent. She'd wanted to check in on a few members of her original team. She'd been separated from them for two weeks, since she'd gotten laid up by some kind of stomach virus. Erin knew their personal lives and had listened to their problems. They'd worked long days together, scouring dishes so everyone on board could be fed safely. That had developed a deep sense of loyalty. Now she doubted she would be allowed down to say goodbye to them. COVID-19 made that too risky.

As Erin left the *Zaandam* the following day, April 29, and stepped off the tender onto the *Emerald Princess*, she looked up at the new ship. It was so much larger and more modern than the *Zaandam* or the *Rotterdam*. Carnival had designated the ship as the one that would repatriate U.S. and Canadian crew members. Dozens were already aboard, and they were headed to Miami.

Erin followed orders and headed to her new cabin, trying to prepare herself mentally for two more weeks of isolation. This was no crew bunk just above the waterline, but a proper guest cabin. It was small but nice, with two twin beds and a small balcony. On the way up the stairs, she caught sight of a colleague from hotel management back on the *Zaandam*. They'd become friends, seeing each other frequently over the years. But when the woman saw Erin, she looked away, pretending as if she hadn't seen her. Erin knew why. She was afraid, as if Erin were bringing the plague. As she closed her cabin door, Erin tried to prepare herself. No one was getting off the ship without doing his or her two weeks. Those were the latest CDC rules.

*

At CDC headquarters in Atlanta, Dr. Cindy Friedman understood how harsh these new rules were. Personally, she felt sorry for the crew, stuck on ships, confined for fourteen, or even twenty-one, days in windowless cabins, shut off from family, friends, and the rest of the world. They'd identified 124 cruise ships languishing in U.S. waters, with nearly 95,000 workers aboard, and getting them off would be a complex task, given all the COVID-19 restrictions.

Dr. Friedman had had a lot to do with creating these rules, and she was convinced there was no other choice. Her cruise ship group had dealt with outbreaks on thirty ships in the first two months of the pandemic. One pattern was clear. A ship's crew was especially likely to spread the virus. It wasn't their fault, she knew. Friedman's boss, Dr. Martin Cetron, head of the CDC's quarantine unit, had explained the challenges early on. Crew on a cruise ship simply could not be isolated or socially distanced. They bunked together, shared bathrooms, ate in cramped mess rooms, worked in confined spaces, frequently with limited ventilation. Once a crew member became infected with COVID-19 from a passenger, from someone on shore, from a relative, he or she spread it fast. Dr. Martin Cetron had declared loudly and publicly that a cruise ship was an ideal environment to spread COVID-19. There were multiple studies to back that up.

Friedman soon detected that the COVID-19 outbreak on the *Zaandam* had a distinct profile, different from what she'd encountered on other ships. Usually, the passengers brought the virus on board, and then crew became a key vector for spreading it. Friedman saw that in case after case, most notably on the *Diamond Princess*. CDC spreadsheets for the *Zaandam* documented COVID-19 cases among crew from the engine room up to the reception desk, as well as among passengers. "You don't see as many cases in the engine room or at the bottom of the ship," she said in an interview. "But in this ship, it looks like there were cases in both, all the way along on the curve."

Somehow, COVID-19 had spread equally among the *Zaandam*'s 586 crew members and 1,243 passengers. This pattern convinced Dr. Friedman and her CDC colleagues that crew members must be isolated until outbreaks could be confined within the ship. Otherwise, they might unwittingly carry the disease from port to port, all the while showing no symptoms. The wide geographical diversity of crew members meant that flying them home would essentially seed the disease worldwide. Dr. Friedman and her colleagues wrote their detailed set of rules to assure that crew members, for the time being, would be allowed off a ship only when they were clear of COVID-19. Public health agencies around the world followed the CDC's lead, leaving tens of thousands of ship workers unwelcome in port after port.

*

Erin knew she would be allowed out of the room for only thirty minutes at a time—to eat. The rest of the day, this cabin would be her world. She was pretty certain this lockdown would be the last. Carnival had clearly planned this out in detail, down to the logistics of sorting the crew by nationality, by ship. They were so close. Getting home would be quick as soon as the quarantine was over. But for now, Erin was determined to make the best of it.

APRIL 30

COVID-19 ICU, AdventHealth Orlando

Carl Zehner remained in the ICU in an induced coma, machines keeping him alive. There was the ventilator, which breathed for him. A feeding tube kept him from starving. Carl had been in intensive care for almost three weeks after being transferred from the *Zaandam* to the hospital in Orlando. Back home in Nashville, his husband, Leo, sat in the living room of their spacious Victorian home, where they'd lived for thirty-eight years. They'd worked so hard to restore the house and fill it with Carl's collections. He'd spent his life collecting things. But the player piano, where Leo sat, was the prize. It was more than a century old and worked perfectly. A hardwood cabinet spanned the far wall of the room, each cubby holding a player piano roll. There were seven hundred of them, each containing a song, making it one of the finest collections in the world. Carl also had dozens of hand-cranked Victrola records, and hundreds more old 78s that he liked to listen to in the waning hours of the evening. Leo didn't have the time or energy to ponder Carl's eccentric collections, as nice as they were. He was consumed with the job of managing Carl's care. Every day, Leo received updates from the doctors or the nurses and analyzed them in detail. Slowly, Carl seemed to be improving.

A few nights earlier, Carl was taken off the ventilator. He could breathe on his own, the ICU doctors concluded. The parameters looked promising as Carl's lungs began working again, the ventilator silenced. The first night, a nurse found him sitting up, watching television, when she checked on him. Carl didn't say anything, and he looked okay, so the nurse let him be. But in the early morning, just before dawn, Carl's vital signs crashed. His blood oxygen fell to a dangerously low level, his organs fighting to function.

The doctors felt they had no choice. They performed an emergency intubation and turned the ventilator back on.

Leo knew this was serious. He tried to put the doctor at ease. "Well, we want to do everything we can do for Carl, but we really don't want to use heroic measures," Leo said.

The doctor cut him off. "We're long past heroic measures."

Leo was stunned. This was much more serious than he'd thought. For several days, Carl's condition worsened. The doctors came back with more bad news. Carl was suffering from acute respiratory distress syndrome, known as ARDS. Carl's pneumonia had advanced to a critical stage, the air sacs in his lungs filling with fluid leaking from the surrounding blood vessels. This form of lung failure, occurring in the most severe COVID-19 cases, meant Carl was fighting for his life, and Leo knew it.

Leo had been so hopeful. "I had been planning a coming-home party," Leo said. "Now I was looking at the possibility of switching to planning a funeral." Leo broke down, the tears coming. Was Carl going to survive?

He called his pastor, Judi Hoffmann, from the Methodist church across the street. She knew all about Carl's illness, and Leo needed to talk. "What's the difference between a funeral and a memorial service?" he asked. She replied, "Well, the funeral has the body, and the memorial service doesn't."

Leo was far away from Carl and had no way to get closer. COVID-19 made that impossible. But he realized someone needed to pray for Carl. Leo called the hospital in Orlando and asked for the pastoral service. "Could somebody go by and say a prayer for Carl?" Leo asked.

"Oh, yes, we can ask him to do that. Are you Catholic?" the man on the phone asked.

"No."

"Is Carl Catholic?"

"No."

Leo understood now. They were tastefully asking if he needed a priest to perform last rites. Leo kept it simple: "Please, can you go by and say a prayer for him?"

MAY 4, 3:32 P.M.
Rehabilitation Unit, AdventHealth Orlando

On a different floor in the same building, Lance Hutton took a break from his physical therapy activity to catch his breath. It was a good day. He'd walked longer than ever, perhaps fifteen hundred feet in all. Three weeks off the *Zaandam*, and Lance had reached his personal goal, completing two laps of the floor. Lance was almost back to where he was before stepping foot on that ship, at least physically. COVID-19 was finally gone; the latest test had come back negative. His lungs were clear of the pneumonia that had nearly killed him. Lance could walk on his own, which was no small feat. When they'd brought him here from the COVID-19 ward, he couldn't take more than a couple of steps. His legs didn't work. His body couldn't maintain any strength.

Lance had always kept himself in pretty good shape, playing golf, walking, keeping active. COVID-19 erased all that. He'd never felt this weak. Once, when he was off the ventilator, he got hit with the chills, shaking so violently that he couldn't stop. The nurse brought blankets, but that didn't help. "I thought I was going to die at that point," he said.

Lance wanted to return home, to put hospital care behind him. It was hard to think of what he'd gone through. The virus attack had been so severe, and so rapid. Then there was the devastating loss of Sharon. Why was she gone but he still here, among the living? He asked the doctor why and questioned what they had done to get him through the worst of COVID-19. "Nothing," the doctor told Lance. "We did not give you anything to cure you. We only addressed the symptoms you were having, until your body was able to overcome it."

Lance paused a moment, letting that sink in. "Why my body did, and Sharon's didn't, is a mystery I'm not ever going to answer."

CHAPTER 15
UNFAMILIAR HORIZONS

APRIL 16, 3:30 P.M.
Batam, Indonesia

The agonizing logistics of Wiwit's death continued even after he was gone. Just hours after he passed away, Anny Doko was forced to make yet another brutal decision. Health authorities in Florida were gripped by a fear that his corpse was still infected with COVID-19 and might infect others, a vector further spreading the disease. It was impossible to find an airline willing to fly Wiwit home to Indonesia. Anny wanted to see him one last time, and the family wanted to provide him a Christian burial. The virus took that from them, too. Wiwit, she was told, must be cremated. Anny had no choice. "I thought things through, and I decided, You know, I don't want him to stay away too long. I want him to come home as soon as possible," Anny recalled.

On April 16, eight days after Wiwit's death, Anny stared as her husband's body appeared on a computer screen. He was wrapped in a white cloth. The funeral home in Florida had agreed to let her view Wiwit one last time, via Zoom. Anny watched, racked with grief, as the attendant slowly revealed Wiwit's face, then gently covered him again before closing the wooden coffin. "We were able to see the final seconds of him being put into the cremation container," Anny said.

It would take another two months to bring Wiwit's ashes home. Anny, helped by Holland America, had to work through maddening bureaucratic hurdles. The global COVID-19 lockdown made every step of the process complicated. Adding to the chaos, no one could find Wiwit's passport. It was missing. Somewhere, in the transfer from ship to ambulance to hospital, it had disappeared. Anny now had to prove that the man she'd watched slowly die was indeed her husband. Month after month, she fought to confirm his identity, but it was futile. In Indonesia, a death certificate for a citizen who dies abroad requires the presentation of a passport. And Anny needed the death certificate to settle his estate. The cruise line blamed the hospital; the hospital blamed the cruise line. Anny had to sort out all the details.

But none of that ultimately mattered to Anny. The love of her life was gone. Her two sons no longer had a father. Anny had always dreamed that she would spend the rest of her life with Wiwit, the man who always had a smile for everyone. His death left a painful void. Wiwit would never come back from the sea as he'd been promising for so many years. They'd had plans to open a little restaurant in the market in Batam. After three decades of Wiwit's working in the cruise industry, they'd been so close to realizing that dream. He'd hoped to retire in another three years.

Anny recalled one of the last conversations she'd had with Wiwit, near the end, after he'd asked her to pray for him. "You know that I really admire what you've done," he told her. "You do everything yourself."

Anny was taken aback.

"You've always been my greatest support," Wiwit confessed. "You always pray for me, and I appreciate that. If I die one day, I'm very confident that God will help you."

A month after Wiwit died, Anny received a huge deposit in the family bank account: one billion rupiah. It was the payout for Wiwit's death on the job. Holland America had deposited the equivalent of $73,355 in her account. Considering that Wiwit typically sent home a thousand dollars a month, it was like receiving six years of salary all at once. Then another deposit appeared.

In solidarity with the much-loved Wiwit, Holland America employees joined forces and collectively gathered donations for Anny. Hundreds of workers on the *Zaandam* donated, as well as Wiwit's former colleagues aboard fourteen other Holland America ships. Additionally, when housekeeping staff members cleaned the vacated cabins on the *Zaandam*, they gathered the coins and forgotten bills—left behind in the passengers' hasty retreat—and donated buckets of cash and coins. The solidarity campaign from employees raised an additional ten thousand dollars for Wiwit's family. Thanks in part to Wiwit's friends at sea, Anny now had the money she needed to open that restaurant.

APRIL 28
Mar del Plata, Argentina

Claudia Osiani arrived at her seaside apartment in Mar del Plata, Argentina, and instead of feeling protected, she felt vulnerable. Nothing felt normal. Her favorite routines were prohibited under the COVID-19 lockdowns. No more swimming with her girlfriends. No more rehearsals with the theater group. Even the smell of her house had changed. Or had she?

Before the *Zaandam* odyssey, before the COVID-19 onslaught, Claudia and Juan had carefully selected an apartment with an ocean view. Their living room windows framed a wide slice of the Atlantic Ocean. Her crow's nest panorama now felt like a mocking reminder, as if she was still trapped at sea. When Claudia looked out her window, she couldn't escape the sensation that she was on the balcony of a cruise ship. After one brief glance into the expanse of the Atlantic, Claudia drew the curtain. *That's enough ocean view for now,* she told herself.

She missed the chance to have a coffee—or two—with her friends. Even the ability to open the door and walk about freely was no longer an option. These were the freedoms she missed, and needed so desperately. "I can't be shut up all day in my house even if I am doing things that I like. There is a moment when I need to get out! I need a bike ride!"

With her years of experience helping others to process traumatic events, Claudia had assumed that she would be able to handle a momentous event. Then reality struck. "Until that edgy situation arrives, you really don't know how you will manage it," she said. "It was just ocean beyond ocean, and we didn't know where we were going," she recounted, describing the ship navigating huge circles, the sun swinging around and around the ship like an enormous pendulum.

Claudia also felt her body change. The intense periods of stress provoked a resistance to insulin, sent her blood pressure soaring, and made her a candidate for diabetes. She also came to understand her own mortality. Aboard the *Zaandam*, a passenger had felt ill, then he showed COVID-19 symptoms, and twenty-four hours later he was dead. "That's when I realized that nothing is really in our hands. Nothing. You can't stop it. You are on vacation and enjoying life, and *bam!*"

She started going to a therapist, and through counseling she was able to confront her fears and lower the levels of stress. As she recovered her inner health, her outlook improved. "I discovered something beautiful. I adore the sea, even though I was locked up at sea. Now when I go out, it's pleasurable; I see the ocean and I don't feel anguish—it helps me. I am constantly grabbing my bicycle, and that is my therapy. I ride my bike close to the ocean, looking at the ocean."

MAY 5

St. Louis, Missouri

On May 5, accompanied by a nurse, Lance went to the airport in Orlando and boarded a flight to St. Louis. He was returning home without Sharon. His daughter, Amy, who'd fought day and night to get him off the *Zaandam* and out of danger, was waiting to drive him home. Lance had already started to make his peace with the horrors he'd endured. His body still had a long fight ahead. Lance could feel the damage this virus had done with every unsteady step, every labored breath, and the exhaustion that unexpectedly crept up on him. But Lance's mind was getting clearer. He was almost eighty-one—maybe the weakness and pain came with the territory. He learned to celebrate the small victories. Never had he been so pleased being able to load the dishwasher.

But Lance could see that Amy was angry, wanting someone to be held accountable for her mom's death and her father's journey to the brink. Amy snapped a picture of her father, Lance, and her husband, Ron, and they looked happy. But Amy couldn't let go. How could the cruise line have missed her mom's symptoms? How could they have left them alone, and then ignored their pleas for help? How could the cruise line have allowed her parents to embark on a voyage as the pandemic spread? How could it play games with refunds? "Amy is mad; she wants them to be held accountable," Lance said from his home in Foristell, an hour's drive west of St. Louis. Amy called a lawyer and talked about suing the cruise line. But Lance didn't want to go that route. "The longer I am away from the cruise, the more I wonder whether it's illegal to be stupid," he said. "I've come to the conclusion that it's probably not illegal. I think they were just stupid about it." Lance wanted to embrace the good things he still had left on Earth. Fighting a giant corporation in court was a journey he chose to avoid. "I don't know if I want to go through that, to bring it all back," he reflected. "It makes me sad."

Several days after returning home, Lance had Amy post a message on Facebook, thanking the people he cared about in this life: "I am on the mend, slowly getting my strength back. It must have been a higher power that laid its hand on me and pulled me through this," Lance wrote. "I am sure that was influenced by the many prayers, good thoughts and just plain rooting for me."

A week after returning home, Lance found a moment for some musical therapy of sorts. He sat in his wood-paneled den with his son-in-law, Ron, and one of his friends. He was happy for company now that Sharon was gone. They'd been hanging out all evening, sipping beer, munching snacks, and now they convinced Lance to pick up that acoustic guitar he'd bought a couple of years back. Ron and his friends were musicians, and Lance always appreciated their jam sessions. Lance sat back and began picking some new notes. Perhaps there was a song here.

MAY 23
Arnhem, the Netherlands

Arriving home in the Netherlands, crew member Anne Weggeman felt as if she had come ashore to a foreign land brimming with riches. At the supermarket, she could choose her own food. At home, she cooked for herself. On the ship, she'd had no such freedoms. "You just got a plate that was put in front of your door. So it's, Can I eat this? Or not?"

Weggeman wandered her neighborhood in Arnhem with her mask on and her ears open, catching up with COVID-19 reality, snapping up snippets of conversation. "I would hear people say, 'We're in quarantine; I'm so bored. I feel the walls coming at me.' And I would be like, *'Really?*

You have a whole house! You have windows. You can open the door and walk outside.'" Having lived with COVID-19 intensely and up close, Weggeman had a "whole new perspective on what it's like to lose my freedom."

As the COVID-19 restrictions eased in the Netherlands, Weggeman analyzed the most intense moments of her time on the *Zaandam* and reflected on the psychological transformation bubbling up inside her. Fighting COVID-19 as part of a team had made it so much easier to bear, she now realized. Yes, she had been alone in her cabin, but she never lacked the loyalty of the team. Her team. Simple gestures, like a housekeeper smuggling her a guitar, a cook delivering a hot tea, or a fellow receptionist sneaking in for a clandestine hug, were lifelines to her sanity. A guitar. A tea bag. A hug. Maybe life wasn't so complicated.

Surviving COVID-19, the young Dutch woman realized, was about the battle inside one's head as much as the physical battle to ward off bodily infection. Fighting for the safety of the group, she felt a tribal loyalty. Her fortune, her prospects, her sanity all depended on the collective behavior (and decisions) of the larger community. Focusing not on her personal safety but on the benefits to the larger group, with an altruistic outlook, Anne had found peace of mind.

Instead of the panic attacks that she'd experienced (due to the stress from the grueling work schedule) before COVID-19 hit, she now felt a tremendous power. She realized that her role translating for an elderly French passenger with a painful broken arm and working side by side with Dr. Hall to overcome the language barrier had provided her with a purpose and a mission. Dedicating her energy to helping others stoked a passionate appreciation for the rudimentary moments of life. "After this really, really hard time, I had the most beautiful time of my life out there," she said, sounding surprised at her own conclusions. "The connection with the other crew, being at sea forever where you only see blue sky and blue water. Life was simple and empty, in a way," she continued. "On the ship, I felt at home. . . . I do not regret it at all. It has given me so much in very different ways."

JUNE 18
Nashville, Tennessee

In mid-June, after seventy grueling days in the hospital—often prone and at times in a coma—in Orlando, Carl Zehner flew home to Nashville on an air ambulance. Leo hadn't seen Carl since they took him off the *Zaandam*, when he'd been knocking on death's door. He was still a long way from recovery. The virus had taken a great toll and devastated Carl's body. He'd lost thirty-five pounds, mostly muscle, he was constantly weak, and his lungs were still fighting the vestiges of pneumonia. He had a persistent cough. "As soon as I sit up, I go plop," he said. "I can't hold myself up. Just absolutely can't hold myself up."

Leo made taking care of his husband a full-time job for months, and that wasn't going to change anytime soon. "There's a post-COVID-19 syndrome that they're just now discovering," Leo said one morning, sitting across from Carl at their kitchen table. Carl smiled, pausing to say hello to his pet parrot in a cage across the room, then explained. "It's fatigue, shortness of breath, and this lingering cough."

Leo placed Carl back into rehabilitation at the Vanderbilt University hospital. Day after day, for two weeks, they coaxed his muscles back to life, strengthened his breathing, helped him regain a sense of balance. But the doctors warned Carl there was only so much they could do. Carl's lungs would never fully recover. At best, doctors explained, he would recoup 70 percent of his respiratory capacity. "When I stand up, it's not okay," said Carl. "It's hard for me to walk; I get short of breath very easily."

Carl's sense of humor, however, never flagged. Back in Orlando, in his darkest days, he'd told jokes to his nurses, and belted out show tunes and an annoying 1960s advertising jingle for Mr. Clean, a household solvent. "Mr. Clean gets tough on dirt and grime and grease in just a minute! Mr. Clean will clean your whole house and everything that's in it!" Carl repeated the jingle again and again, laughing.

"No one ever talks to us," his nurse had exclaimed, "and here we have you singing to us!"

"I want to make life as fun as I can," said Carl, laughing. "And as happy an experience as I can."

Then, in September 2020, Carl had another setback, suffering a heart attack. Years of blocked arteries suddenly shut off blood supply to his heart. Carl went through open-heart surgery. The doctors believe it was unrelated to COVID-19, but Carl isn't sure. A couple of weeks after heart surgery, he had a simple explanation for his miraculous survival: "I'm not going to die."

"You were pretty near it," Leo said.

"No. I'm Carl Zehner. I'm not going to die."

Within a month, Carl was back on his feet, puttering around his house, tinkering with the player piano, enjoying his birds. Carl and Leo then filed a lawsuit against Holland America. They sought damages based on what they believe was faulty medical screening when the passengers first boarded in Buenos Aires. There were the filings and depositions and the frequent check-ins with the lawyer, who happens to live right around the corner from them in Nashville. The suit has progressed, slowly, and is currently in discovery, but details are confidential.

Despite the lawsuit, Carl and Leo started dreaming of booking another vacation on a cruise ship. They needed this. Throughout four decades, this was how they traveled, how they saw the world. "It's like the hotel goes where you want to go," said Carl. "You never have to do all that packing and unpacking. You just open the suitcases once."

The couple appears to hold no deeper misgivings toward the cruise ship employees, the staff of the *Zaandam*, or even the Holland America Line as a corporation. If they win the lawsuit—and even if they lose—they are planning to spend generously on new Holland America cruise extravaganzas.

Leo started looking at cruise offerings for fall 2020 as soon as the cruise lines announced plans to send ships out again. Carl and Leo knew they wanted to travel with Holland America, as the company had always been their favorite. And they wanted their first cruise to be on the *Zaandam*. Maybe it was necessary to put all the trauma behind them. As the cruise lines searched for a way to restart voyages, Carl and Leo booked an eight-day cruise. It was time to head back to sea, time to put those agonizing memories behind them. The idea of cruising felt not only exciting but necessary. A triumph of their own. A victory over COVID-19.

JUNE 8
Ocho Rios, Jamaica

Living in a rustic cabin in Jamaica, Erin Montgomery was still finding her bearings a month after she disembarked. Instead of a porthole to look out at the world, she now had a broken and cracked window. She had run out of money in California and was unable to pay her bills, so she took a leap of faith and flew to the Caribbean, where, she figured, life would be less expensive and less stressful. But it hadn't worked out as planned. From inside her rented room in a shack, she could see the beach, but due to COVID-19 restrictions, she was banned from walking outside.

Erin's journey from celebrity chef to cruise ship officer to suddenly unemployed was brutal. Her job was gone, and the industry was paralyzed. "I lost everything. I have no savings left; I had to sell my car because I couldn't afford payments. I feel like less of a person," Erin said. "I feel very selfish right now, and I'm having a hard time dealing with that. I want someone to hug me, and love me, and tell me that everything is going to be okay."

Erin knew she was far from the worst off. As she tracked the progress of her companions still aboard the *Rotterdam*, she imagined their anguish as week after week they churned east, first to South Africa, where the doctors and nurses disembarked, and then toward Asia, on the final leg of what they mocked as a "world cruise." When the ship arrived in Indonesia, the authorities feared the crew was still contagious, so all the cruise ship workers who got off were tested. The results were devastating. Of the forty-three Indonesians tested, the results all came back positive. Everyone was placed yet again in a fourteen-day quarantine, this time on shore in Indonesia at a hotel watched over by armed guards.

Erin stayed in contact with her team. It had been an unforgettably brutal experience, and listening to the ongoing tribulations of her colleagues, she felt scared and sad. "Nobody on land—I don't care if you are a scientist or whatever—can understand," she said. "I didn't even have the luxury of going outside and breathing fresh air. When you're trapped out there, it's a whole different ball game."

JULY 12

Foristell, Missouri

Lance Hutton diligently worked on his rehab routines and was finally agile enough to pick up a golf club. He had played golf for years, loved it so much that he and Sharon bought a place by the course after Amy moved out and he had retired from his long career as an educator. Before COVID-19, Lance and his friends would play often. They liked to pretend it was for fun, but they were fiercely competitive. Lance figured that after what he'd been through, they'd cut him a break. He started with a few holes, then nine, then eighteen. He was struggling a little, trying to keep up with his previous handicap of eight strokes. "My friends won't give me a break," he joked. They insisted on playing like they always did, so Lance accepted he was going to lose the five dollars they tended to bet on a round.

As summer wore on, Lance Hutton was looking ahead, enjoying what he could, making the days count. He hadn't made it to Machu Picchu, but that was okay. There was one thing he would still need to check off his bucket list. He thought about it every time he needed to drive somewhere. For decades, he'd always had some version of a sedan or minivan. They were comfortable rides that met his family's needs and didn't break the bank, didn't draw attention. That was the sensible midwestern solution. But now his daughter, Amy, was long grown, his grandkids, too. And Sharon was gone.

Lance could afford to think about himself. And he knew how to make it happen. He'd found it online, used but in mint condition: a 2011 burgundy Infiniti convertible. Within a week, the minivan was gone. The Infiniti was there in its place. Lance put on his shades, settled into the leather driver's seat, and headed out. The winding country roads of Missouri were perfect for this car. He crossed rolling, wooded hills and farms for miles and miles around. Lance smiled, opening it up on a straightway, then taking the curve a little fast.

After what he'd been through, this was nothing. He was trying hard not to have any second thoughts, any regrets. Lance Hutton wasn't about to look back. Despite his pain, and the deep guilt about boarding a cruise that took his wife's life and nearly took his, Lance Hutton was certain that life continues.

APRIL 10, 2021

Jakarta, Indonesia

After twelve months of bureaucratic battles to bring Wiwit home, on April 10, 2021, Anny Doko was finally able to lay her husband's remains to rest in the family mausoleum in Jakarta—nearly a year to the day after his death. It was a small service, only a dozen friends and relatives, all wearing masks and keeping their distance, respecting the strict restrictions on gatherings because of yet another surge in COVID-19 cases. Those who couldn't attend watched live, via YouTube.

Anny placed an urn with Wiwit's ashes inside a small white casket. She surrounded the urn with fresh carnations. She spoke to him, but before her good-bye had begun, it was interrupted. She couldn't continue. The pain of his death, of the torturous wait, of a life alone—all this was too much. She broke down. The family pastor stepped in and helped. Anny leaned over, kissed the urn, crying. She held the coffin tight before finally letting go so the attendants could close the lid and take Wiwit to a waiting hearse.

With his coffin removed, all that was left was a large framed photograph of Wiwit impeccably dressed in his elegant navy blue Holland America uniform. At first glance, he didn't look like a stereotypical hero. But real heroes rarely carry the chiseled features of Hollywood icons. They more often look like the rest of us. Like the janitors, bus drivers, and delivery workers who lost their lives to COVID-19 because they continued to work, Wiwit sacrificed his life doing what he'd done for his entire career, serving the paying passengers aboard cruise ships.

Wiwit worked twelve-hour days because he had no choice. It was his job to collect the passengers' dirty linens, press their clothes, sew the uniforms. Wiwit worked day and night, even as the deadly virus was closing in, deck by deck. That dedication to the job on a cruise ship had cost Wiwit his life, and, half a world away, left his family gutted with grief.

For months after Wiwit was gone, Anny Doko remained paralyzed by the pain. She tried to go on without the man who'd been her love since she was a teenager. Near the end of 2020, Anny took a first step. She and her son Matthew set up a little eatery in the central market in Batam. Anny cooked by day, churning out large portions of Indonesian noodles in hearty broth, curries, and deep-fried samosas. In the evening, she sold the fresh food from a small stall at the market, catering to people looking for a home-cooked meal.

Anny and Matthew knew Wiwit would have been proud.

ACKNOWLEDGMENTS

The crew of the MS *Zaandam* deserves special thanks. Their firsthand stories provided the context, look, and feel at the core of this dramatic story. These insider accounts (from dishwashers to dancers to officers) allowed us to capture the bravery, heroism, and human errors that marked this voyage. They revealed to us a deep sense of belonging and care for one another and for the hundreds of strangers who were their passengers, even as the world turned its back on the *Zaandam*.

Thanks also to the passengers of the *Zaandam* who shared their deeply personal stories. The danger, terror, sickness, death, and, in so many cases, hope and redemption that they experienced were critical to paint this portrait of human survival at the dawn of a terrifying pandemic. There are so many others to thank, including experts at the Centers for Disease Control and Prevention, Department of State diplomats, and harbor pilots, who all went above and beyond.

To piece together this work of narrative nonfiction, we relied on dozens of interviews and thousands of pages of documents, many never before revealed. We gave the cruise lines and their executives ample opportunity to comment on material events, without success.

This book would not have happened without the unwavering encouragement of our agent George Lucas at InkWell Management. He saw the importance of this dramatic story about survival at sea well before we did.

Thanks to our stellar editor at Doubleday, Jason Kaufman. Jason was instrumental in bringing a fledgling idea to fruition, by showering the project with encouragement, sharing elegantly effective advice, and sublime editing. Kathleen Cook, our production editor, and Michael J. Windsor, who designed our amazing cover, helped bring it all home. Thanks to Annabel Merullo at PFD for her longtime guidance and keen eye for great stories. Thanks also to Devianti Faridz, who helped immensely as our translator in Indonesia. Bud Theisen, our researcher and loyal collaborator, brought great insight into the development of the story line and helped us sort the most important threads of this complex tale.

*

My seven daughters also lived this book, watching Dad with cruise ship deck plans taped to the walls of the house as he studied the movements aboard this mysterious ship.

To Akira, Kimberly, Maciel, Susan, Francisca, Zoe, and Amy, I am grateful for your enthusiastic support of your globe-trotting dad. Totinha, that your rock-solid confidence in this book made all the difference just as this project launched.

Finally, I would like to thank my high school teachers at Lincoln-Sudbury Regional High School in Massachusetts who so imbued us (the students) with a curiosity that to this day I reflect on those lessons from the early eighties. To teachers Bill Schechter, Don Gould, Tom Thacker, Jean Wentworth, Paul Mitchell, Bob Wentworth, Tom Pulchasky, and especially David Apfel, I send a long-belated note of appreciation.

Jonathan Franklin
Punta de Lobos, Chile

*

This book was born out of my coverage of the *Zaandam*'s voyage for *Bloomberg News*, often in collaboration with two amazing colleagues, K. Oanh Ha and Drake Bennett. That coverage produced an in-depth *Bloomberg Businessweek* story about the *Zaandam* that was masterfully edited by Dan Ferrara, with enthusiastic support from Joel Weber and Jim Aley. Dan helped me find the voice that flourished in *Cabin Fever*. My former editor, John Voskuhl, helped me stay focused on the story.

Thanks to legendary investigative journalist Jonathan Neumann, my mentor and longtime editor. He taught me how to find truth through empathy, digging, and following my instinct.

I found great counsel and humor in my good friends and brilliant journalists Simon Romero, Paulo Prada, and Brad Brooks. *Bloomberg* colleagues Stephanie Baker, Jessica Brice, Lauren Etter, Jonathan Levin, Flynn McRoberts, Vernon Silver, and David Voreacos, were always there when I needed them.

Also at *Bloomberg News*, Bob Blau and Otis Bilodeau, as well as Dan Cancel, Jacqueline Simmons, and Craig Gordon, gave me the space and support to write this book while keeping my day job. Thanks to Reto Gregori, Kristin Powers, and John Micklethwait for granting me the leave I needed to get it done.

Thanks to my kids, Gabi, Pascual, Lucas and Nico for inspiration and support. A simple thanks really doesn't do justice to Adriana, my wife, friend, and eternal font of sage advice. She sacrificed so much to assure I had the time and creative space to co-write this book, amid the chaos of the pandemic, raising our little daughter, Gabi, working like crazy as a *Miami Herald* reporter, and being an amazing partner. I owe you, fofa.

Michael Smith
Miami, Florida

ABOUT THE AUTHORS

MICHAEL SMITH is an award-winning investigative reporter at *Bloomberg News* and *Bloomberg Businessweek*. His long-form stories document financial crimes, the business of narcotics and human trafficking, and environmental and labor abuses in corporate supply chains. Smith's dozens of national awards over his thirty-year career include the prestigious George Polk, Maria Moors Cabot, Robert F. Kennedy, and Overseas Press Club prizes. Recently, he reported extensively on COVID-19 outbreaks on cruise ships. *Addicted to Profit*, a 2020 series about chemicals used to make cocaine and heroin, forced two U.S. companies to halt sales in South America and won a Gerald Loeb Award for investigative journalism. Smith is based in Miami, where he lives with his wife and daughter. *Cabin Fever* is his first book. @SmithMarkets

JONATHAN FRANKLIN is an award-winning public speaker, investigative journalist, and bestselling author. His latest book is *A Wild Idea*, the rollicking biography of the North Face founder Doug Tompkins, who gave up his riches, moved to a remote shack, and became one of the world's greatest land conservation activists. Franklin's previous books include *438 Days: An Extraordinary True Story of Survival at Sea* and *33 Men*, the inside account of the dramatic Chilean mining rescue. A native of New Hampshire, he splits his time between Portland, Maine, and Punta de Lobos, Chile, where he lives with his wife and seven daughters.